TOUGH PLANTS
FOR
TOUGH PLACES

FEB   1999

TOUGH PLANTS
FOR
TOUGH PLACES

How to Grow
101 Easy-Care Plants
for Every Part of Your Yard

PETER LOEWER

Rodale Press, Emmaus, Pennsylvania

Printed in the United States of America on acid-free ∞, recycled ♺ paper

Cover design by Acey Lee

If you have any questions or comments concerning this book, please write:

    Rodale Press
    Book Reader Service
    33 East Minor Street
    Emmaus, PA 18098

Library of Congress Cataloging-in-Publication Data

Loewer, H. Peter
    Tough plants for tough places : how to grow 101 easy-care plants for every part of your yard / Peter Loewer.
      p. cm.
    Includes bibliographical references and index.
    ISBN 0–87857–986–9 hardcover
        0–87596–730–2 paperback
    1. Plants, Ornamental. 2. Plants, Ornamental—Selection. 3. Plants, Ornamental—Pictorial works. 4. Gardens—Designs and plans. 5. Gardens—Styles. 6. Landscape gardening. I. Title.
    635.9—dc20   91–29449
                              CIP

Distributed in the book trade by St. Martin's Press

2 4 6 8 10 9 7 5 3 1 hardcover
2 4 6 8 10 9 7 5 3 1 paperback

What is Heaven? Is it not
Just a friendly garden plot,
Walled with stone and roofed with sun,
Where the days pass one by one,
Not too fast and not too slow,
Looking backward as they go
At the beauties left behind
To transport the pensive mind.

Bliss Carman, *Heaven*

Contents

Preface

Three years ago last July, my wife and I were driving from our home in Cochecton, New York, to visit my sister-in-law in Bethel, Connecticut. As we moved along the interstate, we noticed that highlighting the passing fields were a number of wildflowers in full bloom, even though the area had been suffering from a lack of rainfall for many weeks. In fact, the local weather pundits had warned that we were in the midst of a protracted drought.

"Come to think of it," my wife said, "the garden at home doesn't look half bad either."

"That's true," I said, "and I haven't watered at all over the past few weeks."

"Why should our garden be doing that well?" she asked.

"Because," I replied, "there are a lot of tough plants in our garden and a great number of natives, too. They've been able to exist in adverse weather conditions for thousands of years. After all, this isn't the first summer with poor rainfall and high temperatures."

We drove along in silence for a few seconds, whereupon she said, "It seems to me there's a book idea there."

And for the next 45 minutes, we began to list the plants that we knew for a fact are able to survive both poor soil and bad weather conditions that many fancy perennial garden plants cannot.

By the time we reached Bethel, the list was over 50.

Today this book includes more than 100 plant genera covering hundreds of species and cultivars, ranging from flowering perennials to bulbs, groundcovers, vines, shrubs, and a few small trees. They are all, in my opinion, tough plants and able to survive adverse conditions when given just half a chance to survive. Drawings of each of the plants are also included.

Since that drive to Connecticut, we have moved from our 33-acre country home in upstate New York to 1 acre within the city limits of Asheville, North Carolina. Not only has this move allowed us to deal with more plants, it has also given us experience with two distinct climate zones, both having gardening and weather highs and lows. I have tried to pass this experience along in the following pages. Over the past 17 years of gardening, I have had personal encounters with all the plants listed.

There are also 25 garden plans within these pages, illustrated with black-and-white and color plans. They cover a number of garden ideas and consist of the various plants described in this book. The plans are there to copy directly if you wish or to adapt as you see fit.

The introduction concerns some of the basic tenets of gardening. If you are new to this wonderful pastime, I would ask you to read it. If you are an old hand, perhaps give it a fast glance and go on to the text.

If any of you have suggestions or comments on the contents of this book, please write to me in care of Rodale Press, 33 East Minor Street, Emmaus, PA 18098. I always answer my mail.

Special thanks on this project must go to my wife, Jean, for the original suggestion; to my editors at Rodale, for their advice and council; to Dominick Abel, my agent; and to all the gardeners I have met who always share experiences and plants with a generosity unmatched in any other profession.

Peter Loewer
Asheville, North Carolina

Introduction

Readers of my other garden books know that for years my wife and I gardened on 33 acres of abandoned farmland in upstate New York in the township of Cochecton, not more than one mile from the Delaware River, 1,300 feet up in the Catskill Mountains.

The soil in our original garden consisted of a thin layer of whatever weeds had died that year, on top of a few inches of clay and rock—each winter would see more rocks—in turn covering red shale and huge blocks of granite.

The climate was Zone 5a, having minimum winter temperatures of $-20°$F. But every few winters we would hit a low of $-30°$F. These temperatures were often accompanied by 20 or 30 MPH winds and, for the last ten years, very little if any snow-cover—over the winter of 1987, the ground froze to a depth of 7 feet. But when local gardeners were asked about the climate, they all agreed that although many low temperature records were being broken, the year-to-year climate was getting warmer. The average frost-free period was 117 days.

Some years we would have a surfeit of rain: inch after inch would fall as though Mother Nature was ignorant of actuarial tables. Other years would be dry, with weeks passing with nary a drop. Strangely enough, over a ten-year period, the inches would balance themselves out, and rainfall would be normal when averaged over decades and centuries.

The soil around our new home in North Carolina is basically red clay, but without the rocks found up North. Since parts were gardened before, there are areas where peat moss or compost have been added, and those spots are far better than any found in our original garden.

We are now about 2,200 feet above sea level. The summers are exactly like the summers in upstate New York. The winters are much milder. The coldest month is January, when night temperatures are generally in the twenties and daytime highs about 45°F. The average frost-free period is 195 days. Although some weather experts say we are now in Zone 6, most gardeners—they often have more climatic experience than the weather people—say it's Zone 7. Whatever the final outcome of the battle of the zones, the majority think it's getting warmer.

There has been a drought here for the last three years. This year shows no sign of being any better. Winter and spring see many inches of rain, but summers are basically dry.

In the old garden, we had trouble with deer—they ate everything in sight! In the new garden, deer are no longer a threat. They have been replaced by the activity of squirrels who have a predilection for rare or interesting bulbs. So some things never change!

The garden plans are based on personal experience. In this book, I have mentioned both our old and our new gardens plus any tips and thoughts about a particular genus, species, or cultivar.

The hardiness of plants is also considered. Each plant description includes a hardiness zone number, which indicates the limit of northern hardiness for that plant. The reader may assume that the plant is hardy throughout the indicated zone and in all warmer zones. Plants not heat tolerant enough to flourish in warmer zones are noted as such in the plant description.

It should also be noted that confusion has reigned for years in what could be called the "Great Zone Debate." For decades, the United States Department of Agriculture (USDA) published a map showing 10 climate zones based on average minimum temperatures found in various parts of the United States and Canada. The Arnold Arboretum (AA) also published a map depicting 10 zones. The maps did not match. The USDA listed Zone 5 as −20°F to −10°F while the AA has Zone 5 between −5°F and −10°F. Various books and nursery catalogs would use one map or the other, often not pointing out to the reader which was being quoted. Then to further confuse the issue, in January 1990, the USDA issued a new map that depicted 11 zones. Zone 11 has a minimum temperature above 40°F and is found in two tiny parts of California and the Florida Keys.

Be sure to keep in mind that the first 10 zones on the new map do not match the original map. Take North Carolina, for example. In the old USDA map, that state was in Zone 7 and Zone 8 with the coldest minimum temperatures from 0°F up to 10°F. In the new map it is in Zone 6 and Zone 7. The coldest temperatures are now −10°F to 10°F. This is the result of averaging in some colder than usual winter temperatures over the past few years and possibly a belief by the government that there is no warming trend.

Unfortunately, it will be decades before all the garden reference books, nursery catalogs, and commercial plant lists are reprinted to align with the new 1990 USDA map. Therefore, in the interest of clarity, this book uses the old USDA map reproduced in Appendix C.

And we should mention here the concept of the microclimate. Microclimates exist in every garden. These are areas that are sheltered from the worst of the winter wind or receive protection from a small hill or enjoy extra warmth from a southern exposure. Such areas help marginally hardy plants to survive. One of the marvelous adventures of gardening is experimenting with such plant placement and therefore suceeding with a rare specimen that everyone else in the neighborhood has lost because they did not provide that extra margin of protection.

In the appendixes are lists of suppliers, publications, and growers, but they are far from complete. If you know of a source not on the list, please let me know by writing to me in care of Rodale Press.

On Naming Plants

There is a move on in publishing—especially in popular magazines—to "glitz it up and dumb it down." Many editors and publishers now believe that the public is too ignorant to deal with Latin names for plants; therefore, only popular names should be used. That's fine as long as you are dealing with dahlias and delphiniums (those two common names, by-the-by, are also the Latin names). But as soon as you branch out into unusual annuals and perennials, you will find that common names change not only from region to region, but from country to country.

There are, for example, seven different plants known as snakeroot: common snakeroot, black snakeroot, button snakeroot, Sampson's snakeroot, Seneca snakeroot, Virginia snakeroot, and white snakeroot. They are all different plants belonging to different plant genera.

All the plants known to man are given these Latin or botanical names and each is unique. And they are easily understood throughout the world. Whether in Japan or Saudi Arabia, Russia or Chicago, and regardless of the language spoken by the native gardener, *Cynara scolymus* is the artichoke and *Taraxacum officinale* is the common dandelion.

And there is usually a fascinating history behind many of these botanical names. In this book, I've given the derivation of both the genus and species names. Don't worry about pronunciation, either. Very few people can speak these names with impunity, and you will generally be using them in the written sense alone.

All reference books, most good gardening books and magazines, and nearly all catalogs and nurseries—today even most seed packets—list the botanical name under the common. Four terms are in general use: *genus, species, variety,* and *cultivar.*

In print, the genus and species are set off from the accompanying text by the use of italic type (if the text is italic, the botanical name is set in regular or roman type). *Genus* refers to a group of plants that are closely related, while the *species* suggests an individual plant's unique quality, color, or perhaps honors the individual who discovered it. Some reference books give the species a capital letter when it is an epithet derived from a person's name, a former generic name, or a common (non-Latin) name. Such a practice is still permitted and is followed in *Hortus Third* as a guide to those who wish to continue it but most publications now use only the lower case for species names and we will do so here.

The *variety* is also italicized and usually preceded by the abbreviation "var.," set in roman type. A variety is a plant that develops a noticeable change in characteristics that breeds true from generation to generation. A *cultivar* is a variation that appears on a plant while in cultivation (thus a change either by chance or design). The word is derived from **culti**vated **vari**ety, and a cultivar is distinguished by roman type inside single quotation marks.

Thus, the common biennial garden flower called the foxglove has the botanical name of *Digitalis purpurea.* The genus name is Latin for the finger of a glove and refers to the shape of the blossom, while the species name refers to the usual color of the flower. Biennial means it lives for two growing seasons, as compared to the one season of an annual and the many seasons of a perennial. There is a cultivar called 'Foxy' that blooms the first year.

Around the Garden

Soils and Soil Types

The plants described in this book range from those happy in the damp and the wet to those that prefer the driest of soils. Some are happy in average soil, some like a bit of added humus or compost, and a few will persist in solid clay, if not a red shale bank.

So the first thing a gardener should do is to check the soil for its character: Is it solid clay, rich loam, sandy, or various combinations? Is it well drained or does water stand in puddles even after a light rain?

Clay soils are sticky. If you roll a lump of wet soil between your fingers as though rolling a cigarette and it forms a compact cylinder that does not break up, that's clay. Clay can become rock-hard when completely dry. Instead of sinking into such soil, water simply rolls to the lowest level and sits. Soil with lots of organic matter will drain, and sandy soil drains immediately. Most states have extension services that will advise you as to soil content if you are not sure how to go about it.

Unless a particular plant demands special conditions, try to prepare a garden soil that strikes a balance between clay, sand, and loam. In addition to improving drainage, the organic matter helps to provide food for healthy plant development.

I'm most familiar with clay soil since both our northern and southern gardens feature that soil type. The best thing to do to clay soil is feed it as much organic material as you can find. The more organic material that you add, the better the soil becomes. And take advantage of the weather. Whenever possible, dig your future garden in the fall and let it lie open for the winter, allowing the frost action to help break up the soil.

Finally, remember that many plants do very well in clay soil, and that includes roses. Plants with fine roots or alpine and mountain plants that demand perfect drainage usually perish in heavy clay soils, but plants with coarse roots do very well.

Composting

As I mentioned above, the best way to build good soil, no matter what kind you start with, is to add organic matter. You can add leaf litter from the woods, peat moss, coal ashes, sawdust, shredded paper, wood ashes, shredded bark, grass clippings, weed remnants, or shredded leaves. Best of all is compost, the rich, organic material that is left after the bacterial action takes place in a compost heap.

But there's more to compost than what it does to poor soil. First, it's an easy thing to do. There's no fuss or bother, simply the act of bringing vegetable scraps out to the compost bin and tossing them in. You've immediately cut back on using the garbage disposal and messy and smelly garbage cans. For 20 years, we took all of our vegetable scraps to compost heaps rather than make endless trips to the local dump (like many places out in the country, there was no tax-paid garbage collection).

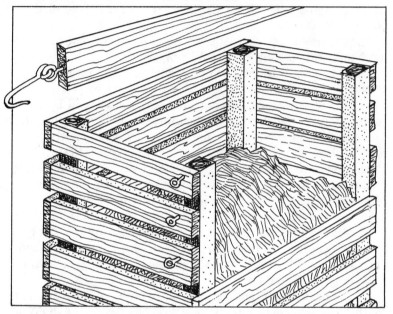

The compost bin pictured above uses pressure-treated, stock 4 x 4's for the posts and 8-inch-wide pine planking for the sides. The wooden pieces are held with aluminum nails, and the removable front sections are held with ordinary door latches.

It's a money saver. All that cash used to buy fertilizers and garden conditioners can go for buying plants.

Plants grown with compost as a nutritional resource are healthier than those grown with artificial fertilizers and plant conditioners, since compost adds valuable nutrients that the commercial products lack.

Choose an out-of-the-way spot for your compost pile, somewhere handy to the garden. The spot should be level and well-drained land with at least a half-day of sunlight. You can either buy a ready-made compost bin or build your own (see diagram). Just make sure that your creation has adequate venting in the sides and bottom to allow free passage of air. If air is lacking, the desirable *aerobic* or oxygen-loving bacteria and fungi will be replaced by *anaerobic* organisms that do not require air to function, thereby slowing the action of decay and producing odor.

Once the bin is set up, you can begin to pile up discarded vegetable matter collected from grass clippings, weeding, kitchen vegetable scraps, and even black-and-white newsprint. Remember, smaller is better. A mature cabbage will eventually break down, but it could take months to accomplish. If broken into small pieces, the cabbage will decay in only weeks.

In a typical compost heap, vegetable matter is alternated with layers of soil. Once a week or so, the pile is turned to keep the ingredients mixed and bacterial decomposition working at high efficiency. Since a dry compost heap will not "work," the gardener must occasionally add moisture. Eventually, the bacteria will break down the collection of organic matter into a rich, beautiful, dark brown humus that is completely free of odor and is manna to the garden.

The only items not suitable for a compost heap are animal feces, bones, any meat products, and plant material that has been dosed with herbicides or pesticides. It is also a good idea not to use material that has been infected with a virus or is seriously diseased.

Checking the pH of the Soil

The pH scale is a method of measuring the relative acidity, or sourness, and alkalinity, or sweetness, of the soil. The pH scale ranges from 0 to 14, with 7.0 indicating that the soil is neutral, neither acid nor base. Soils with a pH less than 7.0 are acidic; those with a pH greater than 7.0 are alkaline. Most plants grow in pH ranges between 5.0 and 7.0, slightly acidic to neutral. Swamps and bogs that have high percentages of peat are extremely acidic; in humid regions, and most woods and forests, the soil is moderately acid to slightly alkaline; arid regions go from a moderate up to a strong alkaline content; and desert areas in the Southwest have vast alkali flats.

Most garden centers now stock an inexpensive paper pH tape. Held against a sample of moist soil, the tape will turn colors to indicate the degree of acidity. Or you can, once again, call your county extension agent about the acidity of local soil.

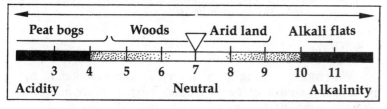

The pH chart above shows the scale used to describe the alkalinity and acidity of soil and where these soil conditions appear.

Mulching

When the hot days of summer arrive in your garden and that sun beats down on dirt and plant alike, the soil and the roots begin to bake and what water there is quickly evaporates. That's the time to apply a garden mulch.

Mulches help slow the evaporation of moisture from the soil and cut way back on the weeding required. They also protect the soil structure and prevent crusting of the surface. Depending on the material used, mulches can also improve the appearance of the garden by giving beds, borders, and edgings a neat and orderly look. Just promise not to use black plastic: about the only thing it's good for is in vegetable garden applications where it keeps the ground warm for crops like melons; it's unaesthetic when used in a formal garden.

Stone mulches are excellent for rock gardens and for drought-resistant plants. A mulch of pea gravel, for example, keeps mud from splashing onto dainty rock garden plants during heavy rains. Stones hold warmth from the sun, radiating it back at night; the condensation produced is excellent for many plants.

If you do decide to mulch your garden, it's often a good idea to use those with an organic base. These essentially plant-based materials gradually decompose, adding organic matter to the soil. I don't advise using peat moss for a mulch since it packs down and repels water with a vengeance.

Mulching Mowers

A whole new generation of power lawn mowers is upon us. They are called mulching mowers and are designed to cut up grass clippings, returning them directly to the lawn. The clippings quickly break down and do not need to be bagged and thrown away. To avoid pile-ups of clippings, never mow the grass when wet and never remove more than one-third of the length of the grass blades in a single mowing. Recent developments in disposing of clippings include a grass clippings compost maker that will turn them into compost in less than 30 days. Clippings can also be used to mulch garden beds.

Watering

Watering is getting to be a very serious business in many parts of this continent. More and more demands are being made on what turns out to be a limited resource. So when you do water the garden, do it well. Use enough to soak into the soil, down where it will do the most good. As water penetrates into the soil, roots grow down to reach it. Plants with longer roots will survive dry spells; surface watering forces roots to grow up where they are easily destroyed by even short periods without water.

According to tradition, gardens need about 1 inch of water per week. That, of course, will vary according to the temperatures and how hard the wind is blowing, since high winds speed evaporation. Soil type is also important. Fast-draining soils dry more quickly than clay. The individual plant's requirements must also be considered. Shallow-rooted plants need water more often than deep-rooted ones, and new plantings also need even, constant moisture to establish new roots. But usually if you get one good soaking rain per week, you will probably not have to water. The best way to tell when the garden needs water is to stick your finger down into the soil. If it feels dry a couple of inches below the surface, it's time to water.

Watering Systems

Overhead sprinklers are the least efficient way to water: pretty to look at but essentially bad business, especially in areas of high sun, high heat, high winds, and porous soils. Soaker hoses are far better, and drip irrigation systems that deliver water directly to the root zone are the best.

Soaker hoses have tiny holes that let water out slowly, soaking the ground. Many kinds can be installed underground or under mulch or laid directly on the top of the soil. Trickle or drip systems use slender plastic tubing with tiny pores that allow water to ooze out slowly. Kits are available that give you all the parts you need. Attach the system to a water source, install a timer if you like, and you're ready to go.

There are various kinds of water timers on today's market. A simple wind-up timer meters any amount of water up to 1,400 gallons from 5 minutes to 3 1/2 hours, then shuts the water off automatically. A computerized control will turn sprinklers or irrigation systems on and off even when you are on vacation and can be programmed for seven days. It operates on two AA batteries.

Pests and Disease

Walk into that section of any garden center that sells pesticides and you will be bowled over by the smell of chemicals that pervades everything on the shelves. Those rows and rows of brightly colored boxes and brown plastic bottles are not full of pudding mix, but heavy-duty formulas that are poison to all concerned. The user is warned in very small type of chances not worth taking. Magazine ads back up the use of these formulas by showing beautiful pictures of perfect gardens and go to great lengths to persuade you that only with chemicals can you have great flowers and a perfect lawn. But there are other ways to garden without resorting to sprays for which you need an 800 number to call if the stuff gets in your lungs.

First, pest control starts with good soil condition, good fertility, adequate watering, and good housekeeping about the garden. Never allow diseased or decaying plant material to lie about. And remember that a healthy plant can fight off many attacks that will kill a weaker cousin. Just as a healthy person is very resistant to disease, so is a healthy plant.

Our worst garden problem has always been slugs, simply one of nature's most disgusting creatures. These are snails without shells that glide about on a glittering trail of slime and chew holes in just about everything. We refuse to use poisoned bait because of possible danger to garden cats (who effectively take care of any rabbit problem). We've tried trapping slugs with pans full of beer but have never found them to work. So I resort to the easiest method by taking a flashlight out into the garden at night, spotlighting slugs, and sprinkling a few grains of salt on their tender bodies, starting the process of reverse osmosis and eliminating them completely.

Japanese beetles are also a problem, but they can be picked off the plant and dropped in a can of soapy water, the resulting mixture buried deep when the can is full. Or you can use one of the new chemical bait traps that lure the males with sex attractants and the females by odor of rose.

Insects like flea beetles, aphids, and spider mites can be controlled by spraying with insecticidal soaps or using insecticides derived from the dried flower heads of the pyrethrum daisy (*Chrysanthemum cinerariifolium*), a plant that resembles the common field daisy. Pyrethrum has two drawbacks: Sunlight breaks it down and reduces its effectiveness. Unfortunately it also kills beneficial insects such as honeybees. Since its chemicals are readily broken down by the action of light, apply pyrethrum in late afternoon. Late afternoon application also reduces its contact with foraging bees.

Rotenone is another plant-based insecticide, manufactured from the roots of the tuba root (*Derris elliptica*) and the lancepods (*Lonchocarpus* spp.), but it can cause severe irritation to humans if inhaled. It also kills beneficial insects. It is sold as a dust and is an extremely potent control for many insects. Like pyrethrum, it safely breaks down in the environment.

Plant Propagation

Seeds

When seeds arrive, you will note that most packs are clearly labeled with explicit instructions for sowing. Do not open the packs until you are ready to use them. Until that time, store the packs in a cool spot—never near a radiator. If seeds need stratification—a period of exposure to about 40°F—before sowing, keep them in the refrigerator for 6 to 8 weeks.

Sow seeds in a sterile medium, either commercial or your own make. A heating cable is helpful to speed germination for some types of seeds. If you are missing information on how deep to plant seeds, use the following rule of thumb: Seeds 1/16 of an inch or larger should be covered by the thickness of one seed; tiny seeds that resemble dust, like begonias, need not be covered at all. Label your plantings carefully with plant name and date; sounds simple, but it's very easy to forget such information. For ease of transplanting, use individual peat pots for most seeds.

Once seeds are planted, put the pots into larger containers, cover with glass or plastic wrap, and place them in a spot out of the direct sunlight. It need not be completely dark unless the instructions for that particular kind of seed specify that darkness is needed for germination. Keep the wrap away from the surface of the medium to prevent condensation from swamping the seeds below. Never let the medium dry out, either before or after germination.

When the first green shoots appear, remove the plastic wrap and move the containers into the sunlight. If you are doing this in

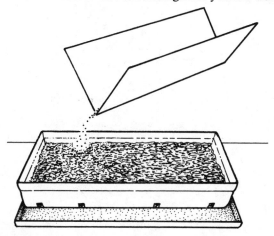

Use a folded piece of paper to distribute small seeds on a sterile medium.

late spring, provide some protection, as the hot rays of a noonday sun can be dangerous to tiny plants. A piece of screening will do fine.

Pot the plants on as they grow. When spring frosts are over and the weather is settled, move the seedlings out to a protected place in the garden.

Cuttings

Late spring or early summer is the best time to start cuttings, since at this time the plant has a good supply of food stored in its cells to keep it going until new roots are formed. Most plants will root later in the season, but the process is slower. It has also been scientifically demonstrated that the younger the stem, the faster new roots will start.

Take healthy stems, 3 to 5 inches long, using a clean, sharp knife or razor blade. Make the cut slightly below the point where a leaf stalk joins the stem, removing any damaged leaves and those near the bottom of the cutting. Fill a peat pot full of moist sand or a commercial rooting medium, and make a hole with a pencil to three-fourths of the pot's depth. Stick the cutting in the hole, making sure that the bottom of the stem touches the medium. Put the whole affair in a plastic bag, sealing the opening at top with a twist-tie. The bag holds the moisture that the leaves give off but cannot replace until new roots are formed. Check to see that the medium stays moist but never soggy. After two

Once a cutting is inserted in a moist rooting medium, set the peat pot and cutting in a plastic bag. Then tie the top closed, and the bag becomes a small greenhouse.

weeks, give the stem a tug to see if roots are forming. If they are not, pull the stem out and check for rot. If all looks well, try again. You can use commercial prepared hormone powders if you wish, but I've always shied away from using them. When new roots grow through the peat walls, pot on.

Division

Most perennials get larger as they grow. Eventually clumps are formed, and often growth diminishes at the center. Early spring is an especially good time for dividing plants, when they are programmed by nature to grow. But the fall is also a good time for such activity because plants are now becoming dormant. Remember if you live in an area where winter appears early, be sure the new divisions can get settled in before frost hits the ground. Dig up the clump, then chop it apart with your spade or hatchet. Make sure a good supply of roots is left with each piece. Replant immediately.

Some plants, especially grasses, produce stolons. These are underground stems that end in a growing tip. If removed from the mother plant, they will root and produce new plants.

Designs for Twenty-Five Gardens

Don't ever let anyone tell you that landscaping and installing a garden is easy work. It isn't. But, at the same time, never let anyone tell you it can't be done without hiring all the work out, including the design. After all, the majority of living rooms in American homes and apartments are quite comfortable and suit the inhabitants; in few cases was a decorator hired to do either the planning or the purchasing. Doing your own garden will take patience and a lot of hard work, but when it's all over, you will have that marvelous feeling of achievement that comes from being involved with a job well done.

Each of the following gardens could be installed exactly as in the accompanying plans or could be modified to fit individual requirements. They all use the garden practices mentioned in the introduction and combinations of the more than 100 plants described in this book. Possible sites for the gardens are also listed.

Some of these gardens are built around particular subjects like a Japanese garden or a desert garden, but these ideas should be matched or adapted to the particulars of your land. Others are gardens created to solve specific problems. All of them are based on experiences that my wife and I plus family and friends have encountered over the past 20-odd years. Where outside help was used—a local firm to haul gravel or to move large rocks—that help is mentioned. None of the gardeners I have ever been involved with up to now have ever hired out the weeding, digging, or any of the labor involved with building the garden itself; choosing those options defeats the whole purpose of home gardening, doesn't it?

Some Hints on Garden Design

It's amazing just how few people design their gardens. Oh, sure, American gardens are neat; the grass is cut and the dead blossoms are removed from the marigolds and petunias. But if trees are planted, they're stuck out in the middle of the lawn or planted in straight lines, and if conifers are used, they become stickless lollipops stuck in orderly fashion along the black macadam driveway. For some reason, the most imagination always goes into the vegetable garden where leaves become a canvas of green dotted here and there with the bright colors of the tomatoes or squash.

So with the following suggestions and designs, I'd like to bring the gardener's imagination out of the vegetable patch and into the garden proper, perhaps to replace some of that endless— and expensive—grass with blooming plants.

- Trust your own aesthetic judgment. After all, it's your garden.
- Many books on garden design talk about the proper matching of color, but it's only really practical in a very large garden with a proper staff of gardeners. Of course a sprig of tiny white flowers under a foot high would be overpowered if surrounded by three sunflowers, each 3 feet tall. But in small gardens, going out of your way to match the proper colors is often overdone. When matching colors, think of intensity or brightness. If you use a hibiscus that bears hot pink flowers, pair it with plants that also produce hot, bright colors—not something with pale lavender bloom.
- Pay attention to the eventual size of a plant, shrub, or tree. Try to visualize what it will be five years from the day you plant it. It's amazing how fast some plants will grow.
- Unless you plan a garden the size of Versailles or Hampton Court in England, avoid too many borders with straight lines. Gentle and sweeping curves usually look better and are easier to keep up.
- Match plants to available conditions. Avoid putting a bush that requires perfect drainage next to one that revels in the damp. You can probably rectify any mismatch, but it is often more trouble than it's worth.
- Use ornaments that are in scale with your garden. In a typical lot, a small Japanese snow lantern holding a candle or low-

voltage light will always look better than a 6-foot marble statue of Venus de Milo. Scaled-down ornaments add depth to a garden rather than overpowering it.

- Never take on more garden than you can take care of. We all have eyes bigger than our garden stomachs, but at a certain point it's best to overcome the collection desire, thus allowing time to sit back and enjoy it all.

- Finally when planning a garden, take paper and pencil and make a sketch of what you hope to do. It need not be a complicated map, so perfectly drawn that framing is a must, but just something to help you arrive at the starting point and save eventual energy, money, and grief.

A Courtyard Garden

This garden design assumes the gardener lives in a ground floor condominium or city apartment, or has an area of the garden especially suited for such a garden room.

Recently I was called to look at a garden—or what was left of a garden—after some ten years of neglect. It was an area in front of a large ranch house, bounded on the left by the full garage, at the back by the house including the front door, on the right by a sloping bank of ground-hugging junipers that eventually became a woods, and the driveway in front. There were three marvelous dogwood trees (*Cornus florida*) and a lot of dead and dying grass and some struggling heathers. This garden, in all practicality, was an enclosed rectangle in partial shade.

I asked the owner if she ever just wanted to sit in a garden and not do anything. Yes, she said. And, she added, her husband hated to maintain this lawn. So we discussed replacing the mostly dead grass with a terrace of flagstones, bounded by ivies and pachysandras, with spring bulbs planted along the edges, and the centerpiece of the plot being a very old garden bench of great beauty that now sat in her backyard, unused.

My own courtyard garden is a 20 by 25-foot rectangle, which because of nearby, very tall trees, gets a half day of sun. One long side is a raised 3-foot wall that is now being planted with a number of vines and rock plants, including an alpine clematis (*Clematis alpina*) and a red passion flower (*Passiflora* spp.) that spends winter in the greenhouse. Along the bottom edge of the wall is an 18-inch-wide bed planted with epimediums (*Epimedium* spp.) and spring bulbs. Because our house and garden sit on the side of a terraced hillside, the other long end of the rectangle is a flat 3-foot-wide bed that contains various daylilies—arranged by cultivar to bloom all summer—a rhododendron called 'Blue Peter', and at one end a star magnolia (*Magnolia stellata*) and at the other, a snowball viburnum tree (*Viburnum × carlcephalum*). The narrow end at the far side of this outdoor room is planted with hostas and ferns, and the narrow end close to the house becomes the entrance, an imaginary doorway defined on one side by some miniature roses and on the other by a specimen hosta 'Frances Williams'. The garden room is carpeted with grass and contains an old concrete bench and, on various pieces of flagstone, greenhouse plants summering outside.

With the installation of low-voltage outdoor lighting along main pathways, this courtyard garden becomes a landscaped entrance to the house as well as a marvelous place to sit on a hot summer day. The same plan could be used to create a garden room almost anywhere on your lot.

A color rendering of the courtyard garden is found on page 9.

A List of Plants:

1. Bishop's weed (*Aegopodium podagraria* 'Variegatum')
2. English ivy (*Hedera helix* 'Manda's Crested')
3. Creeping juniper (*Juniperus horizontalis* 'Glauca')
4. Variegated hostas (*Hosta undulata* 'Albo-marginata' and 'Variegata')
5. Lady fern (*Athyrium filix-femina*)
6. Hostas in pots
7. Spanish bluebells (*Endymion hispanicus*)
8. Barrenwort (*Epimedium grandiflorum*)
9. Small pool with pink waterlily (*Nymphaea* 'Hilary')

A Courtyard Garden

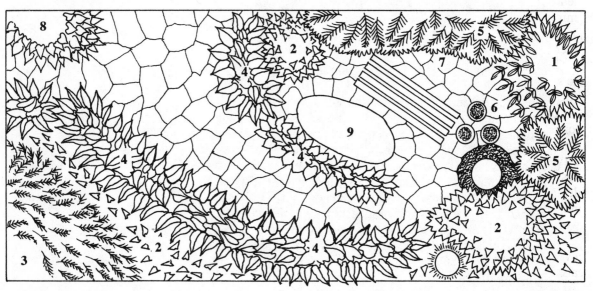

A Garden of Groundcovers

The following two gardens are designed to take advantage of the various groundcovers available on the nursery market today. Here the idea is to have low-growing plants that cover the ground without resorting to continual weeding and mowing in order to give your property a kempt look. The minute that grass grows over a certain height, it begins to look like a rock star that should be sheared immediately. Ivy or ajuga, on the other hand, tumble about like the controlled curls on Madonna's head and are always attractive.

It's not that I'm against lawns; they have their place in the garden, especially English gardens. After all, lawn is from the Middle English word *launde* and originally meant a heath or moor, eventually becoming "lawn" or an open glade. But in England the climate is cool and blessed with a lot of rain, and lawns become velvet carpets that run between gracious perennial borders. Here in most of America the summers are hot, often parched, and unless subjected to extensive artifical watering, lawns turn brown until they perk up again when temperatures fall in autumn.

So groundcovers can be a big help in cutting back on the work of maintaining a lawn. They are also effective in areas of partial shade where lawns begin to look straggly because they are not getting enough sunlight.

For the many Americans who would like to reduce their lawn-care chores, the following two gardens are designed to replace high-maintenance grass. The gardens are designed for partial shade, but the ideas can be adapted to full sun by utilizing plants like carpet junipers (*Juniperus* spp.), bugleweed (*Ajuga* spp.), thyme (*Thymus* spp.), sun-loving, hay-scented fern (*Dennstaedtia punctilobula*), and other plants that thrive in the sun.

The first garden is made of curved lines to emulate the look of the sidewalks and terraces found in many Brazilian gardens; the other uses variations on squares, circles, and rectangles.

The pathway through the first garden is made of loose flagstones. They are set level with the ground; underneath, a few inches of soil have been replaced with some sand. But such a path could just as easily be made of pine needles or chunks of bark, such as most garden centers carry. If brick walkways are used, it's a good idea to use one of the edgings available to hold the brick in place and prevent the groundcover roots from invading the spaces between the bricks.

An excellent reflecting pool can be made of the black plastic cover from a commercial-weight plastic garbage can. The plan also calls for a sundial, but a small piece of garden sculpture would do just as well.

In the first garden you can use a small tree already planted in your yard or purchase any of a number of small decorative trees. In this case I've picked a serviceberry.

The edgings of the second garden can be made of railroad ties, a few layers of flagstones, or stone or brick and mortar. Many garden centers now carry a large selection of bricks and cement blocks that are heavy enough to make a low, easy-care wall.

The floral display is composed of various annual flowers found at garden centers, and the color and plant combinations are changed yearly.

Color renderings of the two gardens are found on pages 10 and 11.

A List of Plants for Garden 1:

1. Bugleweed (*Ajuga reptans* 'Burgundy Glow')
2. English ivy (*Hedera helix* 'Buttercup')
3. Houttuynia (*Houttuynia cordata* 'Chameleon')
4. Candytuft (*Iberis sempervirens*)
5. Existing small tree or serviceberry (*Amelanchier laevis* 'Rosea')
6. Creeping thyme (*Thymus* spp.) or golden sedum (*Sedum acre*)
7. Creeping juniper (*Juniperus horizontalis*)
8. *Pachysandra* 'Silveredge'

A List of Plants for Garden 2:

1. Bishop's weed (*Aegopodium podagraria* 'Variegatum')
2. Creeping juniper (*Juniperus procumbens* 'Nana')
3. Creeping juniper (*Juniperus horizontalis* 'Bar Harbor')
4. *Pachysandra terminalis* 'Green Carpet'
5. Existing small tree or smoke tree (*Cotinus coggygria* 'Notcutt's Variety')
6. Barrenwort (*Epimedium grandiflorum*)
7. Yearly display of annual plants from garden center
8. Horsetails in pot (*Equisetum hyemale*)
9. Small waterlily, perhaps *Nymphaea* 'Marliacea Chromatella'

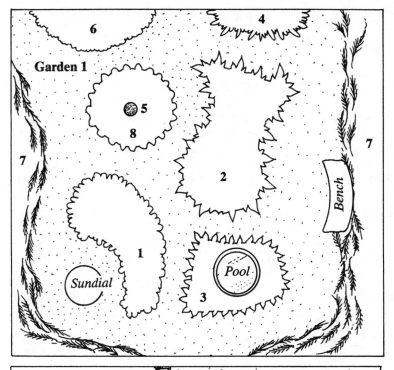

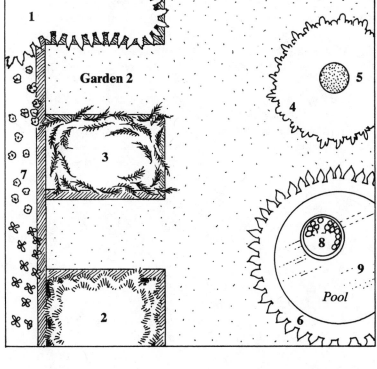

A Garden of Groundcovers

A Postage Stamp Garden

The term postage stamp does not refer to the design of this particular garden but merely to the fact that no piece of land is too small to have a special group of plants—even if it consists of only three pots set on the edge of a sidewalk or on a few pieces of flagstone. When we lived for a number of years in a railroad flat in Manhattan, our gardens consisted of two windowsills in the living room, but gardens they were.

Such small gardens could be built about the smaller spring-blooming bulbs, to be followed by low-growing perennials, chosen either for flowers or for their attractive leaves. And come to think of it, a favorite postage stamp could be copied by the judicial use of plants in the same way that designs are copied from paintings to woven tapestries.

A garden friend lives on a small city lot with a great deal of shade provided by fine old trees, giving him only a small place for a garden. So he made a moss garden in a rectangular space about 3 by 4 feet. Here wood mosses and ground pine (*Lycopodium obscurum*) are cunningly arranged with small stones and even an old black mixing bowl—I think it's Fiestaware—that, full of water and buried to its rim, becomes a small lake. Now the eye can travel over a Lilliputian landscape and almost imagine another world.

And speaking of three pots on a sidewalk, a neighbor up the street from us, who has hardly any garden space at all, purchased five 30-quart plastic tubs of the type used to contain water lilies. Only instead of lilies, he's planted roses and rudbeckias in two tubs, assorted annuals in two, and one large tomato plant in the last.

The following postage stamp garden measures 3 by 5 feet and is located in full sun. By the time the leaves of the surprise lily have ripened and disappeared, the goldenrods and tree mallows have matured. Then in summer the surprise lily blossoms pop up, adding color and maybe some of the same element of surprise you feel when stamp prices go up. To keep the daylily leaves in better shape over the summer, remember to remove the scapes (flower stems) after blooming is over.

A color rendering of this garden is found on page 12.

A List of Plants:

1. Blue fescues (*Festuca ovina* var. *glauca*)
2. Tree mallow (*Lavatera trimestris*)
3. Fall aster (*Aster novi-belgii* 'Alert')
4. Stonecrop (*Sedum spectabile* 'Autumn Joy')
5. Bugleweed (*Ajuga* 'Atropurpurea')

Continued on page 41

This courtyard garden becomes a cool and shady retreat on a hot summer day. Various ferns and hostas will grow beautifully in such a setting. See pages 3 and 4 for a description of this garden, a plan, and a list of plants.

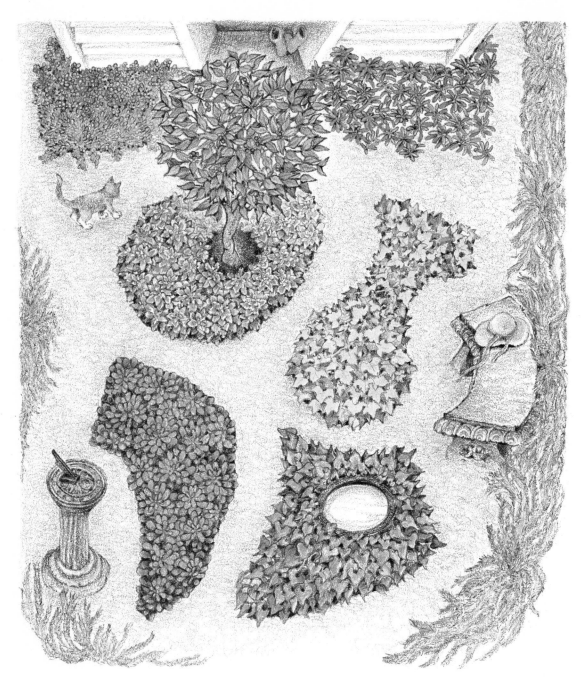

The two gardens devoted to groundcovers are not only attractive, they'll also save hours of garden maintenance and lawn care. The garden on the left is an informal design with curved pathways that echo the edge of a concrete bench, available at most garden centers. The garden at right is more

formal, with straight edging of the beds, in this case landscape ties. For lists of tough groundcovers along with designs for these gardens, see pages 5 and 6.

Although the postage stamp garden covers a very small piece of land—here an area of 3×5 feet—these hard-working plants will provide flowers from early spring well into fall. See pages 8 and 41 for a description of this garden.

Many houses are surrounded by old, valuable trees that provide a great deal of shade. The shade garden above becomes a cool retreat on sunny days and features ferns and wildflowers. Birds will visit the birdbath throughout the garden year. Turn to pages 41, 42, and 43 for a list of shade-loving plants and designs for a shade garden.

An autumn garden can be a blaze of color, especially when it features an American sumac tree (above left) along with ornamental grasses and fall-blooming bulbs. For a description of this garden and a list of plants for fall color see pages 43, 44, and 45.

In winter, this garden becomes a peaceful retreat where the shiny greens of a rhododendron contrast with the tans and browns of the fruiting stems of sensitive ferns, dried grasses, and *Sedum* 'Autumn Joy'. Winter gardens are especially beautiful when covered with a soft mantle of snow. You'll find a list of plants and a design for the winter garden on pages 45, 46, and 47.

Planting a rough-cut bank with plants that will grow on a steep slope—in this case creeping junipers, ornamental grasses, and daylilies—will turn an eyesore into an asset. This garden, described on pages 47 and 48, is especially valuable for dealing with new home landscapes or steep, difficult-to-mow slopes.

Combine an effective design with an unusual mix of plants suited for hot and difficult situations and you have an asset for any landscape. In the stylized gardens, plants are used for both color and

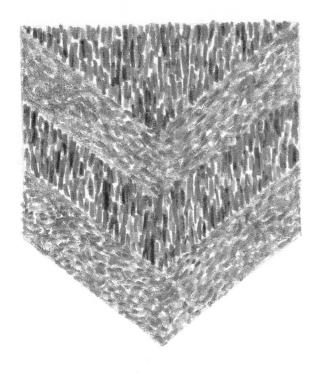

the texture of their leaves. You'll find descriptions and plant lists for four stylized gardens on pages 48, 49, and 50.

Transform the edge of a pond garden with plants that are at their best when growing in or along the water's edge. Such a garden is suitable for a pond of two acres or a small backyard pool. For a plant list and a description of this garden, see pages 51 and 52.

The bog garden includes plants that prefer to grow in moist or wet soil. Dragonflies and other insects will delight in the habitat it creates and watering problems will be held to a minimum. The plan and plant list for the bog garden is found on pages 53 and 54.

Where soil conditions are very poor and drainage slow, it's easier to garden in raised beds rather than import tons of new soil. The flowering plants in the raised bed garden pictured above grow beautifully behind a low retaining wall of fieldstones. See pages 54, 55, and 56 for a description and list of plants to grow in this garden.

For delightful spring color, plant a bulb garden. The garden above, which is described on pages 56 and 57, includes a number of daffodils and tulips for spring bloom, but chives, other flowering onions, and lilies will extend the season well into summer. Only the summer-blooming portion of the garden is shown above featuring naturalized lilies and Chinese chives (*Allium tuberosum*) at right.

This American version of an English perennial border is a mass of flowering plants and shrubs that will provide a long season of bloom. Such gardens can contain dozens or hundreds of plants depend-

ing on the amount of room available. See pages 57 through 61 for a description of this garden, a plan, and a list of plants.

The perennial cutting garden will produce cut flowers throughout the gardening season. In the garden pictured above, which is described on pages 61, 62, and 63, perennials, annuals, and gladioli provide color for both the backyard and for cut-flower arrangements.

The edge of the meadow garden is a perfect place for growing wildflowers. Goldenrod, coneflowers, bottlebrush grass, and Queen Anne's lace, shown above, are only a few of the tough, beautiful meadow plants from which to choose. The beetle at lower right feeds on goldenrod pollen. See pages 63, 64, and 65 for a description of this garden, a plan, and a list of plants.

The native plant garden features wildflowers originally found in the United States. Obedient plant, sea oats, Solomon's-seal, swamp sunflower, and rose mallow are among the many easy-to-grow wildflowers native to this country. For more ideas, a description of this garden, and a plan, see pages 65, 66, and 67.

The wild garden is a place where nature makes the rules, not the gardener. Here a section of the garden is pictured. A wood satyr butterfly confronts, from left, bugbane, globe thistle, bottlebrush grass, plume poppy, cord grass, and baptisia. For a description of this garden, a plan, and more ideas for plants, turn to pages 67 and 68.

Plants in pots and containers make it easy to change the design of a patio garden. In the garden pictured above, red caladiums sit in a Chinese porcelain pot. Houseplants such as clivias—the large plant with long straplike leaves—enjoy summering outdoors in such a garden. For a list of plants perfect for containers and more on this design, see pages 69 and 70.

The shrub and small tree border is especially helpful for a property close to a busy road. To have a garden that looks mature in a short time, buy balled-and-burlapped or container-grown plants. See pages 70 and 71 for a description, design, and more ideas for plants.

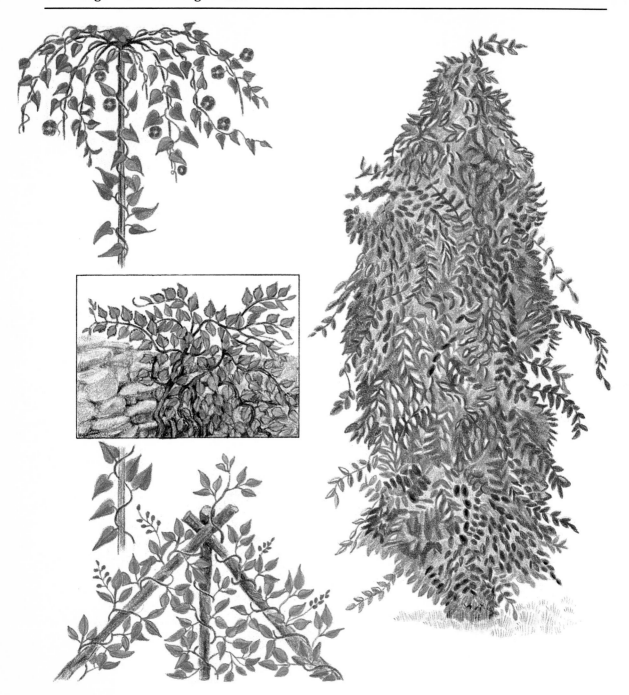

The vertical garden is a place where vines wind their way to the sky above. Four different supports for vines are pictured above, including a *tuteur,* a support often used in the French garden of impressionist painter Claude Monet. These supports, along with tough vines to decorate them, are described on pages 72 and 73.

This Japanese garden features a clear, simple, classic design with a concrete snow lantern viewed from a wooden deck. The plants are chosen for their sculptural quality in addition to their foliage or flowers. See pages 73 and 74 for a description of this garden, a plan, and a list of plants.

For areas with hot, dry summers, this dry garden is ideal. Once established, plants for this garden—including a sumac tree, potentillas, yuccas, purple smoke tree, and the flowering raspberry pictured here, will not suffer from most summer droughts. For a description and more ideas for plants, see pages 74 and 75.

It's possible to have a beautiful rock garden in a very small space, because the plants that grow best when surrounded by rocks and stones are generally all very small. Better still, since they are deep-rooted, they're also generally very drought tolerant. For a list of easy-to-grow rock plants, a description of this garden, and a plan, see pages 76 and 77.

Ornamental grasses require little maintenance and are very drought resistant. In addition, many of these plants produce stately and beautiful flowers at summer's end and well into autumn. The garden above is described on pages 77 and 78.

The dry stream garden represents a solution for properties cut by drainage ditches or dips in the landscape. Above the river of small stones, a small pool made with a PVC liner sparkles in the afternoon sun. See pages 79 and 80 for a description of this garden, a plan, and a list of plants.

Continued from page 8

6. Daylily (*Hemerocallis* 'Eenie-Weenie')
7. Surprise lily (*Lycoris squamigera*)
8. Goldenrod (*Solidago* 'Golden Bush')
9. Goldenrod (*Solidago* 'Crown of Rays')
10. Spiderwort (*Tradescantia* × *andersoniana* 'Snow Cap')

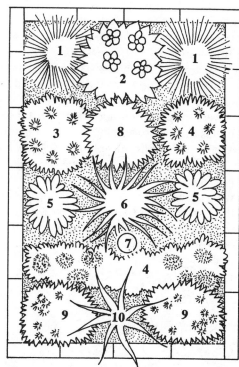

A Postage Stamp Garden

A Shade Garden

In the height of the summer where would you rather be: out in the hot sun, continually blinking your eyes so you can focus on the flowers, or sitting in the cool shade where ferns are dappled with light and the dews of morning are still present?

If you opt for the shade, the following garden could be installed under a canopy of trees or in a spot shaded by a large nearby building. Remove any low-hanging tree branches so a visitor to this garden can walk the pathways without hitting his or her head.

The condition of soil for the shade garden is very important. In full sun, most plants must struggle if they are in dense, poorly drained, clay-packed soil. In shade, that type of soil could be deadly. So shade gardeners must be sure to incorporate leaf litter, garden compost, or peat moss into the soil. In shady parts of our northern garden in upstate New York, we dug down 18 inches, put in a 2-inch layer of pea gravel at that depth, then mixed organic matter with the excavated soil before putting it back.

This plan utilizes a number of groundcovers and ferns; by judicious use of plants, you can grow them either in damp soil or in dry soil. Gardens with seasonal shade from deciduous trees and bushes leafing out will have sunshine available for part of the year. To take advantage of this available light, plant a few bulbs like crocus for early or late bloom.

The amazing thing about combining bulbs and other herbaceous plants in such a seasonal shade garden is their sequence of bloom. Take tulips and hostas, for example. We had a beautiful section in our northern garden consisting of a mix of hybrid fringed tulips including 'Blue Heron' and 'Burgundy Lace' interplanted with *Hosta lancifolia* and the fragrant hosta (*H. plantaginea*). They were all set out underneath a Japanese maple that began to leaf out as the tulips were blooming but before the hostas had hit their stride. As the tulip leaves died back, the hostas spread and covered them up. The result was garden color from early spring to the fall frosts with never a hint of bare earth in between.

The following shade garden is suitable for open shade, a condition that results from tall trees that allow a great deal of bright light to penetrate to the ground below. The areas immediately around the tree trunks are left open for house plants to spend the summer.

A Shade Garden

The pathways can be fieldstone, brick, or pine needles. And at the center of the garden is a birdbath, but this also could be a garden sculpture.

A color rendering of this garden is found on page 13.

A List of Plants:

1. Ebony spleenwort (*Asplenium platyneuron*)
2. Maidenhair fern (*Adiantum pedatum*)
3. Japanese anemone (*Anemone hupehensis* 'September Charm')
4. Jack-in-the-pulpit (*Arisaema triphyllum*)
5. *Astilbe × arendsii* 'Bridal Veil', 'Montgomery', and 'Fanal'
6. *Bergenia* 'Bressingham White'
7. Fairy-candle (*Cimicifuga americana*)
8. Lenten rose (*Helleborus orientalis*)
9. *Hosta sieboldiana* 'Frances Williams'
10. *Ligularia dentata* 'Othello'
11. Honesty (*Lunaria annua*)
12. Gooseneck loosestrife (*Lysimachia clethroides*)
13. Royal fern (*Osmunda regalis* var. *spectabilis*)
14. Alleghany spurge (*Pachysandra procumbens*)
15. Virginia creeper (*Parthenocissus quinquefolia*)
16. Solomon's-seal (*Polygonatum commutatum*)

Other Suggested Plants:

Narrow-leaved hostas (*Hosta lancifolia*)
Christmas fern (*Polystichum acrostichoides*)
Myrtle (*Vinca minor*)

An Autumn Garden

For most Americans, winter, like an unwanted guest, comes early and stays late. Since many parts of the country see the flowers of May quickly wilt in the heat of July and August, the extended—and usually beautiful—weather of September, October, and part of November adds up to more days for gardening than the entire spring.

Even though the first frosts of autumn might have visited your garden by early September, you will note that the days again warm up. During the day crickets still chirp and at night, katydids still talk; only now they direct their comments to the harvest moon. Down at the pool or pond, the dragonflies still dart about. Back in the garden, both honeybees and bumblebees buzz around the still-opening flowers and if caught unaware by a quickly fading sky, curl up in the midst of some asters and wait for the next day's warming sun.

Leaves scutter across the lawn and drying blades of ornamental grasses rustle in the quickening breezes. Chickadees are once again heard at the edge of the vegetable garden—they summer in the deeper woods—and the tiny honks of the nuthatch echo the resounding honks of geese flying overhead. As Coleridge wrote:

"The one red leaf, the last of its clan,
That dances as often as dance it can."

We started our first autumn garden over fifteen years ago, taking advantage of many of the goldenrods and asters that bloomed in the fields surrounding our country home. Over the years the number of plants increased and we've added some larger plants and trees especially for their autumn color, but the asters and goldenrods still made a large contribution to that garden of warm days and chill nights.

A prominent feature of our autumn garden was a staghorn sumac (*Rhus typhina*). These trees are especially good in a small garden because if they're cut back in early spring, they become tropical-like shrubs during the summer and finish the season with a truly great display of flaming foliage in the fall. In our autumn garden plants under the sumac's canopy got filtered sun, but the rest of the garden was in full sun.

Another flower that belongs in every autumn garden is the aster. The fields are full of this glorious flower, and if you have access to such a wild landscape or the permission to remove some plants—they grow like weeds and are not in any danger of extinction—select some of the best colors in the fall, mark the plants well, dig them up the following spring, and move them to your garden. When they are established, cut them back to make them bushier, and look forward to an autumn blaze of color.

A color rendering of this garden is found on pages 14 and 15.

A List of Plants:

1. *Aster novae-angliae* 'Alma Potschke', 'Harrington's Pink', and 'September Ruby'
2. *Aster novi-belgii* 'Snow Fury'
3. *Boltonia asteroides* 'Snow Bank' and 'Pink Beauty'
4. *Chrysanthemum pacificum*
5. Autumn crocus (*Colchicum* 'Waterlily')
6. Winterberry (*Ilex verticillata*)
7. *Miscanthus sinensis* 'Silver Feather'
8. Purple moor grass (*Molinia caerulea* 'Variegata')
9. Obedient plant (*Physostegia virginiana*)

10. Staghorn sumac (*Rhus typhina*)
11. *Rudbeckia hirta* 'Gloriosa Daisy'
12. Stonecrop (*Sedum spectabile* 'Autumn Joy')
13. Goldenrods (*Solidago canadensis* 'Golden Mosa' and 'Nagshead')

Other Suggested Plants:

Purple coneflower (*Echinacea purpurea*)
Sneezeweed (*Helenium autumnale*)
Virginia creeper (*Parthenocissus quinquefolia*)
Variegated obedient plant (*Physostegia virginiana* 'Variegata')
Chinese lantern (*Physalis alkekengi*)

An Autumn Garden

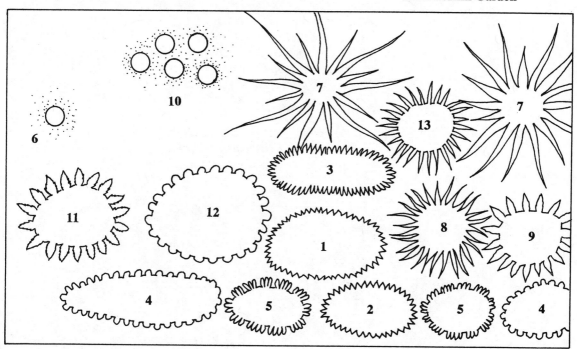

A Winter Garden

We go for many winter walks in the garden. After so many hours at a word processor or dealing with the vicissitudes of life, a walk in the fresh air, no matter how cold that air may be, is a very important thing to do. But a winter garden needs a plan. The majority of perennials that we recognize when the sun is high are frozen solid within the cold earth, and hopefully a layer of snow is providing them a blanket.

Had we world enough and time, I could actually see planting a garden designed just for winter enjoyment, but that really seems to be an impractical suggestion with today's constraints on the uses of land.

We take as much advantage as we can of trees with both interesting winter silhouettes and bark textures. And instead of putting the bird bath in storage, we install a small aquarium heater and find that the birds of winter are delighted to splash in the water, even on the coldest days.

We plant sedums and grasses for their dead but attractive flowers, trees like Russian olives and winterberries for their lively barks and berries, and willows and hazelnuts for their twisted branches. There are ferns with evergreen fronds and, in the right climate zone, lovely things like Lenten roses and evergreen groundcovers, plus ivies of many descriptions.

The cold may chill our noses and that ominous stripe of weak orange light across the western horizon may presage more snow, but it will not stop us from a walk in that winter garden.

A color rendering of this garden is found on page 16.

A List of Plants:

1. Gray birch (*Betula populifolia*)
2. Horsetail (*Equisetum hyemale*)
3. Evergreen wintercreeper (*Euonymus fortunei* 'Colorata')

A Winter Garden

4. English ivy (*Hedera helix* '238th Street')
5. Lenten rose (*Helleborus orientalis*)
6. Creeping juniper (*Juniperus horizontalis* 'Douglasii')
7. Purple moor grass (*Molinia caerulea* 'Variegata')
8. Sensitive fern (*Onoclea sensibilis*)
9. Mountain rhododendron (*Rhododendron catawbiense*)
10. Corkscrew willow (*Salix matsudana* 'Tortuosa')
11. Stonecrop (*Sedum spectabile* 'Autumn Joy')
12. Yucca (*Yucca filamentosa*)

Other Suggested Plants:

Russian olive (*Elaeagnus angustifolia*)
Siberian cypress (*Microbiota decussata*)
Staghorn sumac (*Rhus typhina*)

A Garden for a Rough-Cut Bank

You've seen it endless times, especially around new subdivisions: The developer has taken all the topsoil in the process of removing trees or has cut right through a grade, leaving the new owner with a rising bank of dirt on either side of the driveway. Or right behind the house the land rises up, but unfortunately, all the original plants that held that bank are now gone. The problem with these plots of land is that without expensive terracing using good landscape timbers and high stone walls, the bared earth will continue to erode and eventually more of the bank will fall.

In our New York garden we had such a bank with the bare earth about 6 feet high. Here I set large flagstones into the ground at an angle—starting from the bottom and working up—then interplanted with creeping junipers.

If a bank is not too high, a stone wall can be built in front, then filled with good soil, ready to grow any number of plants. Among the plants that work well in this situation are honeysuckles, wild sweet peas, daylilies, or American bittersweet (*Celastrus scandens*). This last plant isn't covered in the plant descriptions in this book; because it really is such a rampant vine, it's only suitable for the situations described here.

If the slope is at all gradual, the common daylily will do a superb job. I don't mean one of the thousands of immensely popular daylily cultivars, but the wild daylily (*Hemerocallis fulva*), found growing along roadsides throughout America and usually blooming in June and July.

Since there is no one way to predict what the exact physical conditions of a bank garden could be, this garden is presented in a very generalized way.

A color rendering of this garden is found on page 17.

A List of Plants:

1. Hay-scented fern (*Dennstaedtia punctilobula*)
2. English ivy (*Hedera helix*)
3. Common tawny daylily (*Hemerocallis fulva*)
4. Creeping juniper (*Juniperus horizontalis*)
5. Fountain grass (*Pennisetum alopecuroides*)

Other Suggested Plants:

Bishop's weed (*Aegopodium podagraria* 'Variegatum')
Wild sweet pea (*Lathyrus latifolius*)
Staghorn sumac (*Rhus typhina*)
Variegated purple moor (*Molinia caerulea* 'Variegata')
Virginia creeper (*Parthenocissus quinquefolia*)

**A Garden for
a Rough-Cut Bank**

A Few Stylized Gardens

For various reasons, some landscape designers have become the worst of modern artists, producing so-called botanical gardens dozens of acres in size but adorned with only two or three species of plants. Then there are upscale decorating magazines that feature reflecting pools surrounded with gilded concrete frogs; burnt-out automobiles combined with living hedges (I saw such an installation featuring burn-scarred tree branches stuffed into a burned-out Volkswagen at a public garden at the tip of Manhattan); tree trunks and rocks spray-painted with fluorescent colors, including white birch trees banded with fuchsia Day-Glo paint; plastic pipes in unending combinations; and large numbers of artificial plants. These gimmicks look like second-rate album covers for second-rate rock stars, yet intelligent people pay large sums of money for such inappropriate gimcracks. For garden color, nothing beats living plants used in various combinations.

For garden sculpture, you need not have museum quality art. Due to the wonders of poured concrete, a number of today's garden centers stock Japanese lanterns, cupids, and other statues without resorting to garden gnomes. Also look at the number of very attractive concrete drainage tiles available. Finally, seek out the local scrap-iron supplier or someone who deals with ornaments removed from demolished houses.

The following gardens are for difficult situations and include a few very tough plants used in combination with stone, rock, and sculpture. They are for full or filtered sun.

The first is based on a diamond shape and uses sedums and thymes, alternating with charcoal-brown pea gravel and a crushed stone mulch. The second is a cross using ornamental grasses. The third is a chevron made of Japanese blood grass and creeping juniper. The fourth uses yuccas and blue fescues in combination with a large rock.

Color renderings of these gardens are found on pages 18 and 19.

A List of Plants for Garden 1:

1. *Sedum acre*
2. *Sedum spurium* 'Bronze Carpet'
3. *Sedum spurium* 'Dragon's Blood'
4. *Thymus* × *citriodorus*

Other Suggested Plants:

Dwarf Japanese juniper (*Juniperus procumbens* 'Nana')
Sedum kamtschaticum

A List of Plants for Garden 2:

1. Blue fescue (*Festuca ovina* var. *glauca*)
2. Variegated maiden grass (*Miscanthus sinensis* 'Variegatus')
3. Fountain grass (*Pennisetum alopecuroides*)

A List of Plants for Garden 3:

1. Japanese blood grass (*Imperata cylindrica* 'Rubra')
2. Dwarf Japanese juniper (*Juniperus procumbens* 'Nana')

A List of Plants for Garden 4:

1. Blue fescue (*Festuca ovina* var. *glauca*)
2. Yucca (*Yucca filamentosa*)

Garden 1

Garden 2

Garden 3

Garden 4

Stylized Gardens

Edge of the Pond Garden

After we installed our ¾-acre pond across from our garden in upstate New York, we were left with a number of problems. Part of the pond site was excavated and its boundaries were field and fresh meadow; but part consisted of a comma-shaped bank built up of soil taken from the digging. The inside of the comma was water, the top was flat and about 3 feet wide, but the outside sloped down about 6 feet and met the edge of the adjoining woods.

Our first concern was to control potential erosion, so all the bare earth was planted in late fall with a specially formulated mix of grasses recommended by the local extension service (chiefly red fescue, *Festuca rubra*) and with bird's-foot trefoil (*Lotus corniculatus*) to root deep and not mind the potential damp. The next spring we turned to planting the edge of the pond. Although many plants appeared as if by magic (but more from seeds brought in on the feet of birds), they did not always have the floral beauty that we wanted to see reflected in the pond. Therefore we used a number of different plants to bring a casual, yet planned, look to the pond's edge.

We also naturalized many hundreds of daffodils and narcissus close enough to the edge of the pond to produce reflections from most vantage points.

If you have an earth- or clay-bottomed pond planted with waterlilies—especially the wild varieties—keep them under observation because they frequently begin to grow out of control. If they appear to be multiplying rapidly, root some of them up.

And if you have a small garden and want a pool but have no desire to bring in bulldozers or a team of workmen hired to dig a hole and pour concrete, try making your own pond. Dig a small hole and line it with a sheet of the new PVC or butyl rubber pool liners. A 10-by-16-foot liner is available for about $160. This will line a 6-by-12-foot pond about 18 inches deep and hold an incredible 810 gallons.

With a pond this size you can have the enjoyment of planting the pond edges as well as grow waterlilies and other aquatic plants. Just remember that if you want flowering water plants, your pond needs least six hours of sun a day.

One particular wild plant in this pond garden is usually introduced by the bird life and needs some introduction. This is the common rush (*Juncus effusus*). It's not included in the plant descriptions in this book because it is strictly a wild plant that has been replaced in the nursery trade by a number of notable cultivars. These include 'Spiralis', with the usual slender stems twisted like a corkscrew; 'Aureus Striatus', having yellow stripes; and 'Zebrinus', with broadly striped greenish white stems. But none of the cultivars is as tough as the original native plant.

No wild water plant is more beautiful along the edge of a pond than the common rush. The narrow, pointed stems—often with clumps of seed near the tops—become a Japanese print, its lovely reflections echoed in the water beside it. It is common along most back roads with drainage ditches, and you will often find it growing in abandoned pastures and cow fields.

If you have an earthen pond, chances are it's already there, and if you install a small garden pool, try growing it in a large clay pot. It grows well in full sun or partial shade.

A color rendering of this garden is found on page 20.

A List of Plants:

1. *Astilbe* spp.
2. Siberian iris (*Iris sibirica*)
3. Common rush (*Juncus effusus*)
4. *Ligularia stenocephala* 'The Rocket'
5. Maiden grass (*Miscanthus sinensis* 'Variegatus')
6. Prairie cord grass (*Spartina pectinata* 'Aureomarginata'
7. Eulalia grass (*Miscanthus sacchariflorus* 'Robustus')
8. Daffodils and narcissus (*Narcissus* spp.)

Other Suggested Plants:

Hardy geranium (*Geranium maculatum* 'Album')
Japanese iris (*Iris kaempferi*)

An Edge of the Pond Garden

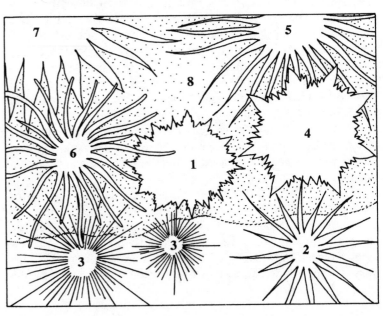

A Bog Garden

Even if part of your potential garden is damp or wet, there is no reason not to have a spectacular place for flowers. Many of the plants listed in the plant descriptions in this book will do quite well when grown in moist or damp soil. Astilbes are a case in point. Although they will struggle along in full sun and dry soil, they grow even better in moist soil. Their roots will adapt to the soil right next to a running stream and produce fine foliage and many flowerings. They should have some shade from the hot noonday sun, especially in the southern parts of the country.

The common rush (described on page 51) is also well-adapted to the bog garden. Also, because a backyard bog garden is usually a limited size and the water stops at the edge of the pond liner, a few very invasive pond plants could be utilized here. These include two types of cattail: *Typha latifolia* 'Variegata', a plant with vertical green and white stripes that is not as invasive and is much more attractive than the species cattail; *T. angustifolia,* the narrow-leaved cattail, which bears graceful, slender leaves that look much more civilized than common cattails.

There are also cultivars of the common canna (*Canna* × *generalis*), called water cannas and developed by Longwood Gardens. The flowers look tropical and colors range from yellow to orange, red, or salmon. Plants adapt to water depths of 0 to 6 inches and grow up to 6 feet in full sun. In colder zones dig up the roots and store them over the winter in a warm basement.

Remember one thing about plants that prefer to live in wet soil: Never let them get dry. So if you're unsure whether your site will support bog conditions, mark the outline of your projected bog garden and excavate the soil at least to a 1-foot depth. Line the hole with a PVC or butyl rubber pool liner—don't use plastic garbage bags or the like since most will break down in a short time. Replace the soil but keep the bog area slightly below ground level so runoff from rain will continue to wet the soil.

If you happen to have an old bathtub or sink and a lot of time and muscle, bury one or the other after sealing the drain. Cover the edge with flat stones or bricks.

A color rendering of this garden is found on page 21.

A List of Plants:

1. Common canna (*Canna* × *generalis*)
2. Horsetails (*Equisetum hyemale*)
3. Rose mallow (*Hibiscus moscheutos* subsp. *palustris*)
4. Siberian iris (*Iris sibirica*)

5. Japanese iris (*Iris kaempferi*)
6. Common rush (*Juncus effusus*)
7. Gooseneck loosestrife (*Lysimachia clethroides*)
8. Variegated cattail (*Typha latifolia* 'Variegata')

A Bog Garden

A Raised Bed Garden

Sometimes the land we must use for gardening is just so poor that the only choice we have to improve the soil is to hire bulldozers and replace a foot or more of soil or bring in the dynamite and blast. If your situation is that bad, consider gardening in raised beds.

Instead of digging down, mark out the area and build it up about 2 or 3 feet above the ground level using pressure-treated railroad ties from the lumberyard (do not use creosote-treated ties). Miter the corners for a neat look. Connect the ties with galvanized nails or drill holes and use doweling for support. If you are not the carpenter type (and few of us really are), hire out the initial work or ask a friend or relative who can operate a circular or chain saw to help you with construction. Another possibility is to build low walls of concrete block, fieldstone, or brick. Fill in the new garden areas with purchased topsoil.

Retaining walls may also be made of fieldstones. In our upstate New York garden I hauled stones for a retaining wall without benefit of tractor or thousands of Egyptian slaves. The motto is: Slow and steady wins the race. Stones for our project came from a tumbledown wall some 500 feet away. But you can also purchase them from nursery centers or, if you live near a large city, one of the many concrete and stone suppliers found there.

In our retaining wall the largest stones went for the bottom of the wall. The back edges of the stones were set an inch lower than the front so the finished wall slanted toward the hillside. In most cases the walls were no higher than 1½ feet.

If you plan to use new raised beds for typical perennials or vegetables, fill them with good topsoil. If you plan to grow many of the typical rock garden or scree plants, plants that require perfect drainage to prevent root rot, for every full load of topsoil add a half-load each of builder's sand and good leaf mold or composted manure.

Remember to allow soil in a raised bed to settle before planting. After the beds are half-filled with the soil, wet them thoroughly to help settle the soil. Let the beds sit overnight before adding the rest of the soil. Then let everything sit for a week or so before planting.

A color rendering of this garden is found on page 22.

A List of Plants:

1. Yarrow (*Achillea millefolium* 'Crimson Beauty' and 'Moonshine')
2. Purple coneflower (*Echinacea purpurea*)
3. Coralbells (*Heuchera micrantha* 'Palace Purple')

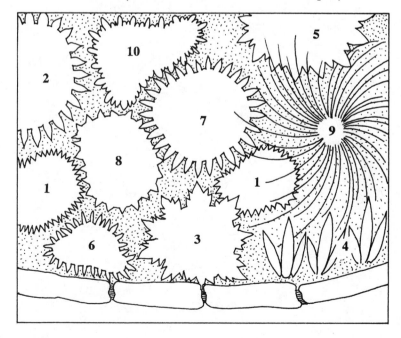

A Raised Bed Garden

4. Iris (*Iris germanica*) in mixed colors
5. Tree mallow (*Lavatera trimestris*)
6. Sundrops (*Oenothera tetragona* 'Fireworks')
7. Garden phlox (*Phlox maculata* 'Miss Lingard')
8. Orange coneflower (*Rudbeckia fulgida* 'Goldsturm')
9. Fountain grass (*Pennisetum alopecuroides*)
10. Boltonia (*Boltonia asteroides* 'Snowbank')

A Garden of Bulbs

One of the most attractive terraced gardens we ever created was a spring bulb garden. The retaining wall for this garden took exactly seventy-two 6-inch-wide fieldstones, some small (about a foot long) and some large (between 1½ and 2 feet long). After installing the wall, we had a grassy rectangular area that measured 16 by 8 feet and was about 20 inches above the original grade at the front.

After the retaining wall was in place, I spaded up the original soil, turning the hunks of turf over, roots up. Next I added ten bags of topsoil (on sale at the nearby garden center) and four bags of composted cow manure (sheep is just as good) that was also on year-end sale. After mixing everything thoroughly, I left it all to settle for a few weeks until the bulbs arrived.

By carefully selecting the bulbs and mixing them with flowering onions and lilies we were able to provide bloom for more than three months. In the spots planted with spring-blooming bulbs,

A Garden of Bulbs

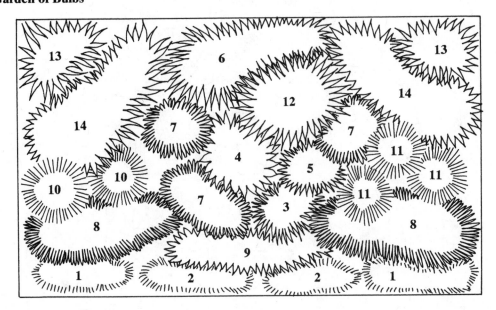

after their leaves had ripened, we planted a variety of annuals, including a great many geraniums carried over from year to year as rooted cuttings.

This plan includes mixtures of lilies for naturalization, something you'll find in many nurseries.

A color rendering of this garden is found on page 23.

A list of plants:

1. *Crocus angustifolius*
2. *Crocus chrysanthus* 'Princess Beatrix', 'E. A. Bowles', and 'Ladykiller'
3. Fireflame tulip (*Tulipa acuminata*)
4. Waterlily tulip (*Tulipa kaufmanniana*)
5. Tulip (*Tulipa tarda*)
6. *Narcissus* 'King Alfred' and 'Mrs. R. O. Backhouse'
7. *Narcissus poeticus*
8. Spanish bluebells (*Endymion hispanicus*)
9. Lily leek (*Allium moly*)
10. Chives (*Allium schoenoprasum*)
11. Chinese chives (*Allium tuberosum*)
12. Chinese trumpet lily (*Lilium* 'Black Dragon')
13. Gold-banded lily (*Lilium auratum*)
14. Lily naturalizing mixture

An English Perennial Border

No matter how much we rail against them, when push comes to shove, most gardeners adore English perennial borders. The problem with bringing such gardens to most of the United States and Canada concerns climate. Except for a few areas along the Eastern Seaboard and parts of the Pacific Northwest, not many areas get the needed annual rainfall, or the cool summers and warm winters that most of the British Isles are lucky to enjoy.

But English borders are as much a matter of design as anything else. The following plans are based on the structure of an English garden, but use tougher and hardier plants to achieve the effect.

The first thing to remember about an English border is the number of plants that it will include. English beds and borders do not have a lot of mulch showing, or for that matter, bare earth. If a prescribed plant has not grown enough to fill in its required area, English gardeners move in temporary potted plants—even greenhouse plants with their pots buried in the earth—or set out annuals until that space is full.

English borders are usually wide—at least 6 to 8 feet—with the taller plants set at the rear. Behind the border is often an old stone wall, a line of shrubbery, or the edge of a wooded tangle to offer the plants a dark contrasting background rather than bright open air. In the border pictured on pages 60 and 61, I've used *Cotinus coggygria* 'Royal Purple', white forsythia (*Abeliophyllum distichum*), and flowering raspberry (*Rubus odoratus*), not only for the flowers but as a fast-growing background, an important thing to plan if you don't have fifty years of time to wait for a line of boxwoods to mature.

Areas where similar colors are grouped, for example a mix of all-white flowers, are best separated from other color combinations by discrete bands of green. The result is similar to a patchwork quilt with color patches on a green background. Colors should be matched by intensity or brightness.

Try to group plants by their time of bloom so you have masses of bloom rather than one peony here and one poppy there, separated by five feet of green. If a spot in our border is a bit blah, I make a beeline for the nearest nursery center and have been known to plant petunias or even marigolds (if nothing else is available) to add color to the green of unblooming plants.

Finally there is the element of surprise. Surprise in the garden is planting something where the visitor or other gardeners would never expect to find it.

In the midst of a bed of cord grass (*Spartina pectinata* 'Aureomarginata'), I placed some *Hemerocallis altissima*. Then in July, the night-blooming daylily blossoms tower on their 7-foot scapes above the mounds of grass leaves. The combination looks like a plant hybrid that could only result from other-world cloning. And it's a garden surprise.

At one end of our perennial border I planted five plants of *Sedum* 'Autumn Joy' in front of a large yucca (*Yucca filamentosa*). When the yucca is in flower, it's spectacular, and when the sedums bloom, that end of the garden is exciting again. But after the yucca blooms faded and before the sedums changed from green to red, something was needed. So I set out some orange glads, their corms timed to bloom in that July period when color was needed.

If you do not have the room for a long, deep border, think about developing a rectangular or circular bed of perennials and at the center make a small terrace of flagstones or even concrete paving blocks. Then find a large terra-cotta pot (there are some excellent plastic imitations at nursery centers), and fill it full of bright annuals. Finally, let a few small ivy plants trail over the edge of the pot. The look is entirely English.

I have used *Allium moly* in the border for spring color. When the flowering is over and the leaves ripen and die, replant this area with pink geraniums.

A color rendering of the English border is found on pages 24 and 25.

A List of Plants:

1. Purple smoke tree (*Cotinus coggygria* 'Royal Purple')
2. Daylily (*Hemerocallis* 'Stella de Oro')
3. Green and Gold (*Chrysogonum virginianum*)
4. Shasta daisy (*Chrysanthemum × superbum*)
5. Korean lilac (*Syringa patula* 'Miss Kim')
6. Thread-leaved coreopsis (*Coreopsis verticillata*)
7. *Allium moly* followed by pink geraniums
8. Columbine (*Aquilegia* 'McKana Hybrids')
9. Boltonia (*Boltonia asteroides* 'Snowbank' and 'Pink Beauty')
10. Knapweed (*Centaurea macrocephala*)
11. New York aster (*Aster novi-belgii* 'Alert')
12. Butterfly weed (*Asclepias tuberosa*)
13. Gold-banded lily (*Lilium auratum*)
14. Purple coneflower (*Echinacea purpurea*)
15. Queen-of-the-prairie (*Filipendula rubra*)
16. Great globe thistle (*Echinops sphaerocephalus*)
17. Orange coneflower (*Rudbeckia fulgida* 'Goldsturm')
18. White forsythia (*Abeliophyllum distichum*)
19. Flowering raspberry (*Rubus odoratus*)
20. Zebra grass (*Miscanthus sinensis* 'Zebrinus')
21. *Phlox paniculata* 'Mt. Fuji'
22. Spiderwort (*Tradescantia* 'Snow Cap')
23. Sundrops (*Oenothera tetragona* 'Fireworks')
24. Stonecrop (*Sedum spectabile* 'Autumn Joy')
25. Stonecrop (*Sedum aizoon*)
26. Daisy (*Chrysanthemum pacificum*)
27. Rose-of-Sharon (*Hibiscus syriacus*)
28. *Hydrangea quercifolia* 'Snow Queen'
29. Balloon flower (*Platycodon grandiflorus*)
30. New England aster (*Aster novae-angliae* 'Harrington's Pink')
31. Yucca (*Yucca filamentosa*)
32. False indigo (*Baptisia australis*)
33. Tree peony (*Paeonia* 'Age of Gold')
34. Plume poppy (*Macleaya cordata*)
35. Texas bluestar (*Amsonia tabernaemontana*)

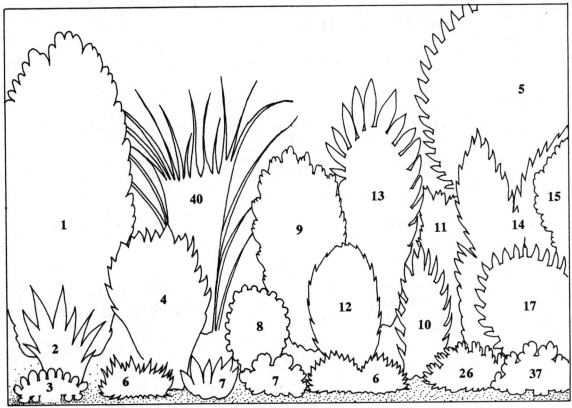

An English Perennial Border

36. Northern sea oats (*Chasmanthium latifolium*)
37. Lady's mantle (*Alchemilla vulgaris*)
38. Willow-leaved sunflower (*Helianthus salicifolius*)
39. Bugleweed (*Ajuga reptans* 'Atropurpurea')
40. Maiden grass (*Miscanthus sinensis* 'Gracillimus')

Other Suggested Plants:

White Meidiland rose (*Rosa* 'White Meidiland')
Japanese anemone (*Anemone hupehensis* 'September Charm')
Goldenrod (*Solidago canadensis* 'Nagshead')

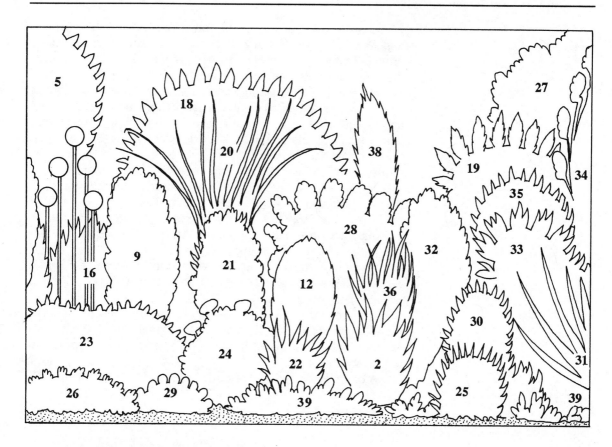

A Perennial Cutting Garden

Flowers are meant not only for garden enjoyment but for cutting, too. Most cutting gardens are built around annuals, but consider having such a garden dedicated to perennial flowers. Then when you have a temptation to arrange a magnificent bouquet for a special lunch or dinner, go to it without harming the perennial beds and borders. Be sure to include a number of daffodils and tulips so there will be plenty of spring flowers.

Remember that a cutting garden is a working garden so any thoughts given to planting arrangements should revolve around *lebensraum* or cultural demands, not considerations of form and color. Leave plenty of pathways so you can easily get to the flowers you want.

Since cutting gardens are usually put in out-of-the-way places, often where the ground has never been used for a garden before, make sure the soil is well-worked and reasonably fertile. But don't overdo with a lot of fertilizers; too much leads to lush growth and fewer flowers. If you are starting a garden in virgin soil—especially if it is very poor soil—work in a few bags of composted manure along with compost from your pile.

Blooming plants use more water than non-blooming plants, so be sure that a source of water is nearby. All those petals unfurl and expand because of the pressure of water moving through their veins. Water regularly and look for signs of wilting. When applying water, be sure to soak the soil thoroughly. If you water only lightly, most of the water evaporates before helping plants.

To conserve water in the cutting garden, use mulches. Bark chips or pine needles—or some locally available mulch like peanut husks or cocoa-bean hulls—will help to hold water in the soil by cutting down on surface evaporation. Mulch extended to your garden pathways makes walking easier and cleaner.

If you have the space, add a few annuals like cosmos (*Cosmos bipinnatus*), sweet peas (*Lathyrus odoratus*), godetias (*Clarkia amoena*), and even some glads.

Another plant that I try to keep in the cutting garden is the giant hogweed (*Heracleum mantegazzianum*), not for fresh flowers but for the dried seed heads, a truly spectacular addition to any winter bouquet.

A color rendering of this garden is found on pages 26 and 27.

A List of Plants:

1. Columbines (*Aquilegia* 'McKana Hybrids')
2. Godetias (*Clarkia amoena* 'Albatross' and 'Brilliant')
3. New York aster (*Aster novi-belgii*)
4. Shasta daisy (*Chrysanthemum* × *superbum*)
5. Fairy-candle (*Cimicifuga racemosa*)
6. Purple coneflower (*Echinacea purpurea*)
7. Sneezeweed (*Helenium autumnale* 'Butterpat' and 'Moerheim Beauty')
8. Giant hogweed (*Heracleum mantegazzianum*)
9. Mixed glads
10. Cosmos (*Cosmos bipinnatus* 'Candy Stripe' and 'Purity')
11. Coralbells (*Heuchera sanguinea* 'Chatterbox')
12. Yarrow (*Achillea* 'Moonshine' and 'Fire king')
13. Sweet pea (*Lathyrus latifolius* 'Fragrant Beauty')
14. *Dahlia* 'Showpiece Hybrids Mixed'

A Perennial Cutting Garden

Edge of the Meadow Garden

Today the meadow garden is as much a garden fashion statement as an attractive way to grow plants and flowers. The concept was first discussed in the late 1800s by William Robinson, the man who suggested planting hardy bulbs in meadow grass and naturalizing wildflowers under trees on great lawns.

But the idea hit the big time in the 1980s with the appearance of endless seed collections selected by various professionals and designed to make meadow gardens look as simple as repotting a geranium.

Well it's a lot harder to establish such gardens than just opening up a can and sprinkling seeds on the ground—as you would discover by reading the small print on the labels. But such gardens are worth the effort, especially when you see how beautiful such a garden can be and how easy it is to take care of, once established.

If you garden at a country house, you may have a nearby meadow, too large for cutting with the lawn mower but perfect for planting suitable wildflowers.

First, consider cloud cutting. Between the front of your meadow and the existing lawn, cut the last swath of grass in graceful curves like the edges of clouds. In the fall of the first year cut only the front third of the meadow. This will also be the edge of your future edge of the meadow garden. The second year, cut the original swath of the meadow plus the next third. Finally, the third year, cut the entire meadow.

The result is that the third of the meadow closest to the house changes the most. But the other parts, when allowed to mature, are open to all sorts of different field wildflowers and grasses from seeds brought by the wind and by birds. This method of cutting looks exceptionally elegant when applied to the side of a hill.

If you are starting a meadow garden by digging into existing meadow, the job is a bit harder. Some of the existing plants that will compete with your additions must be cleared away to give the new plants a healthy start, not only with available sunlight, but with water, too.

If your meadow garden is starting out in a subdivision with bare ground backed by an adjacent field or meadow, you have the easiest row to hoe; the garden plan should be easy to follow, especially when using potted perennials rather than seeds.

Among the wildflowers that are suited for such a garden are Queen Anne's lace (*Daucus carota* var. *carota*), gill-over-the-ground (*Glechoma hederacea*), common daylilies (*Hemerocallis fulva*), chicory (*Cichorium intybus*), wild goldenrod (*Solidago canadensis*), and a fascinating number of wild grasses.

The following plan assumes the edge-of-the-meadow garden will be backed up by cloud cutting. But it would work just as well if the background were a woodland lot, a line of shrubs, or a very steep hillside.

A color rendering of this garden is found on page 28.

A List of Plants:

1. Queen Anne's lace (*Daucus carota* var. *carota*)
2. Gill-over-the-ground (*Glechoma hederacea*)
3. Tawny daylily (*Hemerocallis fulva*)
4. Chicory (*Cichorium intybus*)
5. Wild goldenrod (*Solidago canadensis*)
6. Purple coneflower (*Echinacea purpurea*)
7. Bottlebrush grass (*Hystrix patula*)
8. New England aster (*Aster novae-angliae*)
9. Pearly everlasting (*Anaphalis margaritacea*)
10. False indigo (*Baptisia australis*)
11. Yarrow (*Achillea millefolium*)
12. Butterfly weed (*Asclepias tuberosa*)

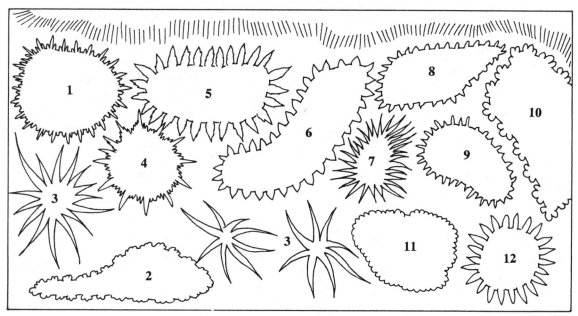

An Edge of the Meadow Garden

A Native Plant Garden

There's a big difference between a native plant garden and a wild garden. The first is evidenced by a use of plants that are native to the area in which the garden appears while the second is more of a philosophy of care than a way of planting.

Climates continually change. Three summers might be wet only to be followed by two that are very, very dry. Look around you as you drive through the area in which you live. When left to their own devices, plants, shrubs, and trees seem to survive almost anything that Nature hands out; obviously the problems begin when mankind starts to civilize the earth and makes artificial gardens.

The garden plan that follows is designed for the East Coast of the United States in areas that have winter temperatures that fall below 35°F. But they could just as easily be designed for any other area.

The first thing to do when planning such a garden is to check with the local county extension agent for a list of native and wild plants found where your garden is planned and for a source of supply. Also check the Appendix B of this book for a listing of regional nurseries that supply native plants.

If you're thinking of going out to collect native plants and wildflowers for your garden—don't! Never disturb any of these plants, especially those that are endangered or protected, unless they stand in the way of a developer's machinery. Each plant that disappears from the wild represents a weakening and impoverishment of our natural world. And never buy wildflowers from the back end of a pickup truck at a farmer's market. The people usually selling these plants have ripped them from the woods and fields, not patiently propagated them over many seasons like the majority of wildflower nurseries do. It takes six to seven years for a trillium to be mature enough to flower. That means a nursery must care for seedlings year after year, and every moment of that time costs money. If you find a trillium for $2.98, turn the other way and hope the pillagers will eventually get the message and stop.

I don't suggest that you turn your whole yard into a native plant garden. You will see spaces in the accompanying plans for a number of plant choices. But the backbone of the garden could be made up of native plants. Thus whatever the fates decree in the way of weather, much of your garden can survive.

A color rendering of this garden is found on page 29.

A List of Plants:

1. Texas blue star (*Amsonia tabernaemontana*)
2. Hardy geranium (*Geranium maculatum*)
3. Northern sea oats (*Chasmanthium latifolium*)
4. Swamp sunflower (*Helianthus angustifolius*)

A Native Plant Garden

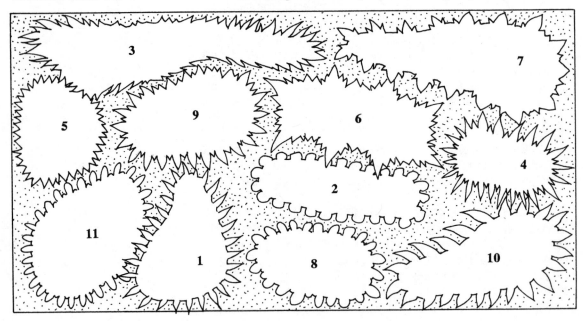

5. Sneezeweed (*Helenium autumnale*)
6. Coralbells (*Heuchera sanguinea*)
7. Rose mallow (*Hibiscus moscheutos* subsp. *palustris*)
8. Creeping phlox (*Phlox stolonifera*)
9. Obedient plant (*Physostegia virginiana*)
10. Solomon's-seal (*Polygonatum commutatum*)
11. Bouncing Bet (*Saponaria officinalis*)

A Wild Garden

Wild gardens are those left entirely to their own devices; work is kept to a minimum. If insects attack, they are only destroyed if everything in sight is threatened. A few chewed leaves are considered changes in texture and not an excuse to spray. The hand of man is always in the garden but it's never directly in evidence.

Wild gardens do not work in every situation. A border of well-known perennials could be allowed to run wild but would eventually fail. Many of the plants used for perennial borders are cultivars bred for color or size of blossom; in the breeding they lose a great deal of their stamina. And while well-maintained front yard gardens are now quite acceptable, it would be a special affront to neighbors who take care of lawn and garden to let your front lawn become an unruly jungle of wild weeds.

Wild gardens are exceptional for a number of reasons, chiefly because they need less fussing and maintenance than their more cultured counterparts. If finding time for gardening is a problem, one of the best ways to reduce the number of hours you spend working in the garden is to grow plants that naturally flourish in the sort of conditions present on your property. That means you should analyze your property by answering the following questions:

- *Is your climate wet or dry?* If you're in a dry area, remember that a wild garden should not be watered unless the weather pattern is really off the norm and failure to water will cause many plants to die. If your climate is wet, choose plants that prefer moist or wet feet.
- *Is there sun or shade?* Many wildflowers bloom in the first rush of spring before overhead trees leaf out and then adapt to shade. Other plants demand full sun in order to perform. Here's a case where a small sketch of your property showing what has sun and what hasn't is a very handy thing to have.
- *Are there natural features that will work to your garden's benefit?* That giant rock at the left of the driveway, that dip in the backyard where the drain from the basement to the back of

the lot settled, or that wooded lot at the corner of your property, are all natural features that could work to your benefit in a garden design. So check your landscape for such landmarks that could be used as a centerpiece to a wild garden.

- *What kind of soil do you have?* Native plants and wildflowers have different requirements when it comes to soil. Some, like black-eyed Susans, will grow in pure clay while others need a soil that is liberally laced with humus and leaf litter. So make sure you match up plant likes and dislikes before starting the garden.

One last note: You will be amazed by the number of fascinating insects that will appear to devour the destructive bugs. If you think butterflies are beautiful wait until you see the shining carapace of a predatory ichneumon wasp.

A color rendering of this garden is found on page 30.

A List of Plants:

1. False indigo (*Baptisia australis*)
2. Knapweed (*Centaurea macrocephala*)
3. Fairy-candles (*Cimicifuga americana* and *C. racemosa*)
4. Purple coneflower (*Echinacea purpurea*)
5. Great globe thistle (*Echinops sphaerocephalus*)
6. Queen-of-the-prairie (*Filipendula rubra*)
7. Bottlebrush grass (*Hystrix patula*)
8. Plume poppy (*Macleaya cordata*)
9. Sundrops (*Oenothera fruticosa*)
10. Variegated cord grass (*Spartina pectinata* 'Aureomarginata')

A Wild Garden

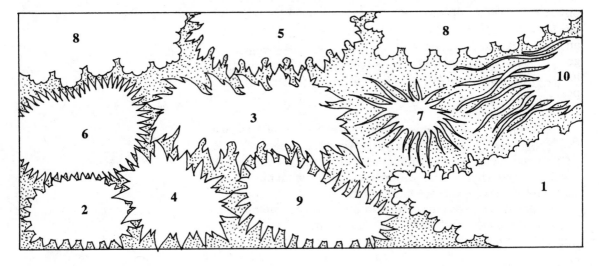

A Patio Garden

Tomb paintings from ancient Egypt show gardens of potted plants. Flowerpots from classical Greece look amazingly like those of the present day and held not only decorative and floriferous annuals and perennials but shrubs and trees as well. The practice of growing plants in pots is just as valid today as it was two millennia ago.

Many people wish to garden but often lack the necessary land or, if living in apartments or condominiums, have at best a small terrace or balcony space. Thank heavens for containers. The plants growing in pots on that terrace can be watered whenever they need it without a great deal of fuss. If you will be away for the weekend, the pots can be moved to a shady spot and given extra watering before you leave. As flowers fade, new plants can be brought in for a change in your flower horizons.

All the pots I use are earthenware, and are washed every fall and used again and again. If you must use plastic pots, hide them in more decorative containers. Use a soil mix with plenty of sand and organic matter and fertilize every three weeks or so. The continual action of water seeping through the soil and out the drainage holes in pot bottoms removes important nutrients.

Another great thing about container gardening is that when the first frosts come in autumn, you can cover the pots with newspapers or old towels for protection. Then on those warm days in Indian summer, your garden will continue to delight when other gardens are through.

And don't forget patio water gardens. I have a very large *Juncus californicus* that sends out stems up to 6 feet high, each stem-tip adorned with tiny clusters of seeds. It's a very attractive plant that in nature must have water up to its crown. So for the patio, I merely set its black plastic pot into a lovely old pottery jar and placed it with my terra-cotta-potted clivia (*Clivia miniata*), a green-glazed pottery jar holding tuberous begonias, and some lovely red-leafed caladiums residing in an old Chinese pot of blue porcelain.

A color rendering of a patio garden is found on page 31.

A List of Plants:

1. Japanese anemone (*Anemone hupehensis* 'September Charm')
2. *Aster novi-belgii* 'Snow Cushion'
3. Assorted daylilies (*Hemerocallis* cultivars)
4. Coralbells (*Heuchera sanguinea* 'White Cloud' and *H. micrantha* 'Palace Purple')
5. Assorted hostas (*Hosta fortunei, H. lancifolia, H. plan-*

taginea, H. 'Shade Fanfare', and *H. sieboldiana* 'Frances Williams'
6. Tree mallow (*Lavatera trimestris*)
7. Stonecrop (*Sedum spectabile* 'Autumn Joy')
8. Blue fescue (*Festuca ovina* var. *glauca*)

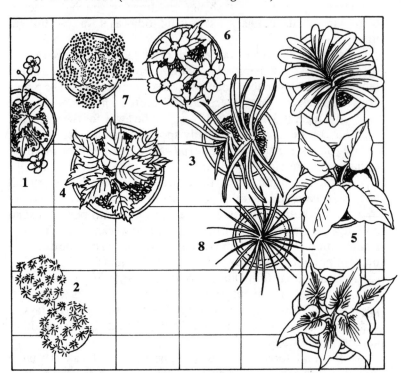

A Patio Garden

A Shrub and Small Tree Border

Shrub borders are perfect foils to use as backgrounds for perennial borders. They are especially suited for land along the edge of a driveway or nearby road. Not only will they filter noise and dust in such situations, they add a bit of mystery to your property.

In our North Carolina garden, the local road has a 3- to 4-foot shoulder before the land drops about 15 feet to gardens below. By planting this slope with various rhododendrons, forsythia, and more unusual small trees and shrubs, we no longer worry about cutting or weeding that bank, yet it provides garden interest all year long. Shrubs in a rough row underplanted with ferns, hostas, or other perennials, or shrubs turned into hedges, make great delineators that bring privacy to various garden areas or create division lines around a property. They also deter dogs and can hide an unwanted view.

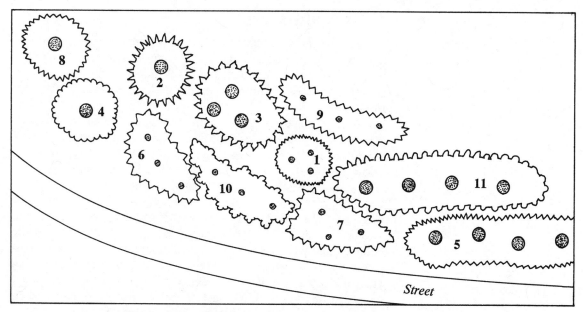

Street

Try to buy balled-and-burlapped or container-grown shrubs. Not only are they easier to plant, they are also easier to arrange. When planting a shrub remember that, once installed, it will be there for a long time. Most shrubs are large enough after a few years of growth to make moving them an impractical pursuit, so the initial planning is very important. It's easy to move a container around if you choose to make changes in a garden plan. Make sure that any prepared holes are large enough to receive the shrub.

A special feature of the following shrub garden is the continual bloom from the white and yellow forsythia of early spring, to the summer's rose-of-Sharon and smoke tree blossoms, to the lasting flowers of the hydrangea.

A color rendering of this garden is found on pages 32 and 33.

A Shrub and Small Tree Border

A list of plants:

1. White forsythia (*Abeliophyllum distichum*)
2. Serviceberry (*Amelanchier canadensis*)
3. Gray birch (*Betula populifolia*)
4. Smoke tree (*Cotinus coggygria*)
5. Russian olive (*Elaeagnus angustifolia*)
6. *Forsythia × intermedia*
7. *Forsythia suspensa*
8. Rose-of-Sharon (*Hibiscus syriacus*)
9. Winterberry (*Ilex verticillata*)
10. *Hydrangea quercifolia* 'Snow Queen'
11. Mountain rhododendron (*Rhododendron catawbiense*)

A Vertical Garden

Every summer I plant moonflowers (*Ipomoea alba*) to twine their way up a trellis set up somewhere in the garden close to the house. Once they begin to bloom, they charm everyone who ever sits on our terrace to look at twilight sky and revel in the cool night air.

A vertical garden is one of the best solutions to the problem of growing plants where space is at a premium. Those walls that surround a city terrace or a suburban patio can be adapted to allow the growth of vines, both annual and perennial.

Square posts of pressure-treated lumber or round posts of cedar or graceful arches made of pipe can be used in the backyard to support many different vines. Plastic trellis of good design and 4-by-8-foot screens of latticed wood are common throughout the country at any number of garden centers. Even squares or rectangles of stock 2-by-4s can be strung with wire to support searching vines. Rolled-up chicken wire packed with sphagnum moss or peat moss can be used to make postmodern columns, which are then planted with ivies or cucumbers and gourds. A tripod of three branches will soon be hidden underneath the burgeoning growth of a honeysuckle or a scarlet runner bean (*Phaseolus coccineus*).

And for gardeners who know about Monet's garden at Giverny and wish to add a French touch to their yards, think about making one or two *tuteurs* for holding up vines. *Tuteurs* means guardians or protectors in French, but in horticultural use they are plant props. They can either be purchased from fancy catalogs or, as city gardeners have discovered, a wind-collapsed umbrella can be set within an upright and buried pipe to make a good imitation *tuteur*.

A color rendering of this garden is found on page 34.

Suggested Plants:

Sweet autumn clematis (*Clematis maximowicziana*)
Virgin's bower (*Clematis virginiana*)
Climbing hydrangea (*Hydrangea anomala* subsp. *petiolaris*)
Wild sweet pea (*Lathyrus latifolius*)
Japanese honeysuckle (*Lonicera japonica*)
Silver fleece vine (*Polygonum aubertii*)

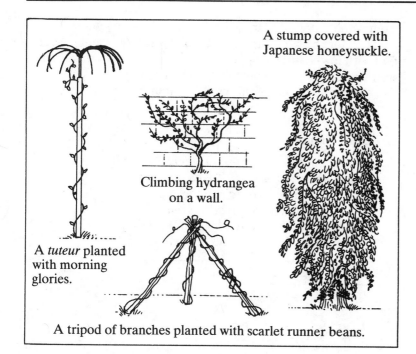

A stump covered with
Japanese honeysuckle.

Climbing hydrangea
on a wall.

A *tuteur* planted
with morning
glories.

A Vertical Garden

A tripod of branches planted with scarlet runner beans.

A Japanese Garden

The Japanese gardener can imagine an entire forest in the branches of one small tree and envision a mountain torrent ending in a waterfall with just a pile of pebbles divided by a tiny stream. Where dozens of flowers are needed to enchant the Western eye, just three flowers can become an entire garden to the Japanese mind.

The lands of Japan have always been crowded with people but even with a very small piece of land, the Japanese can create a garden world unto itself. Stones are used as the backbone of garden design. In Japan, these stones are not seen as mere lumps of granite but are instead endowed with the spirit of nature and represent timelessness, quietness, and stability. There even are correct ways to arrange them: A large stone at the garden's center with a smaller stone at the two o'clock position is good; but if the smaller stone is moved to the three o'clock spot the arrangement is bad. If more than two stones are used, they should be broken into odd-numbered groups of three, five, or seven.

The plan on page 74 features a Japanese-styled concrete snow lantern of the type usually found at any large garden center, a number of stepping stones, and a surface of gravel. The deck is made of pressure-treated lumber but could also be a terrace of flagstones or even of poured concrete. The top of a bird bath can be removed from its pottery post and used as a small reflecting pool.

And for the winter months, the snow lantern can be electrified with low-voltage garden lighting so evening snowfalls can be seen without venturing outside to light a candle.

A color rendering of this garden is found on page 35.

A List of Plants:

1. Maiden grass (*Miscanthus sinensis* 'Gracillimus')
2. *Juniperus procumbens* 'Nana'
3. Fragrant hosta (*Hosta plantaginea*)
4. Balloon flower (*Platycodon grandiflorus*)
5. Horsetails (*Equisetum hyemale*)
6. Star magnolia (*Magnolia tomentosa*)

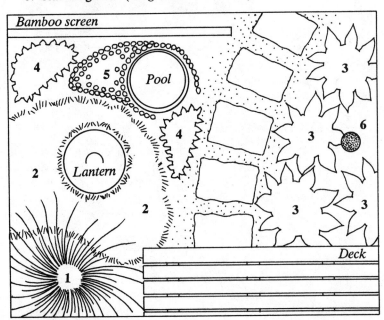

A Japanese Garden

A Dry Garden

After we remodeled our old farmhouse, the first topic of conversation at dinner parties was insulation. Nobody cared about the cost of heat until the first oil crisis of the 1970s—then everybody was concerned with saving money. Today, oil is still usually topic number one, but depending on where you live, close behind—and sometimes in front—is the subject of water. Water is being rationed by many communities and, nowadays, unless you have a deep well that is part of a plentiful water table, watering the garden is considered the same luxury as filling a swimming pool or washing a car.

The garden plan below features plants that, once they are settled, are quite impervious to water shortages whether from the clouds or from the sprinkler.

For mulching a dry garden, the best material to use is crushed stone. The gray color of stones goes well with the plants used in this garden. And crushed stone actually makes a contribution to watering. During the day the stones heat up and at night when temperatures usually fall, moisture condenses on the stones just as it would on a warm window in a cool room.

This garden surrounds a lawn made of a special seed mix for dry summers that includes red fescue (*Festuca rubra*) and buffalo grass (*Cynodon dactylon*). Check with your local extension service to see what drought-resistant grasses are best to use in your area of the country.

A color rendering of this garden is found on page 36.

A List of Plants:

1. Staghorn sumac (*Rhus typhina*)
2. Potentilla (*Potentilla fruticosa* 'Goldfinger')
3. Flowering raspberry (*Rubus odoratus*)
4. Yucca (*Yucca filamentosa*)
5. *Coreopsis grandiflora* 'Sunray'
6. Russian olive (*Elaeagnus angustifolia*)
7. Butterfly weed (*Asclepias tuberosa*)
8. Purple smoke tree (*Cotinus coggygria* 'Royal Purple')

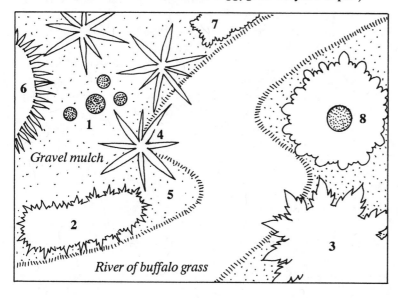

Gravel mulch

River of buffalo grass

A Dry Garden

A Rock Garden

We have always had a rock garden since our life in gardening began. Such gardens need not be large. Even an area of 5 by 10 feet that gets full sun for at least half the day is enough to display a bewildering variety of alpine plants. Choose them from the many small nurseries that offer hundreds of plants or grow your own from the thousands of species offered by the seed exchanges of the various rock garden societies.

The only other requirement is perfect drainage. Unlike other perennials, rock plants and alpines resent the slightest moisture that stays around their roots. Water they need, but it must pass through the soil quickly, or these plants may rot.

When making such a garden, either build a low raised bed or excavate poor soil to at least 1½ feet. Add a layer of rubble like pieces of crockery, bits of brick, stones, and pebbles, then cover it over with the original soil. But for every load of that soil, add a quarter-load of builder's sand, a quarter-load of pea gravel, and a quarter-load of composted cow or sheep manure.

After half the depth is filled with the mix, wet it thoroughly with the hose to help settle the soil between the pieces of rubble. Let it sit overnight before adding the rest. Then let everything sit and settle a few weeks before starting to plant.

A color rendering of this garden is found on page 37.

A List of Plants:

1. Colorado columbine (*Aquilegia caerulea*)
2. *Astilbe chinensis*
3. Bluegrass daisy (*Coreopsis auriculata* 'Nana')
4. Dwarf daylily (*Hemerocallis minor*)
5. Coralbells (*Heuchera sanguinea* 'Matin Bells')
6. Inula (*Inula ensifolia* 'Gold Star')
7. Dwarf bearded iris (*Iris pumila* and *I. pumila* 'Red Dandy')
8. Stonecrop (*Sedum kamtschaticum*)
9. Dwarf goldenrod (*Solidago canadensis* 'Golden Dwarf')
10. Blue fescue (*Festuca ovina* var. *glauca*)
11. Potentilla (*Potentilla fruticosa* 'Sunset')

Other Suggested Plants:

Coreopsis rosea
Hardy geranium (*Geranium maculatum* 'Album')
Balloon flower (*Platycodon grandiflorus* 'Mariesii')

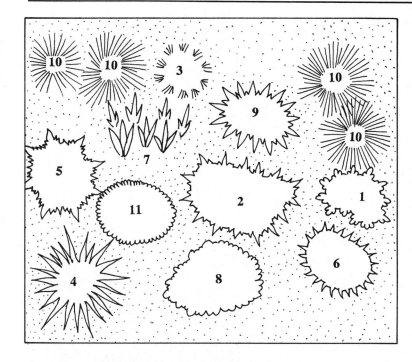

A Rock Garden

An Ornamental Grass Garden

No living garden can get by without some commitment to care and maintenance, but ornamental grasses come as close to being carefree as any plants I know. Grasses are very drought resistant. They are well-suited to growing in less than perfect ground and persist even when set out in the hot sun. As long as they are carefully watered immediately after setting in, they will quickly adapt to conditions that would severely tax other perennials.

When checking the plant listings, you will note that by choosing the proper grasses, you can plan a garden either for a dry plain or hillside or for a damper place where water is about much of the year. And don't overlook the fact that the larger grasses make very effective barriers, screening out unwanted sights and sounds.

When shopping for grasses, first check your local nurseries to see if they have any of the recommended plants growing in containers. Locally available grasses are often a larger size than those obtained by mail order and give the gardener a definite jump on the growing season.

The only real chore in dealing with grasses is the annual pruning of the larger types in early spring. Before the new growth begins, cut the dead stems and leaves to within 6 inches of ground level. The larger clump-forming grasses grow from the inside out,

An Ornamental Grass Garden

and you may notice the plants begin to die in the center after a few years. That is the time to divide the clumps with an axe, and pass on extra plants to other gardeners.

Flowers of ornamental grasses are often quite spectacular and beautiful, not only in the garden, but in dried and winter bouquets as well. If you wish to gather some grasses for such bouquets, pick the stems on a dry, sunny day after the dews of morning have evaporated. Try to pick flowers that have not yet fully opened, cutting the stems as long as you can. Strip off excess leaves and tie small bunches of stems together; then hang them upside down on wire coat hangers in a cool and dry place.

A color rendering of this garden is found on pages 38 and 39.

A List of Plants:

1. Eulalia grass (*Miscanthus sacchariflorus* 'Robustus')
2. Maiden grass (*Miscanthus sinensis* 'Gracillimus')
3. Zebra grass (*Miscanthus sinensis* 'Zebrinus')
4. Variegated purple moor grass (*Molinia caerulea* 'Variegata')
5. Fountain grass (*Pennisetum alopecuroides*)
6. Golden hakonechloa (*Hakonechloa macra* 'Aureola')

7. Northern sea oats (*Chasmanthium latifolium*)
8. Blue fescue (*Festuca ovina* var. *glauca*)

Other Suggested Plants:

> Variegated maiden grass (*Miscanthus sinensis* 'Variegatus')
> Variegated prairie cord grass (*Spartina pectinata* 'Aureomarginata')

A Dry Stream Garden

This particular garden is not for everyone, but it can be adapted to fit a very dry outlook, bringing the feel, if not the actual water, even to a desert. Or it can be used to work around that unwanted but often necessary drainage ditch located at the back of your property.

These drainage ditches are more common than most people suppose. Many large-scale tract developments feature drainage ditches, usually bottomed with water during wet springs, then drying out as summer advances.

Using the proper plants, these ditches can become attractive garden spots. Note that in the accompanying plan, a small pool has been included. For the pool use the new PVC plastic or butyl rubber pool liners at least 30 mil or more thick. There are a number of small waterlilies suited to such small ponds.

I've seen a number of very effective dry riverbed gardens in my travels. In all cases, the owners used local rocks—varying between small pebbles and gravel to large, rounded stones—to emulate a dry streambed.

The first was in eastern Pennsylvania on an acre lot at the edge of Lehighton, with suburbia on one side and a large cemetery on the other. Both areas of land were level but gently sloped to the ditch. By filling that ditch with river stones and planting conifers and grasses along the edge it became an oriental philosophy instead of a garden liability.

Another one was an installation at the Missouri Botanical Garden, where the dry brook curved and twisted along just like its wet brethren would, with large rocks carefully placed along the way to serve as backdrops for a number of drought-resistant plants.

A color rendering of this garden is found on page 40.

A List of Plants:

1. Variegated maiden grass (*Miscanthus sinensis* 'Variegatus')
2. Siberian iris (*Iris sibirica* 'Snow Queen')

3. Yucca (*Yucca filamentosa*)
4. Sundrops (*Oenothera tetragona* 'Yellow River')
5. Zebra grass (*Miscanthus sinensis* 'Zebrinus')
6. Maiden grass (*Miscanthus sinensis* 'Gracillimus')
7. Yarrow (*Achillea ptarmica* 'The Pearl' and *A. filipendulina* 'Coronation Gold')
8. Potentilla (*Potentilla fruticosa* 'Sunset')

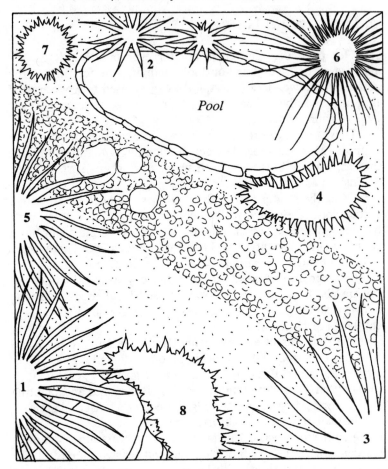

A Dry Stream Garden

Coreopsis verticillata

The Plant Descriptions

Flowering Plants

Botanical name: *Achillea* spp.
Common name: Yarrow.
Habitat: Ordinary garden soil; full sun; tolerates dryness.
Description: Upright perennials with lacy leaves on strong stems, often aromatic when crushed; flat clusters of small flowers in white, yellow, pink, or red; to 4 feet.
Period of bloom: Summer.
Propagation: By division spring or fall.
Zone: 3 to 4, depending on the species.

It's fitting that the first tough plant to be listed is yarrow. Why? Because for thousands of years the stems of yarrow have been tossed, then the resulting patterns read in order to fortell the future. The book used for interpretation is the Chinese *I Ching* or the *Changes of Chou* (according to legend, Confucius himself acted as one of the editors), and any plant that has been around that long has to be a survivor.

The genus is named for Achilles, who, according to legend, was told of the plant's medicinal values by Chiron the centaur. *Potter's New Cyclopedia* lists the common yarrow (*Achillea millefolium*) as being valuable both as a stimulant and a tonic. (The book also reports the taste as insipid, and the odor, feeble.)

Yarrows are equally important in the garden border, the wild garden, or the meadow garden. Their flowers are especially effective when plants are massed. Be warned: Many of the species will crowd out more delicate plants. The flat clusters—made up of many small flowers—are very attractive when dried and used for winter bouquets.

Achillea ptarmica, or sneezewort (wort is an old English word for plant), is an imported wildflower and the parent form of many of today's cultivars. The flower heads are fewer and larger than field yarrow, *A. millefolium,* and the leaves are saw-toothed rather than fernlike. The double-flowered sneezewort is the source of a very old but popular variety, 'The Pearl', a charming plant with clusters of white pompoms on 2½-foot stems, blooming most of the summer.

Achillea millefolium

Achillea filipendulina, the fern-leaf yarrow, has the largest clusters of blossoms—often 5 inches across—on 3-foot stems. Two cultivars are usually offered: 'Coronation Gold' dates from 1952 and has golden yellow blossoms, while 'Gold Plate' has even wider flower heads.

Achillea millefolium is best suited for the wild or meadow garden since it really spreads. The cultivars are a better bet for the garden: 'Crimson Beauty' bears rose-red flowers; 'Fire King' has rich red blossoms; and 'Moonshine' has sulfur yellow flowers. All have 2-foot stems. 'Cerise Queen' has cherry red flowers on 1½-foot stems.

Botanical name: *Alchemilla* spp.
Common name: Lady's-mantle.
Habitat: Ordinary garden soil, but moist in warm areas; full sun to partial shade.
Description: Spreading perennials; lobed leaves with fine hairs that catch and hold drops of water; clusters of chartreuse flowers; to 16 inches.
Period of bloom: Summer.
Propagation: By division spring or fall; seed.
Zone: 4.

One of the most beautiful garden sights is a well-grown collection of lady's-mantle glistening under the rays of a summer sun in morning. The cupped leaves are covered with tiny silky hairs that catch and hold drops of dew that magnify and deflect the light, so that the plants look as though they were bathed in mercury. Add to this the feathery sprays of attractive chartreuse flowers, and here is another plant that should be in every garden.

Lady's-mantle is a European wildflower, with the genus *Alchemilla* derived from the Latinized term for an old Arabic name. The species is *vulgaris,* meaning common or ordinary. The plant has a long history of use in herbal medicine, especially by the Germans who classify it as a "wound medicine." Since it was con-

Alchemilla vulgaris

sidered such an important herb, it deserved a name with a Christian appeal, hence the original "Our Lady's mantle," especially since the leaves seem to be embroidered with pearls. Because the leaves are usually divided into nine lobes, there are many other common names that refer to animal feet, including duck's foot, lamb's foot, and lion's foot.

Use this plant along the front of a garden border or as a groundcover. One of the most attractive displays I ever encountered was the use of lady's-mantle to circle the outside path of a sundial, where it was grown in combination with royal blue delphiniums (*Delphinium grandiflorum*) and pink astilbes (*Astilbe* spp.). The flowers are attractive in the garden or when cut and are also used in dried bouquets. Deadhead to prevent their seeding about. If the plants become too floppy after flowering, shear them back and new leaves will appear and often new flowers.

Alchemilla alpina, the mountain lady's mantle, is a smaller plant reaching a height of 9 inches.

Botanical name: *Amsonia* spp.
Common name: Texas bluestar.
Habitat: Ordinary, moist garden soil; full sun to partial shade.
Description: Bushy perennial American wildflower with narrow leaves and pale blue starlike flowers; yellow fall foliage; to 2 to 5 feet depending on species.
Period of bloom: Spring.
Propagation: By division spring or fall; seed.
Zone: 4.

Bebe Miles, a great American wildflower gardener, first introduced the Texas bluestar (*Amsonia tabernaemontana*) to our garden. That initial plant grew larger every year, eventually becoming a bushy clump festooned in spring with the unique garden color of pale blue blossoms and in autumn with the lovely butterscotch

Amsonia tabernaemontana

the sun always shines brighter here than in England and the flowers turn up to the sky. Another American book advises semi-shade, a condition obviously not entirely to the plant's disliking, although it will produce less flowers. This is one of those rare plants completely ignored by damaging insects.

If the initial flowers are removed as they wither, there is usually a second round of blossoms, less abundant than the first but welcome nonetheless. In our first garden, amsonia grew between some low-growing columbines and our tree peony, where its bushy growth helped to cover up the rough look of the peony's lower branches.

An old species called *Amsonia montana* (really a variety of *Amsonia tabernaemontana*) is new to the market and said to reach a height of 1 1/2 feet.

Amsonia ciliata is a southern species with less flowers on stems up to 5 feet tall. It's best grown in the wild garden.

Botanical name: *Anaphalis* spp.
Common name: Pearly everlasting.
Habitat: Ordinary, well-drained garden soil; full sun or some shade, according to species.
Description: Perennial wildflowers, one American and one Himalayan, with white, wooly leaves; small heads of pearly white everlasting flowers; to 1 1/2 feet.
Period of bloom: Late summer into fall.
Propagation: By seed; division in spring or fall.
Zone: 4.

yellow of the leaves. The plant was named in honor of Dr. Amson, an eighteenth century Virginia physician. The species name is in honor of a sixteenth century German herbalist, Jakob Theodor Muller, who called himself Tabernaemontanus after a mountain near his birthplace.

One mention of amsonia in a popular English book on perennials blames the plant for having too-narrow leaves and somewhat drooping heads of flowers, a problem I've not encountered in American gardens I've seen, since

The autumn is often a melancholy time of the year, since it bridges the gap between the sunny late summer days of September and the first sticking snow and dark afternoons of November. But if you had been fortunate enough to plant an attractive wildflower called pearly everlasting last summer, it would now be evident as a white bouquet shining in

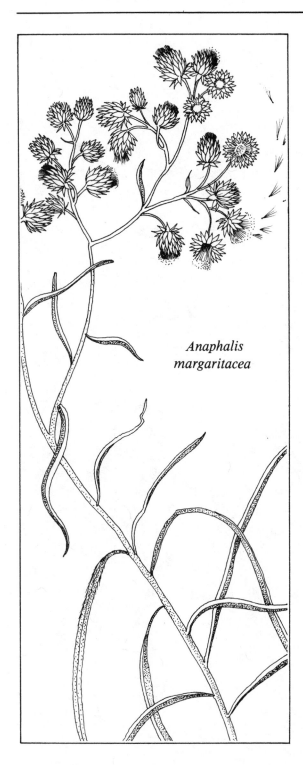

*Anaphalis
margaritacea*

the midst of your garden, unharmed by rains or frost, and waiting for the coming mantle of snow. The petals of everlasting have the ability to dry like tough paper and remain forever pure and durable.

This wildflower belongs to the genus *Anaphalis* (a Greek name for another everlasting flower). The familiar flower of the American field is *A. margaritacea.*

Anaphalis is attractive in the garden proper, especially when three or more plants are used together. It also looks splendid when grown in the wilder part of a rock garden where both flowers and leaves are set off by stone mulch. The attractive gray-green leaf color of both species looks good in the summer garden long before the blossoms appear, and the dried blossoms excel in arrangements for the winter table. Plants are drought resistant, but if kept too dry, the stems begin to bend just below the flowers and look quite forlorn.

The petals are really modified leaves; the true flowers are the tiny yellow or brown florets in the center of each blossom. The stems are covered with a cottony substance meant to prevent wandering ants from stealing the nec-

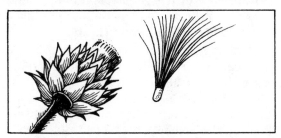

tar kept only for small bees and flies. Flower heads were once used as the ingredients of expectorants in treating colds, but this seems to have been out of favor for the last 80 or so years.

Anaphalis triplinervis is a more genteel type from the Himalayas and shorter in stature. It will adapt to a bit of shade.

Botanical name: *Anemone* spp.
Common name: Japanese anemone.
Habitat: Ordinary garden soil; full sun to partial shade in the North, partial shade in the South.
Description: Perennials with attractive lobed leaves; usually pink or white flowers on wiry stems; to 5 feet.
Period of bloom: Late summer into fall.
Propagation: By division in spring; seed.
Zone: 5.

Anemones, or windflowers, are members of a beautiful genus of plants with both popular names derived from Greek legend. Anemone is from the Greek word *anemos,* for wind; according to Pliny's flimsy speculations in his *Natural History,* anemones do not open until the wind blows. To me, just as plausible an explanation is that the word blow can mean both a big wind and a blooming flower. The seeds are flea-sized, each attached to a tiny bit of fluff, and will fly great distances on the wind. But whatever the derivation, a drift of the autumn-blooming Japanese anemones waving in a September breeze is a magnificent sight to behold.

Many nurseries call these flowers *Anemone japonica* but most of the flowers offered under that name are really *A. × hybrida,* a term first used back in 1849. The true Japanese anemone is *A. hupehensis* but except for three cultivers 'Praecox', 'September Charm', and 'Splendens', the flowers with that name are usually *A. × hybrida.*

In 1956 the first owner of our present garden planted the Japanese anemone 'September Charm'—a deep pink, single-flowered cultivar from an English nursery, first marketed in 1932—on the far edge of the perennial border. Today the flowers are found all over the garden, spread by their windblown seed and, as far as I'm concerned, desirable wherever they alight.

'September Charm'

The cup-shaped blossoms are formed of lustrous sepals, not petals, and surround many golden-tipped stamens that in turn circle a number of pistils. A number of flowers are found on each wiry stem. The large lobed leaves are attractive throughout the garden season.

Plant them about 2 feet apart and allow a season or two before the maximum display is ready, remembering that Japanese anemones look their best when planted in a mass. They are also well displayed when set in front of a low wall or a background of dark green hedging. I dislike the double cultivars and prefer the old-fashioned single flowers.

The black and twisted roots will survive in the heaviest of soils. If a number of plants are needed, simply dig up a plant, chop off the roots, and cut these into 2-inch sections. Spread them about a cold frame and cover with an inch of soil. When new growth appears, pot them up to winter in a cold frame. Plant out the following spring.

These flowers have been popular for over 100 years. 'Honorine Jobert' has 2- to 3-inch white blossoms on 3-foot stems and was first developed in 1858, while the pink 'Queen Charlotte', one of the least offensive doubles, first appeared in 1898. 'Alba' has white flowers on 2-foot stems.

Anemone vitifolia comes from Nepal and is extremely hardy even for an anemone. The cultivar 'Robustissima' is usually offered by nurseries and bears many silvery pink flowers on 2½-foot stems, beginning to bloom in late August and continuing on into October.

Botanical name: *Aquilegia* spp.
Common name: Columbine.
Habitat: Ordinary but well-drained garden soil; full sun to partial shade.
Description: Upright perennial American wildflower and related species with compound foliage; showy, nodding flowers of many colors, usually with spur; to 3 feet.
Period of bloom: Spring into early summer.
Propagation: By division in spring; seeds.
Zone: 4.

For years I drove back and forth along a twisting two-lane highway that wound along the Delaware River between Callicoon and Narrowsburg, New York. At one point a large flat-topped rock, probably left by the glacier of 10,000 years ago, loomed over the road, and every spring it was a carpet of orange-red dots from a colony of the American wildflower, *Aquilegia canadensis.*

The genus *Aquilegia* is from the Latin *aquila,* for eagle, whose claws are said to be represented by the curved form of the petals. The common name comes from the Latin *columbinus,* or dove, again referring to either the birdlike claws or the beaklike spurs of the flowers.

That rocky garden was a clue to the wild columbine's preferences in soil. Given good drainage, the entire clan will adapt to most situations. The compound leaves are attractive in their own right and often remain evergreen in the South. If the leaves get surface tracings resembling unintelligible handwriting by an elf, it is the work of leaf miners. These tiny insects tunnel their way about inside the leaf. Ignore them, as they do not bother the plant.

Since the flowers are attractive and bloom over long periods, columbines are excellent in both beds and borders. Flower season can be extended by deadheading the flowers.

Although many columbines are short-lived compared to most perennials, the flowers self-

Aquilegia vulgaris

sow and hybridize with ease, so there is never a lack of new plants, often in new color combinations. Older plants often develop a tuberouslike root system that does not transplant well, but younger plants recover quickly.

In addition to the wild columbine of the East, there is *Aquilegia caerulea,* the Colorado columbine, which bears sky blue blossoms with white centers on wiry stems growing to 2 feet.

Aquilegia flabellata comes from Japan and is perfect for the rock garden or as an edging in the border, since the plants are usually 14 inches high or lower. 'Nana Alba' has pure white flowers on plants under 12 inches high.

The hybrid columbines are mostly derived from *Aquilegia vulgaris,* the European crowfoot, used in combination with *A. caerulea* and *A. chrysantha* and other species in order to produce a bewildering array of both color and stature. Among the best are the McKana hybrids, with 24-inch plants bearing blossoms of pink, red, maroon, blue, purple, or white; and the Music hybrids, with 20-inch plants having flowers of intense yellow, blue and white, red and white, and pure white.

'Nora Barlow' has fully double flowers; 'Dragonfly' has flowers with longer than average spurs; and the new Spring Song strain has large flowers in reds, yellows, and blues.

Botanical name: *Arisaema triphyllum*.
Common name: Jack-in-the-pulpit.
Habitat: Humus-rich soil, preferably moist; partial shade.
Description: Upright perennial American wildflower with tuberous roots and 3-parted leaves; hooded flower followed by orange-red berries; local variations can reach 4 feet.
Period of bloom: Spring.
Propagation: Usually by seed.
Zone: 4.

When chancing upon a grove of Jack-in-the-pulpits in a shaded woods in spring, it's easy to assume that this is a shy flower devoted to its place on the forest floor and unsuited for travel. But given the right spot in the garden, its good looks command enough respect that even people who love to cut everything down will leave it be.

The common name assumes Jack to be the spadix, the column that bears the tiny flowers, and the spathe to be his hooded pulpit. The generic name, *Arisaema,* means bloody arum and refers to red leaves of certain species. The species name, *triphyllum,* refers to the three leaflets usually overtopping the spathe.

Just as there are differences in preachers, there are differences in pulpits, and sometimes the flowers will be a light green and

Arisaema triphyllum

sometimes a purple-brown. For years, botanists thought the color indicated the sex of the flower, but it is now known that every blossom is unisexual. Tiny male and female flowers share space at the base of the spadix, blooming at different times.

The flowers are not fertilized by bees, for these hardy insects are off foraging in the sunlit fields close by. Deep within the woods, the pollination job is assumed by other insects: fungus gnats, flies, or beetles.

Fertilized flowers shed the spathe, and by high summer, the spadix becomes studded with bright orange-red berries—berries that the Indians would boil along with the tuberous roots to remove the acrid and mouth-burning juices, leaving them to dry and then be ground into meal or used in gruel. One of the local names for this flower is memory-root, an appellation dedicated to the number of students from rural schools years ago who were bidden to bite the berries or roots and became twice-shy.

Do not transplant from the wild, especially in the Northeast, unless plants are in danger of earth-moving equipment or two-legged marauders, since the tuberous roots are often intertwined with the rock that usually lies just beneath the surface of the forest floor.

Provide the plants a shady spot and soil with added humus, preferably in a low spot near a source of water or a site accessible to the hose. Without these niceties, the plants will either refuse to flower or will disappear before producing the beautiful orange-red berries. Handle the tubers with gloves, since they contain an irritating substance.

Often plants become quite large, assuming the stature of minor shrubbery. They are especially effective when underplanted with low and hardy ferns, like the Japanese painted fern (*Athyrium goeringianum* 'Pictum', also called *A. niponicum* 'Pictum').

To grow Jack-in-the-pulpit from seed, collect the berries in the fall, crush them, and plant the seeds immediately.

Botanical name: *Artemisia* spp.
Common name: Wormwood.
Habitat: Ordinary soil, moist or dry according to the species; full sun to partial shade.
Description: Bushy perennials with divided leaves on strong stems; clusters of small white or gray-white flowers; to 5 feet.
Period of bloom: Summer.
Propagation: By division in spring.
Zone: 4.

The artemisias were named in honor of Artemisia, the wife of Mausolus, a Persian governor who designed and eventually occupied the first tomb to achieve international notoriety (hence the eventual mausoleum).

With the exception of mugwort (*Artemisia lactiflora*), these plants are best used for the color of their foliage, usually in various shades of silvery gray. Often found in the poorest of soil, they must have good drainage or the roots will rot. They are extensively used in seaside gardens where summers are hot. But pass these by if you live in an area of continual high humidity and damp, rainy summers.

The larger plants can be used as backgrounds to smaller blooming and foliage plants, and individual wormwoods can be set about the garden to act as foils for white, pink, lavender, or pale yellow flowers. They are excellent when dried for winter bouquets.

Artemisia lactiflora, or white mugwort (*lac* is Latin for milk), is grown for the masses of milk white flowers atop 5-foot stems that bloom in late summer. *Mug,* by-the-by, is an old word for a kind of sheep and might refer to the color of the flowers. This plant is originally from China and prefers a bit better soil than the others, so add a bit of humus when planting. It's excellent when grown as a background for late-blooming daylilies or low-growing asters; in our Catskill garden, it grew on top of a bank with hay-scented ferns below and to the right of a beautiful red-leafed Japanese maple.

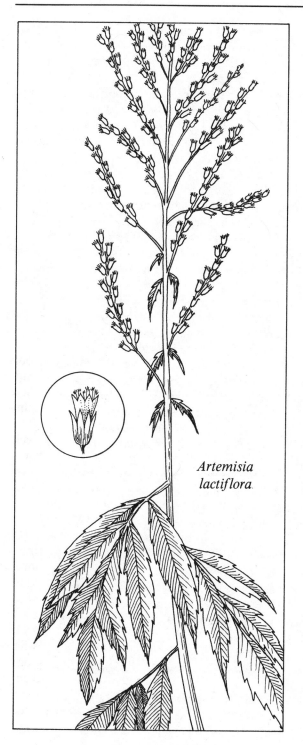

*Artemisia
lactiflora.*

Artemisia ludoviciana, or white sage, is an American original from the West, a very aromatic plant bearing willowlike leaves of the typical silvery white on 3-foot stems and producing gray-white flowers in late summer that blend with the foliage. There are two popular cultivars: 'Silver King' (sometimes termed a variety) is 3 feet tall, and 'Silver Queen' only 2 feet.

Artemisia schmidtiana 'Silver King' is from Japan and grows like a ball with cut foliage, while 'Nana' forms 8-inch mounds of silver-gray, perfect for edging along a sunny path.

Botanical name: *Arum italicum* 'Pictum'.
Common name: Italian arum.
Habitat: Ordinary moist garden soil with some added humus; partial shade, especially in the South.
Description: Perennial tuber producing marbled, arrowhead leaves; unusual flowers like ghostly Jack-in-the-pulpits followed by orange-red berries in early fall; to 1 foot.
Period of bloom: Spring.
Propagation: By division in fall.
Zone: 5.

All the reference books I've checked list this plant as hardy only in Zone 6 or 7, but I found it succeeded in my Catskill garden, where winters could and often did plunge to −30°F. Granted, I used a layer of leaves as a mulch and the plants were backed by a low stone wall, but still they are, I think, worthy of more experimentation.

Arum is the classical name for this genus, first penned by Theophrastus, the Greek philosopher who wrote extensively about plants. This particular species is a tuber with characteristics of growth that seems to be at odds with the rest of the garden, if not the country. Most of the plants offered today are a cultivar incorrectly known as 'Marmoratum' but more properly called 'Pictum'.

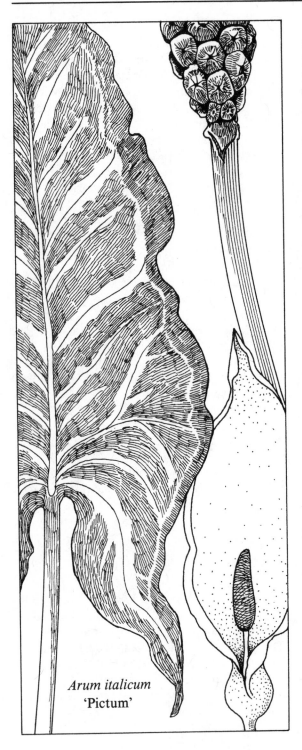

Arum italicum
'Pictum'

New leaves resembling arrowheads made of dark green paper, marbled with veins of a light yellow-green that is sometimes almost white, appear in late fall or early spring according to the severity of the winter. In my northern garden in upstate New York, they pushed through barely thawed soil in late March. In my North Carolina garden, they first appear in late October and remain through the winter.

The flowers appear in early spring. They resemble a Jack-in-the-pulpit, but the spathe does not extend over the top of "Jack," but stands up behind him, like a ghostly white sheet. The flowers are not as inconspicuous as most books say, but, covered by a canopy of their own leaves, they are missed by all but the most intent observers. The flowers and leaves are gone by late summer, leaving stalks topped with clusters of bright orange-red berries, easily mistaken for Jack's. By September's end, the berries are gone and the process begins again.

Italian arum makes a beautiful border plant and a great backdrop for early spring flowers. They are particularly fine when viewed against a stone wall or naturalized at the end of a wild garden. The leaves are especially valuable for winter floral arrangements.

Botanical name: *Asclepias tuberosa.*
Common name: Butterfly weed.
Habitat: Ordinary, even dry, garden soil in full sun.
Description: Perennial American wildflower with narrow leaves on upright stems—but they can sprawl—bearing clusters of intricate small flowers, usually orange; to 3 feet.
Period of bloom: Late spring and summer.
Propagation: Seed.
Zone: 4.

This is a spectacular American flower with the common names of butterfly weed, swallow-wort, chigger-flower, wind root, and pleurisy root. It's the only milkweed that does not have a milky sap. The genus commemorates Asklepios, the Greek god of medicine, and this particular plant has a long history of use in chest complaints and supposedly has a specific action on the lungs.

The flowers are colorful and complex in form. They bloom in large, flat umbels ranging from bright yellow to reddish orange, but usually orange. While few form mature fruit, there are usually one or two pods on any plant, which eventually open to produce ranks of seeds, each with powder puffs of silky threads. There will be variation in color from any packet or pod of seed, so be on the lookout for an exceptionally good color.

While perfectly hardy, the first-year seedlings will succumb to January heaving, so mulch them well the first winter. Once this plant is established in the garden, you can forget any care except for some weeding in its vicinity. Because of their deep-thrusting roots, plants should only be moved when young. If grown in better soil, they tend to grow taller but usually do not require staking except in damp summers when they can sprawl about.

In our garden, we planted butterfly weed around a large clump of plume or Ravenna grass (*Erianthus ravennae*) and, once in place, it gave year after year of summer color.

A cultivar called 'Rosea' is listed in *Index Hortensis,* but I've never seen it offered in this country.

The common milkweed (*Asclepias syriaca*) is great for a meadow or wild garden, but it's too rampant for the formal border. It attracts monarch butterflies and is the only food their caterpillars will eat; as a result of that diet, both larvae and butterflies are toxic to birds and other predators. This plant contains various glycosides, related to the digitalins used in treating some heart disease.

Asclepias tuberosa

Botanical name: *Aster* spp.
Common name: Fall aster.
Habitat: Ordinary but well-drained garden soil, slightly acid, in full sun.
Description: Perennial American wildflowers with strong upright stems and narrow leaves; clusters of daisylike flowers; ray flowers usually blues, purples, reds, or white; yellow disk flowers at center; to 6 feet.
Period of bloom: Late summer to fall.
Propagation: By division in spring; seed.
Zone: 4.

The genus *Aster,* from the Greek for a star, contains over 250 species. According to *The New Britton and Brown Illustrated Flora,* the genus reaches its greatest complexity in the eastern United States, a fact readily evident to anyone who walks the autumn fields surrounded by blooming asters and carrying any wildflower guide. The species have a diverse appearance and, thanks to the insects of the field, hybridize with ease. These are all "daisies," usually with yellow disk flowers surrounded by ray flowers of many colors.

Like our milkweeds, asters need only full sun and good drainage to succeed. And the stems are also just as strong as milkweeds and able to withstand most summer storms and autumn winds. If plants are lightly sheared in early summer before the buds form, they will provide a more compact bloom.

Planted in drifts either in the border or in the wild garden, with the smaller types used as edging, asters should be in every gardener's collection. They even succeed in a rock garden setting and, just as in the field, make especially attractive combinations when mixed with ornamental grasses.

One more thing to remember is that the famous English asters or Michaelmas daisies are really hybrids of three of our native asters, the New England aster, *Aster novae-angliae*; the

Aster novae-angliae

New York aster, *A. novi-belgii*; and the Italian aster, *A. amellus.*

The following cultivars all begin to bloom in September and continue on well into October. Among the New England aster cultivars, 'Alma Potschke' bears salmon-tinged rose flowers on 36-inch stems, and its charm is a definite testimony to Alma, whomever she is. 'Harrington's Pink' has pure pink flowers on 36- to 48-inch stems; and 'September Ruby' has flowers of deep crimson on 40-inch stems.

The New York asters have produced the 15-inch 'Alert', with red flowers; 'Marie Ballard', a 36-inch double with blue flowers; and 'Professor Kippenburg'—another mystery of identification—a 14-inch beauty with blue flowers.

Of the asters of the field, an occasional plant will be a great beauty and, if moved into the garden, will only become bigger. *Aster cordifolius,* or the blue wood aster, is perfect in light shade. The heath aster (*A. ericoides*) has produced the cultivar 'Golden Spray', a 24-inch plant with golden flowers and attractive foliage. *A. lateriflorus,* usually about 48 inches high, is represented in the trade by 'Horizontalis', with tiny panicles of lilac flowers blooming above horizontal branches and leaves that turn coppery purple for fall. This last plant is quite unusual, since the species is an American wildflower called the calico or starved aster (the second description due to the scarcity of leaves and the pronounced stems), introduced into English gardens in 1829. It certainly takes a long time for an American beauty to return home to fame and fortune.

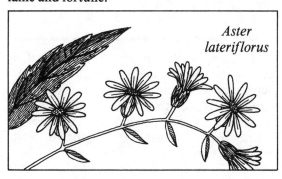

*Aster
lateriflorus*

Botanical name: *Astilbe* spp.
Common name: Astilbe.
Habitat: Ordinary but moist garden soil; best in partial shade, especially in the South, but will take full sun in the North.
Description: Perennials with polished stems and fernlike foliage; feathery plumes of small flowers, usually white, pink, red, rose, or lilac; to 4 feet.
Period of bloom: Summer.
Propagation: By division in spring.
Zone: 5.

Occasionally a botanical name comes along that not only does disservice to the plant described but is frankly not deserved. Such a name is the genus *Astilbe,* meaning *a,* without, and *stilbe,* brilliancy. True, the individual flowers in any panicle are tiny, but because each head contains dozens of branches and each branch bears hundreds of flowers, the total effect is not only brilliant but brightly so.

Most of the astilbes offered today are the result of hybridizing and are listed as *Astilbe × arendsii,* a collective name for a number of hybrids between *A. japonica, A. chinensis* var. *davidii,* and other species. Although the English are considered by many to be the deans of today's gardens, for years much of the most interesting and creative work in hybridizing of plants has been accomplished by the Germans. The hybrids usually called *Astilbe × arendsii* and *A. × hybrida* were originated by one Herr Arends of Ronsdorf and introduced in 1907.

The larger cultivars are best in the garden border as specimen plants, usually planted in groups, and make very effective groundcovers, useful even when not in bloom. The white forms are especially attractive when used against a shrub border or line of bushes. A number of the newer cultivars can also adjust to drier garden conditions.

After the flowers fade, flower heads are best left on the plant since they turn a fine rusty

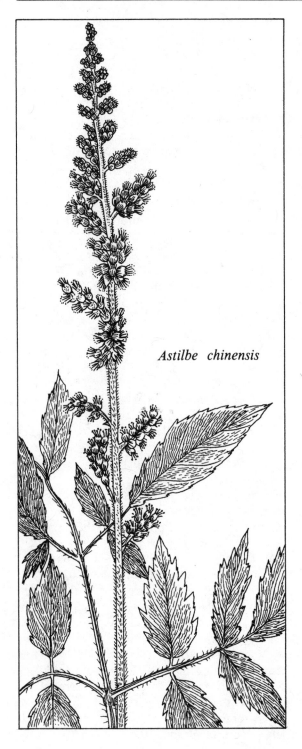

Astilbe chinensis

brown. They are also good cut flowers and are easily dried for winter bouquets. Finally, they can be forced for winter flowering by potting them up in the fall, allowing them to root for about three months, then bringing into heat, giving plenty of water, for midwinter bloom. *Astilbe japonica* is the best for winter flowers. Only the species will come true from seed, so division is the best bet for propagation.

Look for 'Bridal Veil', with pure white blossoms on 24-inch stems; 'Peach Blossom', an unusual shade of salmon pink on 18-inch stems; 'Federsee', carmine rose on 24-inch stems; 'Montgomery', with clear red flowers on 28-inch stems; and 'Fanal', with flowers of garnet red on 2-foot stems.

Astilbe chinensis originally came from China and Japan. The short 8-inch stems are covered with mauve-pink flowers, and plants are well suited as edging plants or in the rock garden, especially since they tolerate a drier soil than the others.

Botanical name: *Baptisia australis.*
Common name: Baptisia, false indigo.
Habitat: Ordinary but well-drained acid soil in full sun.
Description: Bushy perennial American wildflower with attractive blue-green leaves on strong stems; spikes of dark blue pealike flowers, which eventually become attractive seed pods; to 4 feet.
Period of bloom: Late spring.
Propagation: Best by seed, as division of mature plants is difficult.
Zone: 4.

I still remember many of the plants that grew in our first formal garden. Three of the plants that stood in a row on top of the bank were false indigos; they did a great job of holding the soil, looking down on slopes of myrtle and hay-scented ferns all leading down to our red Japanese maple.

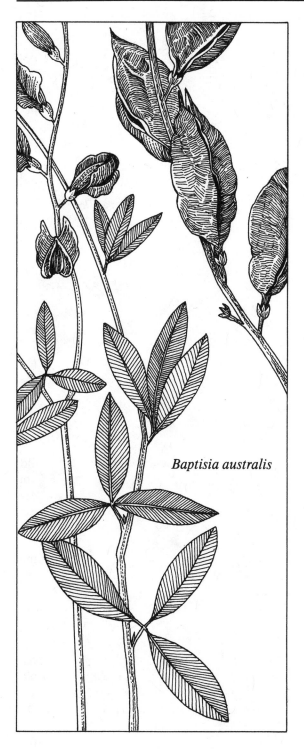

Baptisia australis

They never ceased to amaze. From the flowers of late spring to the seedpods (known commercially as Indian rattles) of fall, it was difficult to believe that this hedge was deciduous and by late fall would be but a memory.

Baptisias are native Americans, first reported in 1758. The genus name is derived from *bapto,* to dye, and thereby hangs a tale (*australis* refers to the American South and not the country). In colonial times, everyone thought these plants would be the substitute for the indigo obtained from species of *Indigofera,* and fortunes were going to be made. Unfortunately, the color from baptisia is not fast, and many fortunes were lost.

This is a plant that needs planning before planting. The root system becomes so extensive that old plants are not easily moved. If using seedlings, set them out by the second spring. In time, each will cover an area of several feet with their graceful foliage.

Because they are legumes, baptisias will grow moderately well even in poor soil and are excellent plants for holding banks of earth and preventing erosion. They will adapt to filtered shade, but the growth will not be as generous.

In the fall, the foliage will turn coal black with frost and is especially striking when planted with goldenrods and little bluestem ornamental grasses (*Schizachryrium scoparium*), grasses that turn a beautiful pinkish tan in the fall.

To save the seedpods, cut them on long stems in early fall before they become too weathered. Place them upright in a dry, well-ventilated spot until needed. The popular name of Indian rattle is well deserved. Thoreau noted in a February entry of his journal: "As I stood by Eagle Field wall, I heard a fine rattling sound, produced by the wind on some dry weeds at my elbow. It was occasioned by the wind rattling the fine seeds in those pods of the indigo-weed which were still closed—like a small Indian's calabash."

Botanical name: *Bergenia* spp.
Common name: Bergenia.
Habitat: Ordinary or moist garden soil, usually with light shade, and protection from bitter winds in coldest areas.
Description: Perennial with thick, rounded, usually evergreen leaves—edged in red during winter—that form clumps; nodding flowers of pink or white; to 1 1/2 feet.
Period of bloom: Early spring.
Propagation: By division in early spring; seed.
Zone: 3.

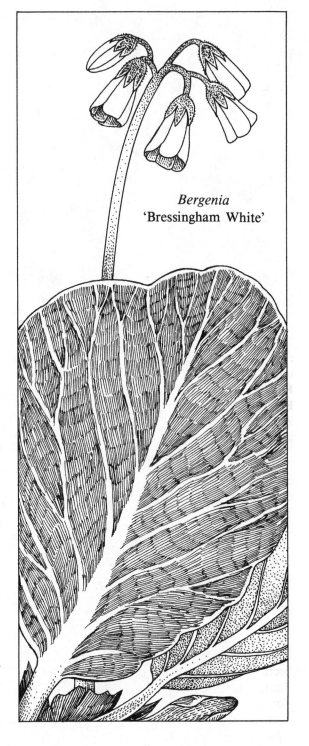

Bergenia 'Bressingham White'

In 1779, Siberian bergenias came to English gardeners. The genus is named in honor of Karl August von Bergen (1704–60), a physician and botanist of Frankfurt. At the turn of the century, bergenias were included with the saxifrages, usually under the name *Megasea.*

Their country of origin should be a cue to their hardiness in the garden, although in Zones 3 and 4 plants should be lightly covered in the winter whenever there is a lack of snow cover, especially if winds are bad. Without such protection, the heart-shaped 10-inch leaves burn around the edges. But when given help, the leaves are evergreen, turning a reddish bronze when temperatures fall. Then, in spring, they produce nodding stalks topped with large white to pink, bell-shaped, 5-petaled flowers. The best stands of bergenia are the result of the roots enjoying partial shade and decidedly moist soil laced with humus, but they will do quite well in full sun.

William Robinson, the English garden writer, recommended their use in naturalizing borders and in plantings at the edge of streams or ponds, especially in company with rocks. Gertrude Jekyll, that maven of garden writing, wrote highly of bergenias, suggesting that one of the best uses was potting up mature plants to share patio space with white and soft pink geraniums. She also suggested using them as filler in open areas between shrubbery and for bordering walkways to soften the hard edge of paving. The leaves are highly valued for winter bouquets.

Over 60 cultivars have been registered over the past 100 years. But the most effective (and available) are 'Bressingham Salmon' and 'Bressingham White', both created by England's Adrian Bloom. The first has compact spikes of salmon-pink flowers on foot-high stalks and leaves that are tinted purple and pink in winter; the second bears blossoms that start out pink and turn white. 'Silberlicht', introduced in 1950, has white flowers tinged pink, with red centers.

Botanical name: *Boltonia asteroides.*
Common name: Boltonia, false chamomile.
Habitat: Ordinary garden soil in full sun.
Description: Tall perennial American wildflower with strong, leafy stems bearing clusters of white asterlike flowers; to 5 feet.
Period of bloom: Late summer to fall.
Propagation: By division in spring or fall.
Zone: 4.

At first glance, boltonias could be easily confused with asters. But one look at the phenomenal number of blossoms should lead nonbotanical gardeners to question that assumption, while the botanist will note that the shape of the disk is a dome or cone instead of the aster's flat surface. The plant is another American native, the genus named in honor of James B. Bolton, an English botanist of the eighteenth century. In nature, boltonias are found in poor or damp soil as far north as Manitoba and as far south as Florida, then west to Texas.

It would seem that boltonia is a new introduction, but William Robinson wrote about the plant at the turn of the century and, in the 1930s, Norman Taylor noted their profuse bloom and suggested their use in autumn gardens. The spe-

Boltonia
'Snowbank'

cies recommended were *Boltonia asteroides,* for its neat daisies in colors from white to lilac, and *B. asteroides* var. *latisquama,* for its larger flowers.

Then in the 1980s, the cultivar 'Snowbank' hit the catalogs, and a new star appeared on the flower horizon with more and bigger flowers of pure white. This seedling selection made by the New England Wildflower Society reaches a height of 40 inches, covered with 3/4-inch blossoms.

Boltonias can be transplanted with ease, as long as you provide plenty of water while they are catching on to their new quarters. Use them also in wild and natural gardens, and to make excellent temporary hedges.

'Pink Beauty' is a new cultivar with flowers of a soft and delicate pink.

Centaurea americana

Botanical name: *Centaurea* spp.
Common name: Knapweed.
Habitat: Ordinary well-drained garden soil; full sun.
Description: Perennials and annuals with stout stems and large, coarse leaves; thistlelike flowers of muted colors; to 4 feet.
Period of bloom: Summer.
Propagation: By division in spring; seed.
Zone: 4.

Centaurea, the name derived from the Greek *kentaurie* because the plant supposedly cured the hoof of a centaur, is a large genus of over 500 species. The common name of knapweed is derived from the hard, knobby heads of the flowers and their ability to raise a nap on fabric. Legend has it that young English girls would remove the expanded florets from a blossom, put the head inside their blouses, and an hour later check to see if new florets had blossomed—if they did, love was on the way.

Knapweeds are tough plants requiring no special attention and belong in the border either as specimen plants or grouped.

The Persian centaurea (*Centaurea dealbata*) is a perennial that will provide rose-purple bloom throughout the summer, its blossoms resembling bachelor buttons on stems up to 2 feet in height. The coarsely cut leaves are gray and hairy underneath and green above. 'Steenbergii' is a cultivar with white inner flowers and purple-red outer flowers. Both species and cultivar will bloom best if not allowed to dry out.

Centaurea macrocephala has no common name. It arrived in the garden world from the Caucasus in 1805. Plants are usually called coarse by English writers and robust by Americans. Either way, the plants have large, rough leaves on stout 3-foot stems that end in the typical thistlelike blossoms of bright yellow, beloved by bees. They make good cut flowers and retain their color when dried.

Basketweed (*Centaurea americana*) is a hardy annual from the prairies and fields of the American Midwest, and it's hard to understand why more of a fuss isn't made over this plant. Interesting in bud and beautiful in bloom, each flower sits alone on a 4-foot stem and opens to 4 inches across. The color is light rose and the flower resembles an open thistle without thorns. The common name refers to the overlapping, spiny, straw-colored segments that wrap the bud and look like woven baskets. Flowers close at night. Make successive sowings for flowers all summer.

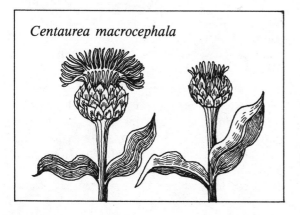

Centaurea macrocephala

Botanical name: *Chrysanthemum* spp.
Common name: Daisies
Habitat: Ordinary garden soil; full sun, but tolerates some shade, especially in the South.
Description: Tall perennials with heavy, scalloped leaves and stout stems; daisylike blossoms up to 6 inches wide, usually with white ray flowers and yellow disk flowers, on strong stems; to 3 feet.
Period of bloom: Summer.
Propagation: By division in spring, usually every other year.
Zone: 4.

Chrysanthemums are members of the daisy family and number over 200 species that have ornamental value. The genus name is from the Greek for golden flower. Of the many species and cultivars, I've had excellent firsthand results with two.

The first is the shasta daisy (*Chrysanthemum × superbum*), a plant developed by Luther Burbank, America's horticulturist and plant breeder extraordinaire. He began with the moon chrysanthemum (*C. maximum*), originally from the Pyrenees Mountains, crossed it with the American field daisy (*C. leucanthemum*), and by dint of careful selection—including an additional cross with the Nippon daisy (*C. nipponicum*)—he eventually produced the shasta daisy (from Shasta, California).

Last June, my uncle showed up at our garden with two cleaning buckets full of shasta daisies just removed from his garden. The day was hot, and it had not rained for weeks. I removed the damaged leaves, got the hose connected, and immediately planted them in unprepared garden soil, in full sun, using a slurry of mud to settle them in. They were in full bloom by July. Obviously no special attentions are required aside from ordinary garden soil, deadheading, and lots of sun. But as my uncle's buckets attested, plants should be divided every other year and are best treated as biennials.

Chrysanthemum × superbum

The large single flowers, up to 4 inches in diameter, have a golden center and are continually produced until early autumn. Use them to fill in the spaces after the peonies and irises are finished. Plant them in groups of three about 2 feet apart. They have shallow roots, so remember to water well in hot and dry weather.

Over 50 cultivars are known, including many doubles, but I still think the best flowers are single. All the cultivars have large blossoms and are pure white, but there are significant variations in height: 'Alaska' bears perfect, snow-white flowers on 36-inch stems; 'Miss Muffet' has flowers on 16-inch stems; and 'Snowlady' blooms on 10-inch stems.

Chrysanthemum pacificum is being touted in the big nursery catalogs as a new Japanese introduction to the garden horizon, but it originally arrived on our shores in 1976. The plant forms a dense, low-growing groundcover with attractive foliage of mid-green edged with a narrow strip of white. Plants bloom in October, with small yellow flowers resembling tansies, and will form a foot-high mat that will spread about 1 foot a year.

Botanical name: *Chrysogonum virginianum.*
Common name: Golden star, green and gold.
Habitat: Ordinary garden soil, well-drained with added humus; partial shade.
Description: Usually evergreen perennial American wildflower with creeping stems and hairy leaves; yellow daisies of great charm; to 1 foot.
Period of bloom: Mostly spring but on through summer.
Propagation: By division in spring; seed.
Zone: 6; Zone 5 with protection.

There are not too many bright yellow flowers that do well in partial shade, but golden star is one of them. From Pennsylvania and West Virginia, then south to Florida and Louisiana, this charming plant is another American native destined to become a very popular plant.

Chrysogonum virginianum

into autumn. The right place in this case calls for good drainage and added humus in acid soil. Use at least three plants spaced about 10 inches apart. In our garden, golden star is used as an edging plant with dwarf hostas to the left and right and a number of hybrid daylilies behind.

Two cultivars are sometimes available. The first, 'Allen Bush', grows more rapidly than the species and is named after the owner of Holbrook Farms, a well-known nursery in Fletcher, North Carolina. The other is 'Mark Viette', a long-blooming form named in honor of one of the owners of the Andre Viette Farm & Nursery, in Fishersville, Virginia.

Botanical name: *Cimicifuga* spp.
Common name: Fairy-candle, bugbane.
Habitat: Ordinary garden soil with added humus; partial shade.
Description: Very tall perennial American wildflowers with strong stems bearing attractive compound leaves and slender wands of tiny white flowers; to 8 feet.
Period of bloom: Late summer.
Propagation: By division in spring; seed.
Zone: 4.

Every gardener has (or should have) a favorite plant, one above all others that he or she would never want to do without. Over the years I've had many, but at this time in my gardening life, the plants that win over all others are most of the members of the genus *Cimicifuga.*

The popular name of fairy-candle is evident when the narrow racemes of white flowers bloom in a shady border. Bugbane refers to the supposed insect-repellent smell of the flowers found on *Cimicifuga racemosa:* The odor is rather rank but nothing to cause anyone to run screaming from the garden. *Cimex* is Latin for bug, and *fugare,* to drive away.

The flowers are numerous and small, have no petals, and the bud covers, or sepals, fall away as they open. The flowers open from the

Named by Linnaeus in 1753, from the Greek, *Chrysogonum* means golden joint and possibly refers to the blossoms rising from stem nodes.

When the plants first bloom, they are only a few inches high, but the blooms at season's end may be on stems up to a foot high. The best show of flowers is in the spring, but when plants are in the right place, they will bloom until well

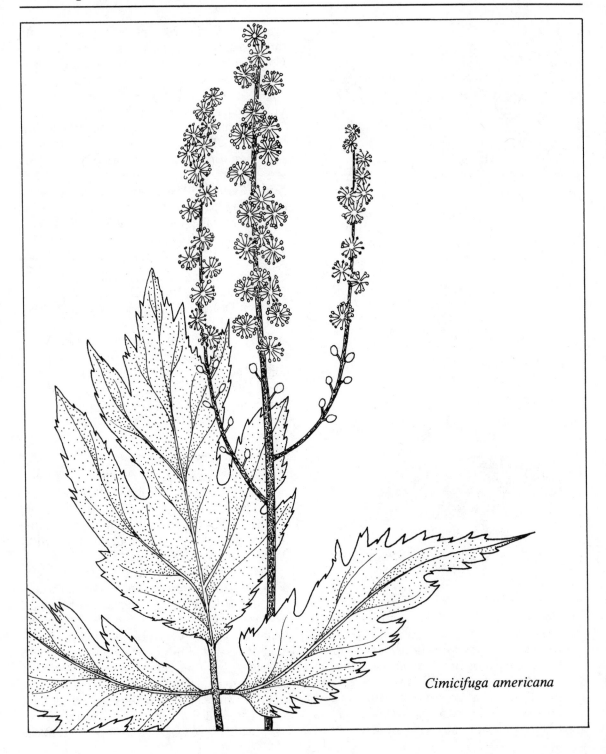

Cimicifuga americana

bottom, and soon the top foot of each 6- to 8-foot stalk is covered with clusters of glistening stamens, like shining, silvery white filaments. The toothed leaves are borne near the ground and are very large and divided. Seedpods form and make a curious rattling sound, hence the other common names of rattletop and snakeroot.

Where soil is continually moist, cimicifugas will take some sun in the North. But south of Pennsylvania, they are best left to shady sites with just a touch of sun in morning or late afternoon. The soil needs some humus and should be on the acid side. Once planted, they can be left alone for years. Both wild species, *Cimicifuga americana* and *C. racemosa,* spread seed about, so there should never be a lack of plants.

A shaded walkway between our garden and the garden next door is edged on the higher side with a long line of *Cimicifuga americana* with its tall spires, all blooming at the end of August well into September and delighting everyone who walks by. Years ago, in our old country garden, I planted one *C. racemosa* so that its flower stalk wound its way through the branches of a Japanese maple and the evening sun reflected red shades on the white flowers. It's interesting to note that Graham Stuart Thomas, one of England's greatest plantsmen, rates *C. racemosa* not only as a truly good garden plant, but one of exceptional beauty. *C. americana* is the shorter of the two American species, with flower stalks to 6 feet.

Cimicifuga racemosa blooms up to 8 feet, depending on soil and moisture. 'Brunette' is a new cultivar with bronzy brown foliage, blooming to 5 feet; 'Atropurpurea' reaches only 3 feet. The species *C. cordifolia* has fewer leaves.

Many native American plants, especially from the East Coast, have counterparts in Japan. Three Japanese species are now on the nursery market. *Cimicifuga dahurica* blooms on 5-foot stalks, and *C. japonica* 'Acerina' blooms in July on 3-foot stalks. *C. simplex* blooms the latest of all, usually well into October. Two cultivars

are usually available: 'Braunlaub', with brown leaves; and 'White Pearl', with unopened buds looking like a pearl necklace.

Botanical name: *Coreopsis* spp.
Common name: Coreopsis, tick-seed.
Habitat: Ordinary garden soil in full sun; drought resistant.
Description: Perennials with wiry stems and small leaves; small, usually yellow or orange daisies; to 3 feet.
Period of bloom: Summer.
Propagation: By division in spring or fall; seed.
Zone: 4.

Consider the poor coreopsis: Bright and shining flowers that are happy to exist in almost any conditions, but saddled with an unfortunate botanical name. *Coreopsis* is from the Greek word for buglike; the common name refers to ticks because the seeds were thought to look like these arachnids.

There are over 100 species from North and South America and Africa, including *Coreopsis tinctoria,* an attractive hardy annual that blooms in a number of bright yellows, pinks, and purples. But the most important coreopsis are the perennials. They are prized members of the bed and border, the wild garden, and even hanging baskets and containers for the porch and patio. Shorter varieties are good for edging along paths and walkways. The flowers are prized for cutting.

These small daisies come in various shades of yellow, orange and, recently, pink. Shear the spent flowers throughout the summer to keep plants blooming until frost.

Coreopsis verticillata, the thread-leaved coreopsis, blooms with 2-inch-wide yellow daisies on wiry stems usually to 3 feet high; the foliage is ferny. These are native American wildflowers, originally from Maryland to Florida and west to Arkansas, and especially adaptable

Coreopsis verticillata
'Moonbeam'

to hot and difficult places. 'Moonbeam', which has been a recent pop plant, bears profuse flowers of an unusual light sulfur yellow; new for the nineties is 'Rosea', with light pink flowers.

Coreopsis lanceolata is similar to *C. verticillata,* with sturdy daisies on 2-foot stems. A European cultivar 'Sterntaler' was introduced in 1962 and has double flowers; 'Baby Sun' has smaller flowers on foot-high stems.

Coreopsis grandiflora is another from Kansas and Missouri, south to Florida, with 2½-inch-wide heads on 2-foot stems. Usually sold are two cultivars: 'Badengold', with large single golden flowers; and 'Sunray', blooming with 2-inch doubles.

Coreopsis rosea is a rather rare creeping wildflower from the eastern coast, fond of damp, sandy soil. It has a dense, bushy habit and pink flowers on 18-inch stems. A dwarf form is valued by rock gardeners.

Finally there is *Coreopsis auriculata nana,* the bluegrass daisy, a lovely form found near Maysville, Kentucky, by Dr. E. Lucy Braun. It bears orange-yellow blossoms, usually on foot-high stems.

Botanical name: *Echinacea* spp.
Common name: Purple coneflower, purple rudbeckia.
Habitat: Ordinary but well-drained garden soil in full sun; drought resistant.
Description: Tall perennial American wildflowers with strong stems that bear coarsely toothed leaves; large daisies with purple ray flowers surrounding a prickly, bronzy brown disk.
Period of bloom: Summer into fall.
Propagation: By division in spring; seed.
Zone: 4.

The problem with naming favorite flowers is that soon after pledging fidelity to one, you find another. A case in point is the purple coneflower or *Echinacea purpurea.*

Echinacea purpurea

In addition to their stalwart beauty, the coneflowers are important ingredients of pharmaceutical compounds, especially in Europe. More than 200 different preparations are manufactured from these plants, including extracts for treating wounds, herpes sores, and throat infections; in addition, present research involves stimulation of nonspecific defense mechanisms. The genus name is in honor of *echinos,* the hedgehog, since the receptacle (the part that holds the flower) is prickly.

The cone-shaped heads of bronzy brown are surrounded by petals (really ray flowers) that begin as horizontal but soon are drooping (the botanical term is reflexed). Colors are varying shades of rose-purple, and flowers bloom on very stout stalks from 2 to 4 feet high, often continuing until cut down by hard frosts. The simple and alternate leaves are very rough to the touch.

Coneflowers are especially beautiful when massed either in the formal border or the wildflower garden. In fact, the more the better. They are excellent cut flowers and able to withstand drought conditions. Remember to deadhead for prolonged blooming.

If growing from seed, it takes about a year in the garden for a large clump to develop, but if started early, they will bloom the first summer. Time divisions for early spring, and pot them up for a few weeks until a new root system develops, as plants resent moving. Once in place, they should not be disturbed for several years.

Echinacea purpurea is the plant usually offered by nurseries and seed houses. John Banister, an English naturalist, sent the first seeds from America to the Oxford Botanic Garden sometime in the mid-1680s. 'Magnus' has broad, nonreflexed petals of rose-pink on 36-inch stems; 'Bright Star' has maroon flowers on 30-inch stems; and 'The King' has large blooms of carmine red on 40-inch stems. 'White Swan' has white flowers on 30-inch stems.

Look for the narrow-leaved coneflower (*Echinacea angustifolia*) for shorter stature—stems are about 20 inches tall, and it has shorter ray flowers.

The pale purple coneflower (*Echinacea pallida*) has narrow reflexed petals on 3- to 5-foot stalks and a long taproot, which enables it to survive most contingencies in the garden. It was used by Native Americans of the northern Great Plains to treat more ailments than any other plant.

Botanical name: *Echinops* spp.
Common name: Globe thistle.
Habitat: Ordinary garden soil; full sun but will tolerate partial shade; drought resistant.
Description: Bold perennials with prickly and toothed leaves; round, thistlelike flower heads, usually metallic blue.
Period of bloom: Summer.
Propagation: By division in spring; seed.
Zone: 4.

Some years ago, while visiting Mohonk Manor, that fine old hotel that sits on the cliffs overlooking the Hudson River above Poughkeepsie, I saw an elegant formal border. There in the midst of a wide expanse of lawn were beds of pale yellow zinnias backed by large clumps of 4-foot-high blooming globe thistles, making a terrific color combination that would last from late August until frost. Like the coneflower, the botanical name of globe thistles is rooted in the word *echinos,* for hedgehog, due to the round and prickly flower heads. All are originally from eastern Europe and western Asia.

Globe thistles are statuesque plants, at home either in bed or border or planted in great groups in a wild garden. Their only failing—if failing it be—is the propensity of the species to cast a lot of seeds, since as soon as the flowers fade the balls quickly fall apart. This leads to an endless supply of new little plants, which bloom the second year. Globe thistles are excellent additions to winter bouquets, but remember to pick the flower heads as they turn a deep blue-gray, before the individual florets begin to open.

E. A. Bowles, the English gardener, once wrote: "I have often recommended them for entomologists' gardens where plants are wished for that can be visited after dark with a lantern, to

Echinops sphaerocephalus

surprise a supper party of noctuid moths." And the gardener will note a continual fluttering of wings around these balls of steely blue.

Although all the plants want full sun, they will adapt to a bit of open shade. The soil must be well drained or the roots will eventually rot.

Echinops sphaerocephalus, or the great globe thistle, is the roughest of the clan, and flower heads can often reach a height of 7 feet.

Echinops humilis or *E. bannaticus* are both credited with the most popular garden cultivar 'Taplow Blue', noted for the bold and intense blue of the flower heads. Since this plant only reaches a height of 2½ feet, it's a good bet for the smaller garden. There is also 'Taplow Purple', reaching 3 feet and bearing violet-blue globes with silver tips that are sterile and will not reseed.

Echinops ritro only grows 2 feet high with flower heads that have good color long before the florets open. Nurseries usually carry 'Veitch's Blue', with flowers of an intense blue.

Botanical name: *Filipendula* spp.
Common name: Queen-of-the-prairie, prairie meadowsweet.
Habitat: Moist to wet garden soil; full sun or partial shade.
Description: Large perennial American wildflowers with compound leaves and stout stems; clusters of many small, fragrant, pale to deep pink flowers; to 7 feet.
Period of bloom: Summer.
Propagation: By division in spring; seed.
Zone: 3.

Shades of the circus: The tall blooming stalks of Queen-of-the-prairie (*Filipendula rubra,* sometimes sold as *Ulmaria rubra*) look so much like cotton candy they lack only a fleet of clowns and a Ferris wheel to be a complete entertainment. The botanical name is derived from *filum,* thread, and *pendulus,* hanging, in reference to root tubers that hang on the fibrous roots of one member of the genus, the dropwort, or *Filipendula vulgaris* (a white-flowered member from Eurasia reported as an escapee in the Northeast). In the species, *rubra*

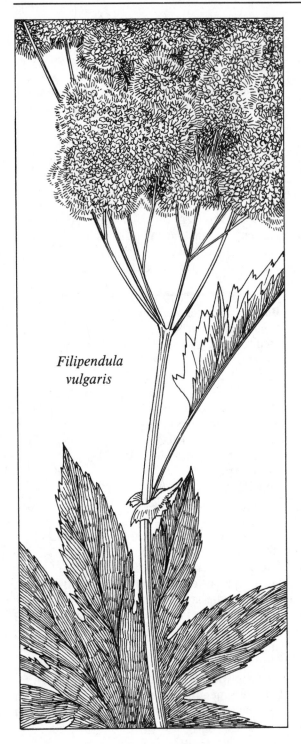

*Filipendula
vulgaris*

means red. The common name was not named for meadows but for mead because the European species, *F. ulmaria,* was used for flavoring herb beers. The leaves, when crushed, have the fragrance of sweet birch.

These are plants of the low woods, wet prairies, and meadows from New York to Minnesota and south to North Carolina and Kentucky. They were introduced to Europe in 1765.

The clusters of tiny flowers are often confused with the genus *Spiraea* and upon close examination are easily recognized to be allied to the rose family. They also act as magnets to innumerable tiny bees and flies. A large clump in full bloom is indeed a showstopper. The foliage is large, lobed, and jagged with uneven teeth, attractive even when plants are out of flower. The roots spread by rhizomes and can become a large clump. Plants will usually not bloom until the second summer after transplanting.

The Queen, while surviving in drier soil, does not do so with grace. Moist to wet soil is required for a full show of flowers, and the plant is perfectly suited for a bog or the edge of a pond or pool. In our northern garden in upstate New York, she sat in front of a low and white picket fence directly in front of a gutter downspout, in turn fronted by various red and orange midseason daylilies; during periods of drought, I never forgot to water.

The cultivar 'Venusta' (often called 'Magnifica') produces 6-foot stems covered with bright pink plumes blooming in midsummer. *Filipendula vulgaris* (also sold as *F. hexapetala*) is usually offered in the form of a double-flowered cultivar 'Flore Pleno', which has foot-high stems covered with tiny double white flowers.

Botanical name: *Geranium* spp.
Common name: Hardy geranium.
Habitat: Slightly moist garden soil with added humus; partial shade.
Description: Perennials with finely cut leaves and wiry stems; loose clusters of lavender-purple to pink flowers.
Period of bloom: Late spring.
Propagation: By division in spring or fall; seed.
Zone: 4.

These are not the geraniums of hot reds and oranges, planted in pots and boxes in American small towns or used to decorate cemetery plots—those plants are *Pelargonium* spp., originally from South Africa. No, these geraniums are hardy plants best suited for the perennial border or the wild garden. The botanical name is Greek and derived from *geranos,* or crane, and refers to the similarity of the seedpod to a crane's bill.

A number of hardy geraniums are used today in the garden, many originally popular plants in England. Most nursery catalogs list a number of species and cultivars. But for naturalizing or the wild garden, nothing beats another American native, *Geranium maculatum.* Loose clusters of pink to lavender-purple, 5-petaled flowers sit atop 1- to 2-foot stalks, themselves adorned with finely cut leaves. There is a white form called 'Album', but it's not too common.

Although most hardy geraniums prefer partial shade, some sun during the day is readily accepted in the North. Where winters are not too frigid, the basal leaves are nearly evergreen. They grow from a tough rootstock, so plant individuals about 1 foot apart and once planted let them be. If plants must be divided, be sure each piece of root has several eyes.

By mulching the soil around the geraniums to keep them weed-free, plants will be encouraged to grow and will eventually form a large clump of specimen plants.

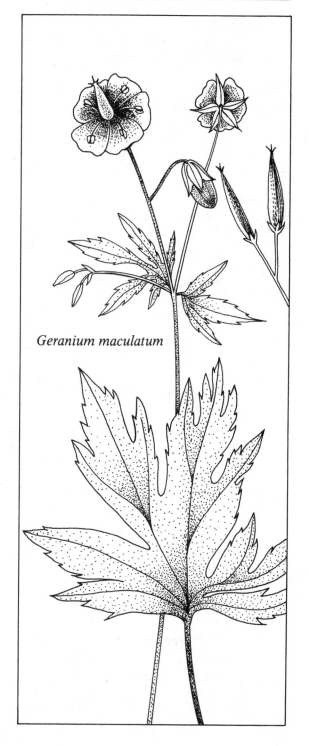

Geranium maculatum

Geranium robertianum is a biennial but will usually flower the first year from seed. Native both to Europe and America, the common name is herb Robert, red robin, or red shanks. Neltje Blanchan, writing in *Nature's Garden,* supposes that the Robert for whom this "holy herb" was named is either St. Robert, a Benedictine monk, or Robert Duke of Normandy. This is a plant of damp, poor, and shady soil, and it will soon spread to the cracks in stone walls. Plants are covered with small pinkish violet blooms from early summer until frost. When the green stems mature, they turn red, and eventually the palmate leaves are stained with crimson. The various rock garden societies occasionally offer a white form, 'Album'.

Never topping 10 inches in height, herb Robert is an attractive groundcover and edging plant and, once established, will continue to self-seed. In fact, when ripe, the little seed containers go off like little guns, and the seed will fly! Many authorities claim that the plant has a foetid odor when touched. I wouldn't suggest rolling around in a patch, but you will probably never be bothered by any smell.

Botanical name: *Helenium* spp.
Common name: Sneezeweed, Helen's flower, swamp sunflower.
Habitat: Ordinary moist garden soil but plants appreciate added humus; full sun.
Description: Large perennial American wildflowers with narrow leaves; clusters of small yellow daisies on stout stems branching toward the top; to 6 feet.
Period of bloom: Late summer into early fall.
Propagation: By division in spring; seed.
Zone: 4.

There are about 40 species of sneezeweed native to North and South America. The botanical name refers to Helen of Troy, but the original plant that was said either to reflect or enhance Helen's beauty is unknown; one story is

Helenium autumnale

that they sprang up where her tears fell. The common name refers to the heavy yellow pollen easily seen falling from the flowers and the unfortunate fact that the notorious ragweed (*Ambrosia artemisiifolia*) blooms at the same time, its tiny green flowers tossing to the winds the yellow dustlike pollen that causes hayfever.

Helenium autumnale is found growing on moist, low ground from Quebec to Florida and west to British Columbia and Arizona. The round heads of small yellow disk flowers are surrounded by bright yellow, 3-scalloped, turned-back ray flowers on stout stems that can reach 6 feet. Plants have evergreen basal rosettes where winters are not too harsh. The species name gives a clue to blooming time: These glorious plants provide flowers from late August well into September.

During periods of drought, give sneezeweed a good hosing; that extra water in midsummer means good flowering in the fall. By pinching back the growing tips in spring, the gardener can create smaller and bushier plants. Every few years, divide the plants to keep them from getting too rangy.

The only problem with the species is its size, somewhat large for a small garden, but the problem is solved by shopping for the various cultivars that produce brighter flowers on shorter stems. Since the lower part of the stems are often bare, brown, and open, plant sneezeweed behind other shorter plants or in the midst of a group of talls.

A number of sneezeweed cultivars are available, all about 4 feet tall. 'Butterpat' has clear yellow flowers, while the petals of 'Crimson Beauty' and 'Moerheim Beauty' are a beautiful bronze-red. 'Kugelsonne' (or sun sphere) has bright yellow 2-inch petals around a chartreuse disk.

Helenium nudiflorum is similar to sneezeweed, but the floral buttons are deep purple and the leaves have fewer teeth. The plant reaches a height of only 3 feet.

Helenium hoopesi comes from the Rockies. It begins blooming in early August and only reaches 2 1/2 feet in height. The flowers are a rich yellow.

Botanical name: *Helianthus* spp.
Common name: Sunflower, perennial sunflower.
Habitat: Ordinary garden soil in full sun.
Description: Perennial American wildflowers with sturdy stems bearing large, often toothed leaves and topped with bright yellow daisies; to 10 feet.
Period of bloom: Summer into fall.
Propagation: By division in spring; seed.
Zone: 5.

A number of European gardeners call most of the members of this plant genus coarse, rough, and weedy, but they would only appear that way to eyes accustomed to the regimentation of European floral displays and the implied peacefulness of age-old shady walkways. They are, instead, akin to many American originals: tough, rugged, and like the American skyscraper, tall and bold. The botanical name is from *helios,* sun, and *anthos,* flower.

When sunflowers are mentioned, most beginning gardeners think of the giant annuals (*Helianthus annuus*), plants that produce foot-wide flowers with disks crowded with seeds arranged in patterns best analyzed as Fibonacci numbers, grown commercially for oil and the delicious edible seeds and by many gardeners just to see how tall a plant will get. (Fibonacci, called Leonard of Pisa, was an Italian mathematician who discovered a mathematical relationship in the spiral of seeds on a sunflower disk or in the screwlike arrangement of leaves around a stem.) But there are a number of sunflower perennials perfect for the garden, providing bloom during the waning days of summer and on into fall. Their wants are slim: ordinary soil and full sun. In return, they will

Helianthus decapetalus

bloom until cut down by a killer frost. Although some are best in the wild garden, others become welcome additions to the back of the border, and one, the willow-leaved sunflower, adds an elegance that few other plants provide.

Helianthus angustifolius, or the swamp sunflower, blooms from late September into October with 2-inch flowers that crowd the tops of 8-foot-high plants; even the leaves are attractive. Although this plant does well with damp feet, it will adjust to the ordinary garden but needs additional water when rain is wanting. If pruned in late June, the plants will be bushier.

Helianthus decapetalus is the thin-leaved sunflower found in the wild from Maine to South Carolina and west to Wisconsin and Iowa. Once again, European nurserymen have taken a particular plant and developed a number of radiant cultivars. Look for 'Capenoch Star', developed in Germany in 1938, which produces 4-inch-wide bright yellow flowers from August to early September, and 'Flora Pleno'. This last cultivar is often listed in catalogs as *Helianthus × multiflorus* and was derived from a cross between *H. decapetalus* and the annual sunflower, resulting in a plant that blooms in late summer with 5-inch wide bright yellow double flowers on 3-foot stems.

Helianthus grosseserratus came to me from a seed exchange at the American Horticultural Society in the early 1980s. Like its annual relative, this perennial can reach a height of 13 feet when given a happy situation of full sun and average soil. Blossoms are 2 ½ inches in diameter and up to 20 of them can top a stem, blooming in early October, and smelling deliciously of cocoa. The leaves are usually (but not always) edged with coarse teeth, hence the botanical name of *grosseserratus*.

I first saw the willow-leaved sunflower, *Helianthus salicifolius* (*Salix* is the genus for willow), in a 1975 book entitled *The Personal Garden* by Bernard Wolgensinger and Jos Daidone, but due to a problem with translations,

Helianthus salicifolius

the plant was not identified. Then, five years later, I picked up a used book, *Garden Guide* by Ludwig Koch-Isenburg, and there, in a small black-and-white photograph, the same plant graced the corner of a small garden pool. This is a must—the graceful bend of the 4-foot stems adorned with such elegant leaves becomes a foil in any garden plan. Small flowers appear in late September and are but icing on a lovely cake.

Botanical name: *Helleborus orientalis.*
Common name: Lenten rose.
Habitat: Ordinary but moist garden soil in partial shade, especially in the South.
Description: Perennial with attractive long-stalked, usually evergreen, deeply cut leaves; clusters of 5-petaled (really sepals) flowers in shades of off-white to purple-brown; to 1 1/2 feet.
Period of bloom: Early spring, but last for weeks.
Propagation: By seed; careful division in late summer.
Zone: 6; Zone 5 with protection.

Hellebores have been cultivated for centuries, the botanical name being bestowed by Hippocrates and used by other Greek writers. Today the most commonly grown plant is the Lenten rose (*Helleborus orientalis*), so named because it usually blooms in the early spring. Drooping, long-lasting flowers of cream, light green, or many shades of purple to brown are often suffused with maroon spots. Dozens of foot-wide palmate leaves on 1 1/2-foot stems arise from a central crown and can make a 4-foot circle. The plants interbreed like the gods of ancient Greece, the baby plants visible under the plant's leafy umbrella. Your garden will eventually support new plants, some with flowers that are classically beautiful and others with color that is a bit of a bore. It's up to the gardener to choose the best. And the gardener should be warned. All the parts of this miracle plant are very poisonous.

Make no mistake about it, the Lenten rose is a superb landscape plant and should be one of the highlights in many gardens. In addition

Helleborus orientalis

to plants scattered about various parts of our garden, one large plant resides at the top side of two low stone steps and acts as a focal point throughout most of the year.

The soil should be well drained and enriched with leaf mold or compost. All species appreciate a neutral to slightly alkaline soil and do especially well when planted near mortared steps or walls. In the North, protection is needed, especially from sleet and ice storms or heavy weight of snow. A thin layer of leaf mulch is beneficial, since it helps to keep the roots cool in summer and protected in winter. The spent leaves from the previous season should be removed in early spring.

When planting hellebores, dig a good-sized hole so the roots can be carefully spread apart, placing the crown about 1 inch below the soil surface. While care is necessary in transplanting Lenten roses, plants that naturally start from seed will do well even in soil of heavy clay.

Flowering plants will develop from seed in about three to four years and should be left undisturbed so they can become large specimen plants. If division is needed, carry out the deed in early fall, keeping at least five growth buds to each division.

Botanical name: *Hemerocallis* spp.
Common name: Daylily.
Habitat: Ordinary garden soil in full sun, but partial shade in the South.
Description: Perennials with clumps of narrow, sword-shaped leaves—some evergreen—and stout floral stalks; 6-petaled lilylike flowers in all colors but pure white and blue.
Period of bloom: Depending on type, late spring into fall.
Propagation: By division in spring.
Zone: 4.

When gardeners talk about rugged plants, the first one usually mentioned is *Hemerocallis*. *Hemero* is Greek for day (each blossom opens and withers in 24 hours), and *callis* means beautiful—but the common name is daylily, and the common perception is tough!

When settlers came to America from England and Europe, they brought along the common tawny daylily (*Hemerocallis fulva*) to brighten colonial gardens. Since a settler's time was at a premium and life was difficult, any plant that made the trip had to be hardy and able to withstand a good deal of neglect: in essence, a beautiful weed. Almost every home had tawny daylilies and a clump of lemon lilies (*H. lilioasphodelus,* once called *H. flava*).

The tawny daylily came to Europe from Asia in the Middle Ages. The plants are self-sterile and known today as the cultivar 'Europa'. All of the daylilies that line the backroads of America are descendants of those plants. They were not spread by seed but either by advancing rhizomes or pieces of them, pushed about by plows and bulldozers or just thrown out with the rest of the garden trash. Now that's tough.

In the late 1800s, plant breeders in Europe saw the remarkable qualities of the daylily and began to develop new cultivars for the growing number of people interested in gardening. When horticultural research was slowed in Europe as a result of the two World Wars, America took up the banner, and from a humble beginning with but a few species, it is estimated that there are well over 30,000 cultivars with more on the way.

Daylilies are virtually care-free. They will hold dry, rocky banks together or grow with perfect ease in moist soil by a lake or steam. They have no monstrous diseases, harbor few if any insect pests, and are perfectly hardy throughout the country.

Entire gardens can be created using these plants: There are dwarf types for rock gardens, species and cultivars for beds and borders, and types for perfect edging plants.

By a careful selection of species and cultivars, you can have daylilies in bloom in your garden from mid-June until the beginning of November. In fact, in warmer climates, some

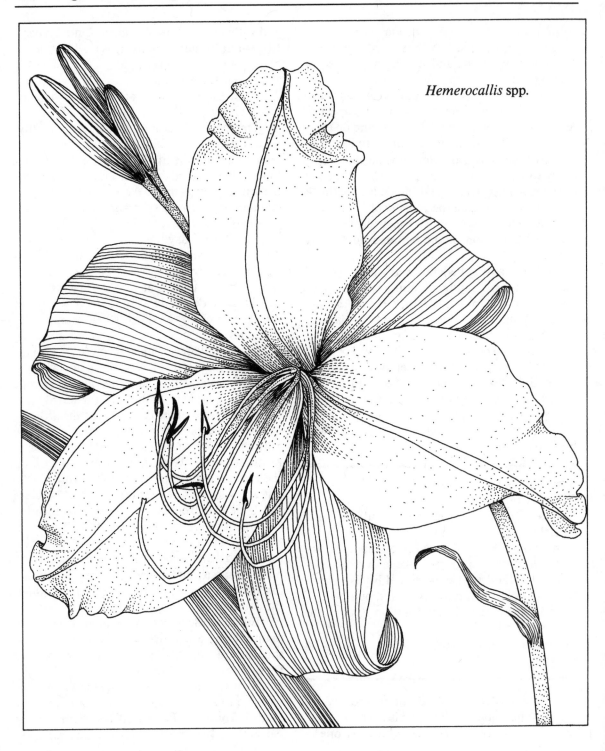

Hemerocallis spp.

are even evergreen. They prefer full sun in the North and partial shade in the South.

Propagation is by division for the wild daylily (as it does not set seed) and by division or seed for the domesticated plants. A plant can be divided into sections of convenient size with a sharp knife or trowel; each section should have a bit of crown with roots attached.

Plants may be left in one place for many years, but once blooming starts to decline and the plants become overgrown, it's time to divide. With reasonable care, they may be transplanted at any time in the season, but the best time is in early spring before growth hits its stride.

Daylilies are excellent subjects for interbreeding, as the flowers are large enough to easily transfer pollen (the yellow powder made up of male sex cells) from one blossom to the female stigma (the fuzzy, flattened top of the long rod that stands above the six surrounding anthers) of another, thus starting the process of setting seed. Start early in the morning. Before you transfer pollen, remove the six surrounding anthers and their pollen from the designated flower, using care to prevent self-pollination. Use a cotton swab to transfer the pollen from a flower of one variety to the stigma of another. After pollinating, cover the blossom with a small paper or plastic bag to keep any wandering bees away. Maintain careful records of your crosses; otherwise, you will never remember.

After a few days, remove the bag and watch the growth of the seed pod. As it matures, the pod swells, lightens in color, and dries. When it is fully ripe and appears ready to split, carefully remove the shiny black seeds within. Seeds may be germinated indoors in peat pots in a cool (40° to 60°F) area over the following winter. Or they can be planted outdoors in the autumn so that they will germinate in the coming spring.

There are literally hundreds of new introductions of daylily cultivars every year. Check the source lists for nurseries that specialize in these flowers.

Hemerocallis citrina blooms in summer with arching 3½-foot leaves and fragrant yellow blossoms on 4-foot stems that open in the early evening and last through the following day. *H. fulva* is the tawny daylily, too rough for today's formal gardens, but still an excellent choice for the wild or meadow garden. *H. lilioasphodelus* is the old-fashioned lemon lily, with fragrant blossoms in late May and early June, and *H. minor* is a dwarf species with fragrant yellow flowers and grasslike leaves reaching a height of 1½ feet.

Botanical name: *Heracleum mantegazzianum.*
Common name: Giant hogweed.
Habitat: Ordinary moist garden soil; full sun or partial shade.
Description: Biennial of heroic proportions; stout celery-like stems with large, deeply cut leaves; flat heads of tiny white flowers like a cartwheel; to 12 feet.
Period of bloom: Summer.
Propagation: By seed.
Zone: 4.

From out of the Steppes of Central Asia comes a plant that is the kung fu master of the flower kingdom, the stationary kudzu—the giant hogweed! Known as *Heracleum mantegazzianum,* this statuesque member of the parsley family has had a home in my garden for a number of years, originally grown from seed obtained in England. In our backyard, it's never topped 10 feet—but a botanist in Vancouver, B.C., reports his plant next to the front door reached 20 feet the first year. The name commemorates Herakles, using the Greek form of Hercules, and it's aptly chosen.

Short or tall, this imposing plant has been grown for decoration in English gardens for years, but unfortunately it escaped from cultivation, invading Battersea Park and other sites around London. Now it's doing the same in the States, with the first infestation reported in west-

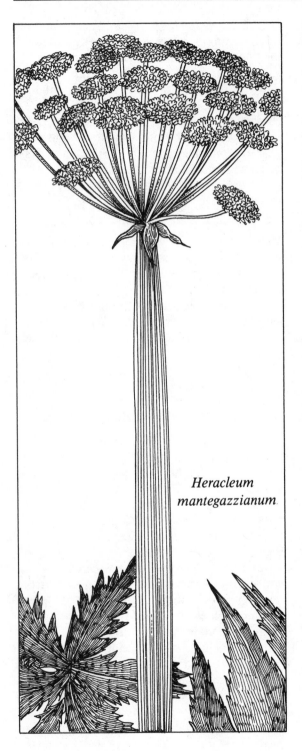

*Heracleum
mantegazzianum*

ern New York. It probably spread from Highland Park in Rochester, where it was grown as an ornamental since 1917. But it is easily kept in check by removing the seed heads as they form or pulling up small seedlings.

Since the plant is a biennial, it will grow only leaves the first year, flower the second, then die. It can be kept under control by cutting off the flower head before the seeds form, just letting a few seeds self-sow to eventually provide bloom every summer.

The stems are hollow and about 1 inch thick. Each stem section can be up to 2 feet in length. The sap contains a chemical, psoralen, which—when exposed to sunlight—produces a painful irritation known as phytophotodermatitis, a blistering affair. Because the sap is activated by sunlight, it is advised that you cut down the plant on a cloudy day or at night.

Not for the small garden, giant hogweed is so imposing, especially when in bloom, that it makes a wonderful addition to the wild garden or specimen planting at the edge of a pond. The large seed heads are spectacular in winter bouquets.

Botanical name: *Heuchera* spp.
Common name: Coralbells, alumroot.
Habitat: Ordinary well-drained garden soil with added humus; full sun in the North, but partial shade in the South.
Description: Perennial American wildflowers with gnarled roots and low-growing attractive lobed leaves; wiry stalks up to 30 inches high, bear bell-shaped flowers, usually in shades of red.
Period of bloom: Late spring into summer.
Propagation: By division in spring; seed.
Zone: 4.

Another American original, coralbells are largely western wildflowers usually found growing in the mountains and on cliff edges and rough terrain in general. The genus is named in honor of Johann Heinrich Heucher, 1677–1747, a professor of botany at Wittenberg. The common name alumroot refers to the astringent properties of the roots.

If your summers are hot, then coralbells can take a little filtered shade, but these are really plants for sunny spots. Although the flower stalks can reach a height of 2 feet, the individual blossoms are so small that to see five well-grown plants in full bloom is to experience a red haze before your eyes. To watch a hummingbird lunch at a single tiny bell-shaped blossom of a red coralbell is a garden treat.

Deadheading provides for more blossoms, so remember to remove developing seeds. The one thing that plants hate is wet feet, so be sure there is good drainage and enough humus in the soil. Every few years, break up the bigger plants or they will eventually crowd themselves out and blooming will suffer.

After a number of years devoted to hybridizing the various wild species, usually working with *Heuchera sanguinea,* both American and English nurserymen have produced a number of superior cultivars that provide both brighter flowers and longer bloom.

Among the many cultivars available, look for 'Chatterbox', with dozens of bright pink flowers on 18-inch stems; 'White Cloud', with dainty white flowers on 20-inch stems; and 'Matin Bells', with bright coral-red flowers on 18-inch stems.

In addition to the above, watch for *Heuchera micrantha* 'Palace Purple', a foot-high plant bearing reddish bronze foliage and off-white flowers on 18-inch stems. This coralbell is such a striking addition to the garden that the Perennial Plant Association has named it Plant of the Year for 1991. Although the parent plant ranges naturally from British Columbia to central California, it's hardy to −20°F. It does resent heavy clay. Use it for border edging, in the rock garden, or mixed with wildflowers. Oddly enough, plants may not be sent to California. Flowers are self-sterile, so they need the gardener to cross-

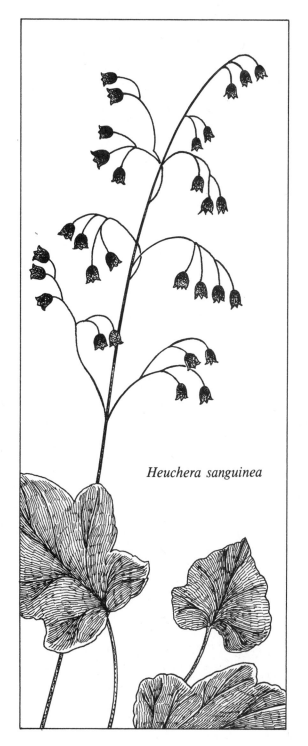

Heuchera sanguinea

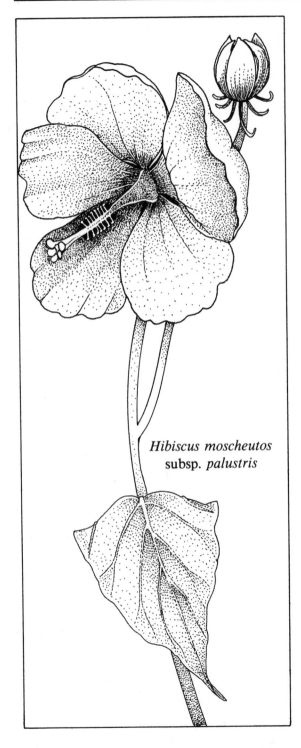

Hibiscus moscheutos
subsp. *palustris*

pollinate them for seeds. When reviewing seedlings, choose the plants with the darkest leaf color.

Botanical name: *Hibiscus* spp.
Common name: Mallow, rose mallow, giant mallow.
Habitat: Ordinary moist garden soil in full sun.
Description: Perennial with strong stems bearing coarse leaves below and 5-petaled, usually pink flowers; to 8 feet high.
Period of bloom: Summer.
Propagation: By division in spring; seed.
Zone: 5.

In other parts of the world, the hibiscus species are used for fiber, food, or to make medicinal products, but here at home they are generally used for ornamental purposes. The genus *Hibiscus* is Latin for marsh mallow. *H. cannabinus,* or Indian hemp, is used to provide a good fiber, much like jute and used for the same purposes; *H. sabdariffa,* or Jamaica sorrel, is famous for being the main ingredient in carcade, a beverage that Mussolini wanted all Italians to drink.

Hibiscus moscheutos subsp. *palustris,* the rose mallow, is yet another American wildflower, inhabiting the coastal areas of Massachusetts to North Carolina, then inland to New York and Ontario. They are so tropical in appearance that it's difficult to believe they will survive winters in Zone 5.

The 8-inch leaves are often shallowly lobed and rather coarse; the stems are strong. The hollyhock-like flowers bloom most of the summer and, in the species, are 4 to 5 inches across. Colors are pink, purple, or white with a red eye. In nature they often reach a height of 8 feet, but they are usually shorter in the garden unless provided with plenty of water or a swampy place. Mulching is suggested in areas of little snow and bitter winter winds.

In the wilder end of our garden, I dug out a 3-foot area—the plants will make large clumps over time—then lined the hole with heavy black plastic, thus making a potential swampy area. Here I planted the species. If starting from seed, begin in early spring, since it takes at least five months from sowing to bloom.

Since the cultivars are more civilized and certainly more robust in look, they are relegated to the formal garden. Here they adapt quite well to drier soil, but I remember to water well during long periods without rain.

'Ann Arundel' bears huge 6- to 8-inch flowers of glowing pink and was bred in Iowa by Robert Darby; 'Lady Baltimore' is a 4-foot plant having flowers just as large as the previous cultivar, only this time the petals have the quality of pink tissue paper and sport a contrasting red center; and 'Southern Belle' is a 3-foot plant that is smothered with 10-inch flowers in shades of white, pink, or bright red.

Hibiscus rosa-sinensis, the Chinese hibiscus, is a beautiful tropical shrub with 5-inch-wide flowers of rose red, often double. Hardy only to Zone 9, it has limited garden use and is best planted in patio pots.

Botanical name: *Hosta* spp.
Common name: Hosta.
Habitat: Ordinary moist garden soil in partial shade, although a few cultivars will take sun.
Description: Perennials with clumps of very attractive basal leaves of varying shapes and colors; usually tall stalks of bell-like flowers; to 3 feet.
Period of bloom: Late spring to early fall.
Propagation: By division in spring.
Zone: 4.

Next to daylilies, hostas are the miracle plants of gardens in the waning days of this century. Originally from China and Japan, they have been cultivated for centuries. The Japanese grow them in gardens, in pots, in deep shade and in full sun, in rock gardens, and in temple gardens.

Young leaves are wrapped around meat or rice as a substitute for cabbage; young leaves and cut-up young shoots are used in stir-fry; and the flower buds can be washed, dried, dusted with flour and batter-dipped, then deep-fat fried.

In 1894, William Robinson called these plants *Funkia.* They were named in honor of a German doctor, Heinrich Christian Funck (1771–1839). By the turn of the century, the name had been changed to *Hosta* in honor of Nicolaus Host (1761–1834), another German doctor.

As to the plants, they are the mainstay of a shady garden. One of the large cultivars, *Hosta* 'Big Daddy' (I apologize for some of these cultivar names that make the garden sound like a place for Barbie and Ken), has large, puckered leaves of a deep blue, reaching 2 1/2 feet in height and 3 feet in circumference. If space is limited, there is *Hosta* 'Shade Fanfare', with cool, green leaves banded with a creamy margin, and growing about 1 foot high and 2 feet wide.

There are few perennials that can be dug up and moved without showing great signs of stress. Hostas are one such plant. Back in 1986, I was called to a house in a nearby town where a garden of 40 years' standing was about to be demolished for a parking lot. Under a stand of maple trees were clumps of ready-to-bloom hostas (*Hosta fortunei*). They had not been touched for years. I dug deeply, dividing some plants as I went along. Later that afternoon, I set the hostas underneath a white ash tree. Within a week (with watering every day), they settled in and began to bloom, producing dozens of scapes with lavender-blue drooping bell-shaped flowers.

Only the late-blooming fragrant hosta (*Hosta plantaginea*) poses a problem, since its sweet-smelling white flowers usually appear in late summer or early autumn and can be killed by an early frost if they are not protected.

Hosta plantaginea

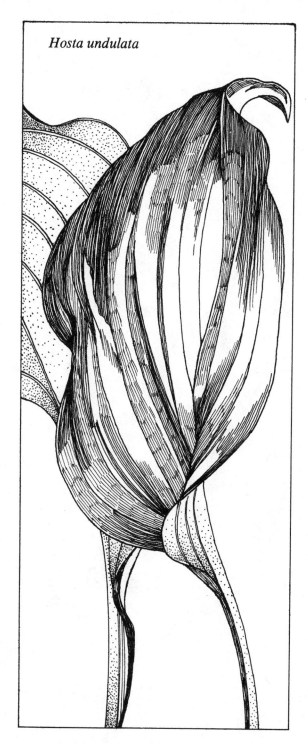

Hosta undulata

Many hostas will tolerate some exposure to sun, but unless they have been offered by the grower as adaptable to sunlight, keep them in light shade. As to pests and diseases, these plants are very tough. Only slugs present a problem; if left unchecked, they can turn leaves into a wonder of lacework.

Today there are hundreds of cultivars derived from some 40 species. Among the ranks, I think the following are particularly attractive.

Hosta lancifolia was introduced from Japan in 1829. Dark, glossy green, pointed leaves grow about 1 foot tall and form eventual 2-foot circles. Deep lilac flowers bloom in late summer. Plant them in groups to make an effective groundcover for shade or along the edge of a pool or stream.

Hosta plantaginea arrived from China sometime in the late 1700s. It would be grown if only for the bright green and glossy, heart-shaped leaves, but come early autumn, the long, waxy white trumpet flowers appear, opening in the late afternoon and on into evening, exuding a delicious honeysuckle fragrance. My plants in my upstate New York garden were given the protection of a high tree, in case I forgot to check for an early frost. In the South, they have the benefit of early morning and late afternoon sun but are protected by tall oaks during the worst of the day's heat.

Hosta sieboldiana 'Frances Williams' is a star even among a family of stars. The 1½-foot-high puckered leaves are a medium green with an uneven edge of yellow and form a 2½-foot circle; flowers are pale lavender, blooming early in the summer. In our garden, this plant sits in front of a low wall next to a set of stone steps, shaded from noonday sun by a viburnum of great age. It is a stunning plant.

Hosta undulata 'Albo-marginata' is a cultivar of a plant introduced to gardens in 1834. Oblong, waxy green leaves up to 8 inches long have a narrow white edge and soon make a spreading groundcover with blue-violet flowers in July.

Hosta venusta is a small plant from Korea with slightly wavy, green, heart-shaped leaves, 1 inch long and 1 inch wide, blooming with violet flowers in early summer.

Hosta 'Blue Angel' should be used as a specimen plant, for its huge clump of blue leaves have an ageless look about them. When the white, hyacinth-like flowers appear in summer, the effect is doubly grand. Three-foot-high leaves will soon form a 4-foot circle in open shade or with partial sun. They are especially beautiful when planted in the shade of a maroon smoke tree (*Cotinus coggygria* 'Purpureus') and near a group of maroon daylilies.

Inula ensifolia

Botanical name: *Inula ensifolia.*
Common name: Inula.
Habitat: Ordinary garden soil in full sun.
Description: Perennials with narrow leaves on thin stems; bright yellow 1 1/2-inch-wide daisies.
Period of bloom: Summer.
Propagation: By division; seed.
Zone: 4.

My original plants came from seed supplied by a traveling friend who brought the packet back from a German supermarket. I had no idea what they were and expected to find a rather coarse plant like another species in the genus, the elecampane (*Inula helenium*), but I was pleasantly surprised.

The genus is supposed to be an ancient Latin name used by Horace, but some authorities say it's a corruption of *hinnulus,* a young mule, since elecampane was reported to be good for either man or beast. The sap and roots of these plants contain *inulin,* a tasteless white semicrystalline substance that resembles starch.

Inula ensifolia is a clump-forming plant with thin, narrow leaves (*ensifolia* means swordshaped, referring to the leaves), usually about a foot high but up to 16 inches. It produces single, deep yellow daisies on wiry stalks. The blooming period is six weeks in summer but can be extended by carefully deadheading the spent blossoms.

Inulas want only that sunny spot to succeed. Seeds planted very early in the spring will flower the first year, but never with the show you can expect the second season. They are excellent planted along edges or massed in the front of the border and are great along the edge of a wall.

If you can't find plants, seed is always available and usually sold as the cultivar 'Gold Star', producing 2 1/2-inch flowers.

Botanical name: *Iris* spp.
Common name: Iris.
Habitat: Ordinary garden soil in full sun with minor variations listed below.
Description: Perennials, usually with rhizomes, that bear crowns of sword-shaped leaves; beautiful flowers on strong stems, representing most of the colors of a rainbow.
Period of bloom: Spring into summer.
Propagation: By division in spring or summer.
Zone: 3.

There are over 200 species of iris, native mostly to the Northern Hemisphere, and most of those from Asia. The name is ancient Greek and some authorities think it's derived from Iris, the rainbow goddess, alluding to the multicolored flowers.

Most irises have fanlike basal leaves that usually grow in two ranks, arising from a stumpy rhizome that resembles a horizontal carrot. Others grow in clumps, producing fountains of leaves that are attractive even without flowers.

There are three groups in the rhizomatous species: Bearded iris have little beards or hairs that appear on the rounded part of the falls, or lower petals (the upright petals are called standards); the crested iris has a crest like a cockscomb on the falls; and the beardless iris

naturally lacks this beard. The petals come in white, then shades of pink, yellow, orange, blue, lilac, purple, to brown and almost black. There are no true reds.

Most of the irises need full sun. Except for those that grow directly in water, they prefer a good, well-drained garden soil with added humus, but many will grow in poor soil and still bloom.

In the North, the rhizomatous irises should have the "carrots" showing when planted; in the South, they should be lightly covered. After flowering, the tips of the leaves usually begin to brown; these can be neatly trimmed (the sign of a well-run iris bed is the attention to such detail). They are best divided and replanted from midsummer to fall, after blooming is through.

When irises are mentioned, most people think of the tall bearded iris (*Iris germanica*), which are hardy in Zone 4. The fanlike leaves are gray-green, and flowers come in a multitude of color combinations, usually seen in garden magazines and full-color nursery ads. There are cultivars that bloom both in the spring and the fall. The tall irises are over 25 inches tall; intermediates are between 16 and 27 inches; the standard plants are between 8 and 16 inches; and the miniatures under 8 inches tall. Perhaps the best introduction to the seemingly unlimited colors available is to order a mix of colors from a nursery special offer.

Iris cristata, the dwarf crested iris, is a wildflower hardy in Zone 5, blooming in early spring and delighting in early season sun followed by the open shade provided by burgeoning deciduous trees. The species is lavender-blue with a 2-inch yellow crest on a 6-inch stem. A white form is 'Alba'. These irises should be mulched in areas with little snow cover.

Iris foetidissima has leaves that produce the distinct smell of raw meat when bruised, but the species name is overdoing it just a bit, since the smell is not offensive. Hardy in Zone 6 and wanting partial shade, this iris is grown not for the pale blue flower but for the beautiful

Iris sibirica

shining orange-red seeds that burst out of the pods in autumn.

Iris kaempferi is the nursery name for the Japanese iris and *I. ensata* is the botanical name. The huge blossoms are often over 6 inches wide, held aloft on stiff, 8-inch stems, blooming in June and looking for all the world like layers of colored linen waving in the wind. They prefer evenly moist soil and are especially happy at the water's edge. There are too many color choices to list, but you can't go wrong with a pure white semi-double called 'Great White Heron', or the Higo strain from Japan that includes 'Nikko', with petals of pale purple-blue and a gold throat.

Iris pallida, or the orris iris, is grown primarily for the foliage and produces fragrant lilac flowers on 3-foot stems. The rhizome is used in the perfume industry.

Iris pumila, the dwarf bearded iris, grows about 6 inches high, blooming in early May, and is best in the rock garden with a spot in full sun. 'Red Dandy' is a lovely cultivar with wine-red flowers.

Iris sibirica, the Siberian iris, does well in Zones 3 through 8. Flowers are 3 to 4 inches on 30-inch stems emerging from marvelous clumps of swordlike leaves. They need full sun and prefer a good, moist soil. Here, too, there are many colors available, but look for 'Snow Queen', a lovely pure white; for a small garden, try 'Little White', with blossoms borne on 15-inch stems.

Finally there is the Japanese roof iris, *Iris tectorum,* supposedly once used as a living binding material for thatched roofs in the Orient. Plants are hardy in Zone 5, grow about 1 foot high, and are covered in June with 6-inch-wide lilac-blue flowers. They, too, prefer a moist soil with mulch added in winters where there is little snow.

Botanical name: *Lavatera trimestris.*
Common name: Tree mallow.
Habitat: Ordinary garden soil in full sun.
Description: An annual of great beauty, like a small bush; attractive leaves; covered with 5-petaled, hollyhock-like flowers of pink or white; to 3 feet.
Period of bloom: Summer.
Propagation: By seed.
Zone: Any zone.

Lavatera trimestris

The tree mallows are mostly summer-flowering perennial plants and shrubs hardy only to the warmest spots of Zone 6, but one species, *Lavatera trimestris,* is a magnificent annual that brings a remembered grace to any garden. The genus was named in honor of the somewhat famous Lavater brothers of Zurich, seventeenth century Swiss naturalists and physicians. The brother Johann Kasper is best remembered for his work with physiognomy, the art of reading character from facial structure (one wonders what he would have thought of today's politicians).

We first grew the mallows in our northern garden in upstate New York, along the edge of a white picket fence and backed by a row of peonies, where they reveled in the hot summer sun and succeeded in the poorest of soil (only the peonies had been given a good start).

Plants grow to 3 feet or more and are generously covered with dark green, alternate, lobed leaves topped with trumpets that glisten like satin. They bloom from mid-July until cut down by frost. The species flowers are pale pink, veined with purple, and up to 4 inches in diameter. Because of their growth habit, mallows look more like shrubs than garden annuals and are truly beautiful when massed toward the back of the border.

The roots resent disturbance, so start the seeds in early spring where the plants are to grow, allowing 15 to 20 days for germination, or sow the seeds individually in 3-inch peat pots. Space plants 2 feet apart.

There are a number of cultivars: 'Loveliness' has deep rose-pink trumpet flowers on 3- to 4-foot plants; 'Silver Cup' is a smaller plant and bushier, covered in glowing pink flowers; 'Mont Blanc' has glistening white flowers that bloom against dark green leaves; and a new selection is 'Ruby Regis', with 4-inch flowers of a brilliant cerise-pink.

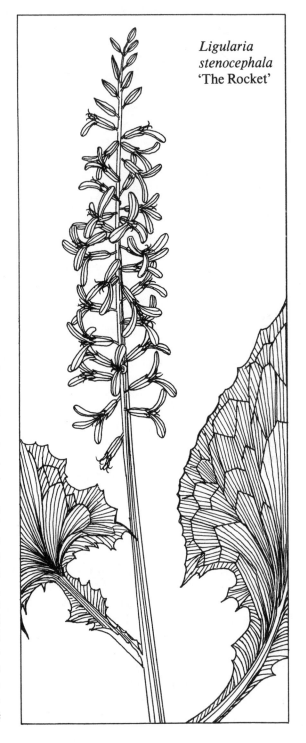

*Ligularia
stenocephala
'The Rocket'*

Botanical name *Ligularia* spp.
Common name: Ligularia.
Habitat: Ordinary garden soil, but prefers moist site in partial shade.
Description: Bold perennials with large rounded leaves on stout stems; tall spires of yellow or orange daisylike flowers; to 6 feet.
Period of bloom: Late summer.
Propagation: By division in spring or fall; seed.
Zone: 5.

When first I heard the word ligularia, I immediately thought of a rare bird or perhaps the title of one of Shakespeare's minor plays, somewhere between *Cymbeline* and *The Rape of Lucrece.* Upon learning that two important cultivars in this genus of plants were called 'Desdemona' and 'Othello', I was sure of it.

But no. The plant's name comes from the Latin word *ligula,* which means "little tongue" and refers to the tonguelike shape of the large petal on each of the ray flowers surrounding the central "eye" of the simpler disk flowers. This genus includes some 150 handsome species, the first plant (*Ligularia dentata*) arriving in Europe late in the nineteenth century, collected in Japan by a Russian plant explorer, Carl Maximowicz. These plants are desirable perennials for a number of reasons: They can be grown with ease in wet, almost boggy conditions, and they thrive in nearly all soils, including those thick with clay. Their leaves are large and well proportioned; they are, for the most part, tall and graceful, yet have stems that are strong enough to withstand heavy rains and winds without staking. The flowers are bold and beautiful and some of them have an attractive scent—*L. dentata* smells of cocoa—and in my northern garden in upstate New York, they would bloom from middle to late summer until the killing frosts of autumn cut them to the ground.

Their only fault is the alarming habit of wilting on hot days, even when they are growing in plenty of moisture. But with the approach of evening, they recover their former glory. Slugs are a problem, and all the sap-sucking beetles enjoy chewing their way across that vast expanse of leaf, so I use a pyrethrum spray to keep the bugs under control.

All the species are easy to grow from seed by starting in early spring using bottom heat of 60°F. Plants can be moved to a sheltered spot by early fall and will flower the following year. In late November, I break up the soil around each plant and cut off the leaf stalks at ground level, just before the ground freezes, then mulch with leaves and pine branches.

Ligularia dentata grows about 4 feet high and often that wide. Its somewhat kidney-shaped leaves are about a foot wide and coarsely toothed. The flower heads have 12 to 14 bright orange ray-flower petals, measuring 2 inches long. 'Desdemona' and 'Othello' both have a purple cast to the leaves, but the second is a shorter plant.

Ligularia stenocephala 'The Rocket' begins to bloom in July and on into August. A large clump of triangular-shaped and deeply incised dark green leaves seems to balance tall spires of bright yellow flowers. Each individual blossom is only 3 inches wide, but in unison, they are a glory of yellowish gold. The column often tops 6 feet.

Ligularia veitchiana needs more room than the rest; as a mature plant, it can reach a height of 6 feet and spread to 4. The leaves are almost round, lightly serrated, and nearly a foot wide. The flower heads are bright yellow and cluster on a stalk some 2 feet high.

Botanical name: *Lunaria annua.*
Common name: Honesty, money plant, moonwort.
Habitat: Ordinary garden soil in partial shade or full sun.
Description: Biennial with coarse leaves on strong stems to 3 feet high; sweet-scented purple to white blossoms in late spring, followed by round silvery pods used for winter bouquets.
Period of bloom: Late spring into summer.
Propagation: By seed.
Zone: 5.

Honesty is a hardy biennial that will flower from seed in the first year if started early in the season. The purple- or white-flowering plants are used in formal flower beds all over Europe but have yet to be popular for that use in America. The name of the genus is from *lunar,* pertaining to the moon. The name refers to the nearly round, silver-white replum, the parchmentlike disk about 1 1/2 inches wide that holds the seeds.

Honesty has been in cultivation for over 400 years, and a vase of the seedpods, although viewed by many as a clich, is still beautiful. According to Pizzetti and Cocker in their charming book, *Flowers: A Guide for Your Garden,* these plants reached their maximum popularity with the Victorians, and occasionally the small moonlike disks would be hand-painted with fanciful designs. The common name of honesty goes back to the Middle Ages and refers to the transparency of the pod allowing the seeds within to be seen.

The sweetly scented flowers are varying shades of reddish violet, about 1 inch wide. There is a white-flowered form called 'Alba'. The upper leaves are almost without stalks, and

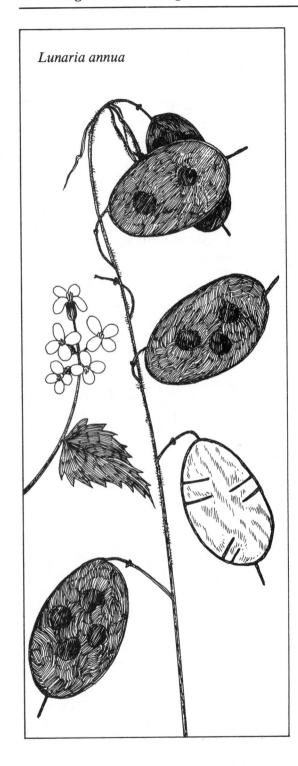

Lunaria annua

the lower leaves are coarsely toothed and rough to the touch. There is also a form with variegated leaves; it is not particularly attractive but just a curiosity.

The fruits are almost elliptical, with silvery, translucent valves, or walls, initially covered with a brownish membrane that is best removed by rubbing it between your fingers.

I always thought that honesty did its best in full sun but was surprised to learn that in its original home in southern Europe, it's a plant of woodlands. While it does well in full sun, honesty prefers partial shade, especially in the American South.

Once a bed is started in the wild garden, they will reseed, and soon there will be flowers and fruits every year. In our garden, a large clump blooms at the edge of a fernery guarded on either side by large purple rhododendrons.

Botanical name: *Lysimachia* spp.
Common name: Loosestrife.
Habitat: Ordinary but moist garden soil in full sun or partial shade; provide some shade in the South.
Description: Perennials with simple leaves on stout stems; either nodding whorls of small white flowers or yellow starlike flowers along the stem; to 3 feet.
Period of bloom: Summer.
Propagation: By division in spring or fall; seed.
Zone: 5.

The loosestrifes are a large group of plants belonging to the genus *Lysimachia,* a name used by the Greeks and probably derived from Lysimachus, the king of Thrace, a country memorialized in the famous line: "I was banished to Thrace, thrice."

Plants spread by underground stolons, so set them at least 2 feet apart or they will join forces in one growing season. If these plants are given the moist garden soil they prefer, they will quickly spread, so isolate them either by containing the roots with a barrier or setting them in a part of the wild garden. But don't confuse these plants with the infamous purple loosestrife (*Lythrum salicaria*), one of the most invasive plants in the Northeast, unfortunately bearing the same common name.

Originally from Japan and China, *Lysimachia clethroides* has the very descriptive common name of the gooseneck loosestrife. A number of these plants in bloom look exactly like a gaggle of geese arching their necks and ready to honk at intruders. The plants grow about 3 feet tall with simple alternate leaves on stout stems

Lysimachia clethroides

ending in nodding whorls of small, white, 5-parted flowers that bloom in summer.

In our northern garden in upstate New York, the goosenecks were backed by a low rise planted with a climbing hydrangea (*Hydrangea anomala* subsp. *petiolaris*) and kept from invading a grass path with a line of bricks set on end. All were in the high open shade of a very old white pine. In order to provide adequate water, I lined the bottom of the trench with heavy black plastic before setting in the plants; thus they had the boggy conditions they prefer.

Lysimachia punctata, or the garden loosestrife, came to England from Asia Minor in the 1820s, where it quickly became established as a ditchweed. It has now been reported as a weed in parts of Quebec and New York. Still, it's an attractive plant with 30-inch stems bearing whorls of leaves and dozens of 5-parted, bright lemon yellow flowers blooming up and down the top 15 inches. The plants resemble a native wildflower, *L. quadrifolia,* but are far more attractive. This plant is especially effective when massed in a border, and the electric punch of the masses of flowers will elicit comments from all garden visitors.

Botanical name: *Macleaya* spp.
Common name: Plume poppy.
Habitat: Ordinary garden soil in full sun or light shade.
Description: Bold perennials with beautiful, deeply lobed leaves, gray-green above and wooly-white beneath; plumelike blossoms; to 8 feet.
Period of bloom: Summer.
Propagation: By division in spring; seeds.
Zone: 3.

Gardeners, especially estate gardeners, often complain about weedy plants. I find the complaint is in direct proportion to the amount of hired help the gardener has.

"Can't seem to control this area," they say, and point to a luxurious clump of bamboo that

Macleaya cordata

most gardeners would love to fight. "But I'll have the crew in here tomorrow and they'll clean it up!"

A case in point is the plume poppy. Yes, it's a spreader. Yes, it's aggressive. But it's also beautiful with a number of attractive assets. A well-grown line of these plants will cover a multitude of sins—including undesirable fences—yet one look at those two-toned leaves waving about in an updraft will delight the gardener's heart. The genus is named in honor of Alexander Macleay (1767–1848), secretary for the Linnean Society.

Many authorities suggest keeping plume poppies at the back of the border, but this plant is too beautiful to hide. It makes a great specimen plant surrounded by lawn or groundcovers. It does well in a pot and can be moved about during the season and set where its tropical beauty is to the best effect. The plumes are comprised of many flowers, lacking petals, but having up to 30 stamens each.

There are two species, and most nurseries now offer both. *Macleaya cordata* (*Bocconia cordata*) is listed by most as the running perennial up to 8 feet high and bearing buff-colored plumes. According to *Hortus Third,* the other species, *M. microcarpa,* differs in having only 8 to 12 stamens per flower but otherwise being the same. Yet nurseries credit the second plant for the new and shorter cultivar 'Coral Plume', only 7 feet high, with salmon-tinted buff flowers.

Graham Stuart Thomas, writing in *Perennial Garden Plants,* says that *Macleaya cordata* is the better of the two and does not have searching roots, while *M. microcarpa* is the more active of the two. Either way, the gardener is ahead.

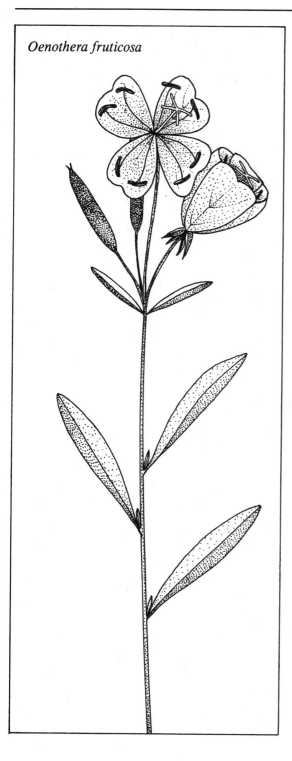

Oenothera fruticosa

Botanical name: *Oenothera* spp.
Common name: Sundrops, suncups.
Habitat: Ordinary garden soil in full sun.
Description: Perennial American wildflowers with strong stems and narrow leaves; topped by brilliant yellow, 4-petaled flowers; to 2 feet.
Period of bloom: Summer.
Propagation: By division in spring; seed.
Zone: 5.

There are two types of evening primroses: the day-bloomers, called sundrops, and those that only bloom in late afternoon or evening, the true evening primroses. Unfortunately they both share the common genus *Oenothera.* The name is from the Greek words *oinos,* meaning wine, and *thera,* to hunt, because of confusion regarding these flowers and still another genus of plants with roots possessing the aroma of wine.

For many years we had a sloping bank in front of our old farmhouse that was covered with wild daylilies (*Hemerocallis fulva*), but between the lilies and the lawn we kept a long, narrow bed of sundrops (*Oenothera fruticosa*). Memories come and go, but I suspect that no matter how many years pass by, the sight and smell of a summer garden after a morning rain will remind me of these bright, bright golden yellow flowers.

The plants have simple leaves and are easily missed in the garden until coming into bud and bloom in high summer. For then the unassuming plants are topped with clusters of bright red buds and yellow-gold flowers.

The species are perfect in the wild garden and can hold their own at the edge of a meadow. For the formal garden, the cultivars are best, as they have more and larger flowers. But a bed of any sundrops in bloom is as close as you can get to a pool of molten gold.

Care is minimal. Sundrops ask only for full sun and well-drained soil; dryness is no problem. Gathered in early winter, the seed heads of the sundrops make interesting additions to winter bouquets.

Oenothera fruticosa is the wildflower from the eastern U.S. The flowers are about 2 inches across on stems between 1 and 2 feet high; basal rosettes are evergreen south of Philadelphia. Although this plant is a rapid spreader, it's easily controlled, as it is shallow-rooted. 'Youngii-lapsley' bears brighter flowers on 24-inch stems.

Oenothera tetragona is often confused with the first species but has been subject to much more hybridizing. 'Sonnenwende' is a 2-foot plant with beautiful orange-red buds that open to brilliant flowers, with foliage that turns red in the fall; 'Yellow River' has 2-inch flowers on 1½-foot plants, and its foliage turns a reddish-mahogany in the fall; 'Fireworks' is bright yellow on 1½-foot plants.

Botanical name: *Paeonia* spp.
Common name: Peony and tree peony.
Habitat: Ordinary but well-prepared garden soil with added humus; full sun in the North, but partial shade in the South.
Description: Perennial shrublike plants with large, attractive, compound leaves; large, showy flowers with many petals; to 7 feet.
Period of bloom: Late spring to early summer.
Propagation: By division in spring; seed.
Zone: 5.

My mother was an avid gardener, and I remember well our backyard when I was a teenager in the late 1940s. There were a number of lemon lilies, a whole bed of various wildflowers collected from what was then woods instead of shopping centers, and a long line of peonies. According to the elderly next-door neighbors, those peonies were planted by the original owners of our house right after the First World War, so they were then 30 years old. Today, some 40 years later, they are still blooming. So when it comes to perennial, the peony is right up there among the leaders.

There are two different kinds of peonies: The herbaceous types are shrubby plants and die down to the ground in winter; the tree peonies have branches covered with bark that remain in the garden all year long.

Not only do both have beautiful flowers, the plants themselves are attractive with their glossy green compound leaves on reddish stems. Both types bloom in late spring and early summer with lovely flowers, which are followed by interesting seedpods. They were named for the Greek physician Paeon, who first used the plants for medicinal purposes (for centuries the roots have been used to treat epilepsy and spasms). The ants usually seen patrolling the stems and buds of peonies are interested only in the sweet sap and do not damage the plants in any way.

The best time for planting is late September or early October, depending on your climate zone. This is another plant for which the old axiom of a five-dollar plant in a ten-dollar hole is particularly apt: The hole should be large enough to receive the plant without crowding the roots. The soil should be rich with added humus. If soil is excessively acid, add one cup of lime per plant. Keep manure and added fertilizers away from direct contact with the roots. Plant with the "eyes," or growing points, to the top, about 1½ inch below the soil surface. Water well. Mulch the first year where winters are excessive. With tree peonies, it's a good idea to cover the plant with a large bushel basket for the first winter.

Every so often the branch of any peony will wilt without any obvious cause. It's usually a fungus blight called botrytis. Quickly sever the wilted branch and burn it. Pick up any leaf litter around the plant, since botrytis usually does not bother plants that have good drainage and plenty of air circulation.

A number of herbaceous peony cultivars are available, with single to fully double blossoms. Some of the more attractive are 'Bowl of Cream', with pure white, double blossoms 8 inches across; 'Emma Klehm', bearing double, deep pink flowers that bloom late in the season; 'Coral Sunset', with flowers of intense

Paeonia suffruticosa

coral; and 'Sarah Bernhardt', whose flowers have deep pink petals that lighten toward the edge and have a lovely fragrance.

Paeonia mlokosewitschii, or the Caucasian peony, bears one of the more unpronounceable names in the botanical world. It was named in honor of one Herr Mlokosewitsch, a plant explorer apparently so little known that even *The Royal Horticultural Dictionary of Gardening* does not list his first name. He discovered this herbaceous peony with 5-inch single sulfur yellow flowers on 3-foot stems in the Caucasus sometime in 1907. I'm familiar with this plant since I coveted it for years, grew my own from seed, waited five years for flowers, and they turned out to be pink. Oh, well, gardening is basically patience and I will try again.

Paeonia suffruticosa is the Japanese tree peony, originally from China but refined by the Japanese, and actually a bush, usually reaching a height of 5 feet with a spread of 6 feet. The flowers are between 6 and 8 inches across.

Tree peonies are expensive, so shop around for the best price. The plants are grafted onto herbaceous peony roots. The graft junction, or joining, should come about 6 inches below the ground level, so the graft will develop its own root system. For a time your tree peony will send up two kinds of leaves: The deeply cut leaves are the tree peony, while the others are shoots from the herbaceous root and should be cut off at ground level.

All tree peony cultivars that I have seen in the U.S. are exceptional plants. But among the more beautiful are 'Age of Gold', with large, double, golden yellow blossoms; 'Gauguin', with yellow petals inked with rose-red lines; and 'Marchioness', featuring a soft yellow suffused with shades of apricot, all surrounding yellow stamens.

Botanical name: *Phlox* spp.
Common name: Garden phlox.
Habitat: Ordinary moist garden soil but prefer added humus; full sun or partial shade.
Description: Perennials with strong stems and simple leaves; terminal clusters of long-lasting, very fragrant, 5-parted flowers arising from a narrow tube; to 4 feet.
Period of bloom: Summer into fall.
Propagation: By division in spring or fall; seed.
Zone: 3.

Every country home worth its salt had the original garden phlox in the border. The botanical name for this important American wildflower is *Phlox paniculata,* and it grows in open woods and bottomlands from New York to Iowa and Kansas and southward to Georgia, northern Mississippi, and Arkansas. Since phlox have been cultivated in gardens for centuries, plants have escaped from cultivation into the wild in many other parts of the country. The genus name is from the Greek word for flame, referring to the bright colors of some species.

Use phlox for cutting—we always keep additional plants in the cutting garden so the border is not disturbed—and for garden color in general. In addition to the color, the sweet-scented flowers (some people find them too sweet) attract butterflies and sphinx moths all day long and evening moths as the sun goes down.

Garden phlox want full sun to light shade and well-drained but moist garden soil, best produced by working in added humus. Since the leaves are prone to powdery mildew, keep the individual plants at least 2 feet apart to provide for good air circulation. Divide the plants every three years to keep them vigorous, and deadhead to prolong bloom and prevent unwanted seedlings. Thin the weaker shoots on plants every spring, and pinch back the front shoots for lower flowers and a better display.

Phlox stolonifera

The 5-parted tubular flowers of the garden phlox are usually white to pink to purple-magenta, but with many variations between. These variations have been utilized by breeders and have led to many cultivars, chiefly by Captain B. Symons-Jeune; many nurseries carry the cultivars that he created.

The Symons-Jeune strain was developed both for strength of the stems and a resistance to fungus. Notable colors are 'Bright Eyes', with pink flowers and a rich red eye; 'Dramatic', with salmon-pink flowers; and 'Dodo Hanbury Forbes', with clear pink flowers, worth having for the name alone. All are about 3 feet high.

Probably the most beautiful phlox in our garden is 'Mt. Fuji' (sometimes called 'Fujiyama'), bearing large heads of lovely snow white flowers on up to 5-foot stems—especially if they are well-watered—which will bloom until frost if the spent flowers are removed. It is a cultivar of the original wild-flower. Among the other lovely colors are 'Starfire', a brilliant red on 2½-foot stems; 'Orange Perfection', with orange-salmon flowers; and 'Blue Boy', the nearest flower to true blue, both on 3-foot stems.

Probably the longest-flowering phlox is 'Miss Lingard', created over 50 years ago either from *Phlox maculata,* the wild sweet William, or *P. carolina.* 'Miss Lingard' will begin blooming in early June and will continue throughout the summer.

Phlox stolonifera, the creeping phlox, was nominated the Perennial Plant Association's flower of the year for 1990; quite an honor for an American woodland flower. The plants crawl along the ground and bear purple or violet flowers on 6-inch stems in late spring. Five cultivars provide white ('Bruce's White'); pink ('Pink Ridge'); blue ('Blue Ridge'); purple-blue ('Sherwood Purple);' and lavender ('Irridescens'). Plants want a slightly acid soil with some humus and spring sunshine to succeed. Since they are the most shade tolerant of the group, they are perfect for edging.

Botanical name: *Physalis alkekengi.*
Common name: Chinese lantern.
Habitat: Ordinary garden soil in full sun or partial shade.
Description: Perennials with heart-shaped leaves; inconspicuous flowers followed by bright orange balloonlike pods; to 2 feet.
Period of bloom: Late summer.
Propagation: By division in spring; seeds.
Zone: 3.

Physalis alkekengi

These plants tumble about, and many gardeners view them as being too undisciplined for the formal garden. But their orange pods are so beautiful and bright, Chinese lanterns should be given an area somewhere in the backyard or in the wild garden.

Even nongardeners are familiar with this plant—almost every still-life painting of flowers done in the 1920s or the 1930s included these pods in the arrangement. For years, my mother had a tea tray decorated with Chinese lanterns.

The genus name is from *physa,* the Greek word for bladder, and refers to the 2-inch-long inflated calyx, or sepals, of the spent flower, which surround an edible but insipid scarlet berry. The flowers are 5-parted, off-white in color, and hidden beneath the leaves.

Pick the stems in the fall as the lanterns start to turn from green to orange, remove the leaves, and hang the stems upside down in a dry place. If left in the garden, the pods soon become skeletonized.

Seedlings will produce lanterns the first summer if started early in spring. Germination takes three or four weeks. Once in the garden, they can be left as is for years.

Physalis alkekengi var. *franchetii* has larger leaves and the 3-inch pods are also longer and taper to a point. 'Gigantea' is even larger.

Some English garden books mention a dwarf form, var. *nana,* but I've never seen it offered in commerce.

Botanical name: *Physostegia virginiana.*
Common name: Obedient plant.
Habitat: Ordinary moist garden soil in full sun; ordinary soil in shade.
Description: Perennial American wildflower with strong, square stems; terminal spikes of usually rose-pink flowers, like small snapdragons; to 5 feet.
Period of bloom: Late summer into fall.
Propagation: By division in spring; seeds.
Zone: 4.

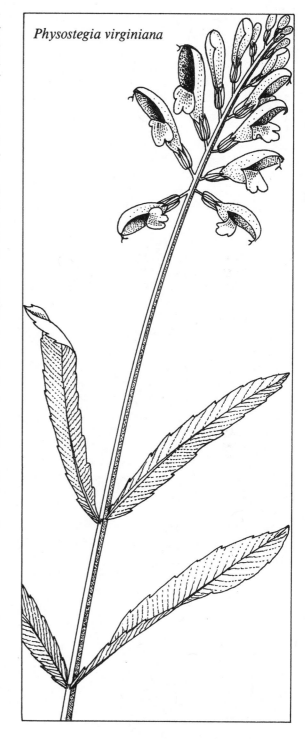

Physostegia virginiana

The common name of obedient plant is well deserved. Move each blossom back and forth or up and down and it will stay where it's placed. Flower arrangers have long known about this oddity, and children are also amused by this seeming power over a flower. In nature, this ability allows the blossoms to face away from a storm; since insects such as bees or bumblebees land against the wind, the flowers have the advantage for pollination. The flowers keep their position due to friction of the flower stalk against the surrounding bracts; remove the bracts and the flowers are limp. The genus name is from *physa,* for bladder, and *stege,* for covering, referring to the inflated floral tube.

Because obedient plants are somewhat invasive, moving about by creeping roots, they naturalize with ease. But if they transgress, simply pull them up. They are beautiful either massed in a formal border or allowed to wander a wild garden. Since they do spread about, plan on dividing plants every three years.

Seed is an excellent way to find plants with pleasing colors. Start seed in early spring. The seedlings will exhibit a wide range of color from magenta to pale pink; keep the best, then propagate by division in future.

There are a number of attractive cultivars. 'Bouquet Rose' has rose flowers on 3-foot stems; 'Crown of Snow' and 'Summer Snow' have white blossoms and usually grow about 2½ feet tall; 'Vivid' has deep pink flowers on 2-foot stalks; 'Variegata', with 3-foot stems, is a truly beautiful plant that has leaves edged with creamy stripes and lovely rosy pink flowers.

Botanical name: *Platycodon grandiflorus.*
Common name: Balloon flower.
Habitat: Ordinary well-drained but moist garden soil in full sun or partial shade.
Description: Perennial bearing strong stems with white sap and attractive leaves; flower buds resembling balloons, opening to bell-shaped, usually blue flowers; to 2½ feet, but usually 2 feet high.
Period of bloom: Summer.
Propagation: By division in spring; seeds.
Zone: 4.

There is only one species in this genus, a perennial herb native to eastern Asia. Although the roots are considered to be poison, in China it's called *Chieh-keng* and used in combination with other herbs in the treatment of influenza and sore throat; in Japan the name is *Kikyo.* The genus means *platys,* broad, and *kodon,* bell, referring to the balloon shape of the unopened flowers.

Their common name is perfectly chosen, for they do resemble a team of hot-air balloons floating above a forest. The oval leaves are a glaucous blue beneath. Since they bloom from summer into fall, they are garden stars. Excellent as cut flowers, their stems should be seared with a match before being placed in water.

Balloon flowers form clumps and do not spread, so they can be left in place for years. They are among the last plants in the garden to break dormancy, so mark their position with care. Seed is readily available but will not flower for two or three years.

In our garden, a bed of blue balloon flowers shared a space with sweet Williams (*Dianthus barbatus*) and blackberry lilies (*Belamcanda chinensis*).

'Album' has white flowers; 'Blue' has deep blue 2-inch flowers; 'Double Blue' has double flowers with dark veining that look more like love-in-a-mist (*Nigella* spp.) than balloon flowers; 'Shell Pink' is, as named, a soft shell pink and grows best in partial shade; 'Komachi' is unusual since the flowers hold the balloon shape after opening; and 'Mariesii' has pastel blue flowers on foot-high stems, perfectly scaled for the rock garden.

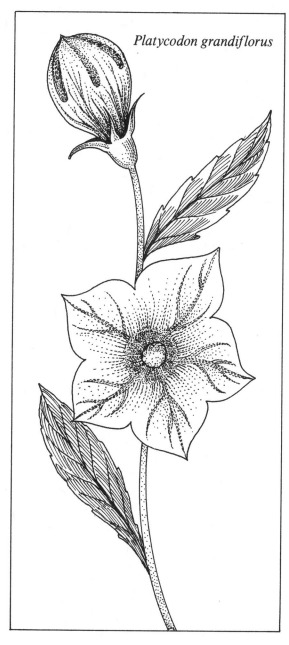

Platycodon grandiflorus

Botanical name: *Polygonatum commutatum* (sometimes listed as *P. giganteum).*
Common name: Solomon's-seal.
Habitat: Ordinary moist garden soil with added humus; shade.
Description: Perennial with tall, arching stems with attractive oval leaves and clusters of small creamy bells hanging beneath; to 8 feet.
Period of bloom: Late spring.
Propagation: By division in early spring; seed.
Zone: 5.

In the wrong place, Solomon's-seal will not survive, since hot sun and dry soil are double sins. But given a spot in the shade with moist soil, this plant will grow and spread with ease. It's not grown for the flowers, which, though pretty, are small, but for the effect of the gracefully arching stems. Clothed in attractive 7-inch leaves, they can reach a height of 8 feet.

The genus is very old, derived from a name used in ancient Greece meaning *poly,* many, and *gonu,* a knee joint, referring to the many-jointed rhizome. The common name comes from the seal-like scars that are left on the underground rhizomes where the branches originate—scars that do resemble the waxen images used to ensure the authenticity of ancient documents. In nursery catalogs, *Polygonatum commutatum* is often listed as *P. canaliculatum,* although *P. canaliculatum* is actually another name for a shorter species, properly called *P. biflorum.* The rhizomes have been utilized in folk medicine for centuries, especially as an astringent, a tonic, and for pulmonary complaints.

Use plenty of humus when planting the rhizomes. If summer rains are sparse, remember to water these plants in order to keep the foliage fresh and green. The plants can sulk after moving, so give them a year to recover unless you begin with container-grown nursery plants.

A good undercover planting for Solomon's-seals would be any of the shorter native

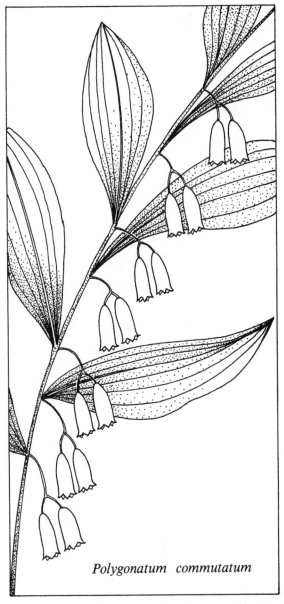

Polygonatum commutatum

ferns, including lady fern (*Athyrium filix-femina*), maidenhair fern (*Adiantum pedatum*), or Japanese painted fern (*Athyrium goeringianum* 'Pictum').

Unlike a number of wildflowers, Solomon's-seals persist throughout the summer. The leaves turn yellow in the fall, and the flowers are followed by blue-black berries.

Botanical name: *Rudbeckia* spp.
Common name: Coneflowers, including black-eyed Susans, brown-eyed Susans, and gloriosa daisies.
Habitat: Ordinary well-drained or slightly moist garden soil in full sun.
Description: Perennials with coarse leaves on strong stems; topped with large daisylike flowers, usually orange or yellow.
Period of bloom: Summer into fall.
Propagation: By division in spring; seeds.
Zone: 4.

The coneflowers are as all-American as hot dogs, root beer, and the dog days of August. Originally classified by the father of modern botanical nomenclature, Linnaeus, the genus *Rudbeckia* is named in honor of Olaf Rudbeck (1660–1740) and his son, both professors of botany at Upsala University in Sweden.

The genus includes the orange coneflower (*Rudbeckia fulgida*), the black-eyed Susan (*R. hirta*), *R. laciniata,* and the brown-eyed Susan (*R. triloba*). All are tough, drought-resistant plants that revel in full sun and seem to bloom forever.

In the last decade, the popularity of the coneflowers has continued to grow, especially since they work so beautifully with the many popular ornamental grasses. In fact, the combination of coneflowers and variegated maiden grass (*Miscanthus sinensis* 'Variegata') has almost become a garden cliché. Whether in the formal border or the wild garden, these are workhorse flowers.

The plants begin to bloom in July with 3- to 4-inch flowers and will continue well into fall. They are easy to grow from seed, flowering the first year, and can also be divided. Divide plants every three years to keep them robust. All are excellent cut flowers.

Rudbeckia fulgida, or the orange coneflower, is a reverse carpetbagger that journeyed up to the North from the South. It's usually

Gloriosa daisies

offered as the cultivar 'Goldsturm', a magnificent plant with 2½-foot stems bearing dozens of 3- to 4-inch flowers that bloom throughout the summer into fall. 'Goldsturm' and the species are not identical: The cultivar is a more uniform plant and if you grow it from your own

collected seed, you will get a mix of seedlings. 'Goldsturm' only comes true when propagated asexually.

Rudbeckia hirta, the black-eyed Susan, is a wildflower performing as an annual, biennial, or short-term perennial, depending on both soil and climate conditions. It is well-suited for the wild or meadow garden, but the plants are not large enough and do not have enough flowers to be in the formal garden. Their genetic offspring, the gloriosa daisy, is another story.

Gloriosa daisies have an amazing resistance to drought, and even badly wilted plants will perk up before your eyes if given a minimum of water. They can, in fact, be moved in full bloom. Dr. A. F. Blankeslee is credited with their development. He took the original 2-inch-wide flower and turned it into blossoms often 7 inches in diameter with varying colors of orange, yellow, gold, tan, brown, and dark red.

'Irish Eyes' has a green eye instead of black, and 'Goldilocks' has double, golden yellow flowers on 15-inch stems.

Rudbeckia laciniata is a native coneflower, first described in 1753, often reaching a height of 10 feet in the wild. It's not particularly attractive in the border, but to the rear of a wild garden it has great color and charm. Around old farmhouses and in abandoned gardens, the double-flowered cultivar 'Golden Glow' still survives, having been in cultivation since before 1913. Often reaching a height of 7 feet, the plants usually need staking and have a propensity to spread about. There is a cultivar (introduced in 1951) known as 'Goldquelle', which seldom tops 2 1/2 feet and is not invasive.

Rudbeckia triloba, brown-eyed Susan, has 2-inch flowers of golden yellow around brown centers, on 4-foot stems. These plants are native from southern New England to Minnesota and south to Georgia and Oklahoma. Listed both as a biennial and a perennial, they self-sow with ease and are excellent for naturalizing in the wild garden or at the edge of a meadow.

Botanical name: *Saponaria officinalis.*
Common name: Bouncing Bet, soapwort.
Habitat: Ordinary garden soil either well-drained or moist; full sun.
Description: Perennial, imported wildflower with simple leaves on strong stems; topped with clusters of fragrant pink or white, 5-petaled flowers arising from a tube; to 3 feet.
Period of bloom: Summer.
Propagation: By division in spring or fall.
Zone: 4.

Bouncing Bet is an immigrant from Europe that escaped from cultivation and is now classified as a weed of the roadside and railroad beds throughout most of temperate North America. In fact, the largest colony of these flowers that I ever saw was on a bank just below the railroad tracks in the center of Callicoon, New York.

The genus is named from the Latin *sapo,* or soap, referring to the mucilaginous juice that forms a lather with water. In addition to its uses as a detergent, the leaves and roots were also used as a remedy for scrofula and skin diseases in general. The chemical concerned is saponin, which easily forms a froth when stirred in water. The lather has been recommended for restoring ancient and delicate fabrics and old tapestries: Dried plants are placed in muslin bags, then boiled in distilled water. The solution is used cold.

The fragrant pink or white flowers bloom throughout the summer and are especially sweet-smelling at night. They are frequently visited by sphinx moths and, in late afternoon, clear-winged hawkmoths that are often mistaken for hummingbirds.

The plants are spreaders and can adapt to many soil conditions, but they need full sun. They are valuable in both the wild garden and the border and can be used to carpet a bank.

'Rubra Plena' has fragrant double pink flowers on 2-foot stems. There is also a white form,

'Alba', usually found only in the various seed exchanges, and a variegated form, 'Variegata'.

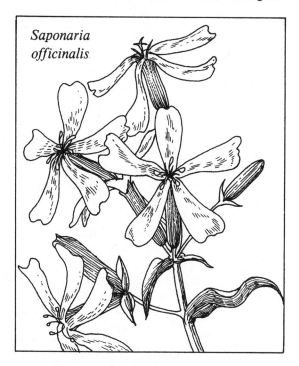

Saponaria officinalis

Botanical name: *Sedum* spp.

Common name: Stonecrop, orpine, sedum.

Habitat: Ordinary well-drained garden soil in full sun or light shade.

Description: Perennial with crisp stalks and fleshy leaves; topped with rounded clusters of small star-shaped flowers; to 2 feet.

Period of bloom: Summer into fall.

Propagation: By division in spring; cuttings; seed.

Zone: 4.

The sedums include plants suited for the perennial garden and for the rock garden. There are about 500 species in this genus, with most of them coming from the North Temperate Zone and a few from mountains in the Tropics. The genus may be from the ancient Latin word *sedere,* to sit, referring to their low-spreading habit, or from *sedare,* to quiet, referring to their supposed sedative properties.

The 4- or 5-petaled flowers are small but colorful. The leaves are succulent, and the stems are strong. They withstand drought and do amazingly well in poor and thin soils.

The smaller sedums brighten up areas between paving stones and the edges of walls. They make excellent edgings along walkways or colorful groundcovers. The taller types become specimen plants or clumps of all-season color in the border. Most make fine cut flowers.

There are enough variations among the species that some authorities have divided them up into eight groups, some tender and some hardy. Many species are available at nurseries and some of the rarer types are carried by the various seed exchanges.

Sedum acre, the golden sedum, is an evergreen creeper up to 5 inches high, with bright yellow $1/2$-inch flowers blooming in early summer. The plant will swiftly naturalize itself, becoming a beautiful cover for both stone and soil.

Sedum aizoon reaches a height of 12 to 14 inches, bearing flat heads of yellow to orange starlike flowers in summer.

Sedum kamtschaticum is only 4 inches high with deep green scalloped leaves, and orange-yellow flowers from July to September.

Sedum 'Ruby Glow' (*S. cauticola* × *S. telephium*) has flower heads that begin in midsummer as rose pink and darken in color as they age. The gray-green leaves are edged in wine red. After the flowers fade, the seed heads still remain, adding interest to the plant. The reddish stems will amble over low walls and rocks.

Sedum spectabile 'Autumn Joy' was once known as 'Indian Chief' and 'Herbstfreude', but by any name it's a super plant in any garden. The succulent leaves are bright green on thick stalks. The flowers begin in spring as tightly packed heads of green buds that resemble broc-

Sedum
'Autumn Joy'

Carpet', with leaves tinted bronze and bearing pink flowers, and 'Dragon's Blood', with dark red flowers.

Botanical name: *Solidago* spp.
Common name: Goldenrod.
Habitat: Ordinary garden soil in full sun or some shade.
Description: Perennial American wildflowers of stout character with coarse leaves on strong stems; topped with clusters of small, usually golden yellow flowers; to 6 feet.
Period of bloom: Late summer into fall.
Propagation: By division in spring or fall.
Zone: 4.

---

coli. As the summer progresses, they expand and turn into pink, rounded flower clusters on top of 2-foot stems. Then, as colder nights approach, the spent flowers turn an appealing shade of mahogany, persisting into the coldest months and making fine dried flowers for winter bouquets. 'Meteor' has gray-green leaves and small flowers of carmine-red and is often used in pots on a terrace.

Sedum spurium is another creeping evergreen sedum best used for covering ground or tumbling over rocks. Two cultivars are 'Bronze

Talk about bad press and plants, and goldenrods are sure to be mentioned. For years, these plants have been blamed for much of the autumn hayfever problem when the real culprit is ragweed pollen. The rangy and unkempt ragweed plant throws bushels of allergy-irritating pollen to the winds and unfortunately blooms in the same fields and waste places as goldenrod. Ragweed's tiny green flowers are missed by most observers, but goldenrod, with its spires of bright golden-yellow blossoms, is easily spotted in the dangerous plant lineup, and goldenrod gets the blame—a case of mistaken identity that continues today. Ragweed has the unusual, lovely genus name of *Ambrosia,* meaning immortal or divine, a name applied by Linneaus for an unknown reason, while goldenrod's genus, *Solidago,* is from the Latin *solido,* to make whole, from its supposed healing qualities.

Not only are goldenrods perfectly acceptable plants for the perennial bed or border, they are excellent as cut flowers and very attractive in late fall after flowers have faded and gone to seed, especially when the gray-brown floral sprays are dusted with snow. And they are perfect naturalized in the wild garden. If taller plants are not wanted, cut them to about a foot

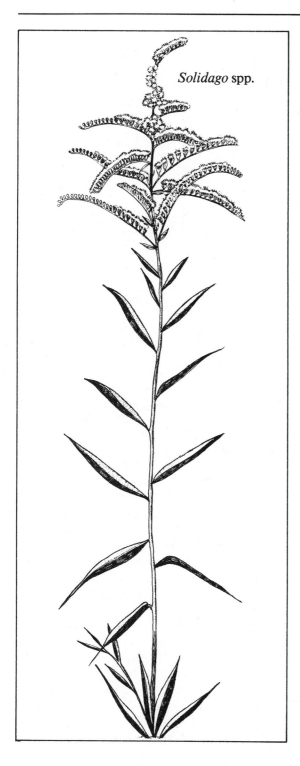

Solidago spp.

in early summer, and they become shorter, bushier plants.

Goldenrod is another native plant that is spoken of as a weed by most Americans, yet adopted by English gardeners. They took it to their beds and borders and applied hybridization and keen eyes to produce a number of beautiful and useful cultivars; *Index Hortensis* alone lists 30 cultivars. *Solidago canadensis* has been one of the parents for most. Cultivars include 'Golden Baby', a compact plant about 24 inches high with upright sprays of golden flowers (it blooms the first year if seed is started early in the spring); 'Golden Dwarf' (sometimes called 'Goldzwerg', German for gnome or dwarf), with yellow flowers on foot-high stems; and 'Cloth of Gold', with golden blossoms on 18-inch stems, blooming in late August. 'Crown of Rays' is bright yellow on 18-inch stems; 'Golden Mosa' is lemon yellow on 30-inch stems; and 'Nagshead' is golden yellow on 40-inch stems.

Solidago rugosa, the rough-leaved goldenrod, grows about 4 feet tall in the garden but taller in nature. The golden blossoms are clustered on the tops of arching stems.

Solidago rigida, the stiff goldenrod, bears flat-topped golden yellow flower clusters on top of perfectly straight stems and is especially suited to groupings in the wild garden.

In addition, goldenrods hybridize in the wild to the identification dismay of all but trained botanists. If you spot a particularly attractive specimen in a nearby field and the owner has no objection, dig it up and move it to your own garden.

Botanical name: *Tradescantia × andersoniana.*
Common name: Spiderwort.
Habitat: Ordinary well-drained garden soil in full sun or partial shade.
Description: Perennial American wildflower with succulent stems; narrow sword-shaped but floppy leaves; 3-petaled flowers, usually in shades of purple, lasting only one day; to 2 ½ feet.
Period of bloom: Summer.
Propagation: By division in spring.
Zone: 5.

Tradescantia × andersoniana

Back in the mid-1600s, John Tradescant, as a subscriber to the Virginia Company, received a number of American native plants for his English garden. He was the first to grow the Virginia creeper (*Parthenocissus quinquefolia*), the columbine (*Aquilegia canadensis*), and the spiderwort or widow's-tears (*Tradescantia virginiana*), the ancestor of today's garden plant.

Spiderwort has flowers that last only a day, but they are replaced by new ones over a long period of time. The hairs on the stamens have long been used in botany classes, since each stamen is composed of a line of single cells easily observed while still living. It is these hairs that give the plant the common name of spiderwort (*wort* is the old English word for plant).

Along with lilacs, ribbon grass (*Phalaris arundinacea* var. *picta*), and a number of shrub roses, spiderworts are often found in abandoned and forgotten gardens. The three petals are usually shades of purple and blue, but rose, pink, and even white forms are found. In order to identify the species, it's usually necessary to examine one of the three sepals under a hand lens.

Although happy in the full sun, spiderworts will adapt to some shade up North and open or partial shade down South. They are handsome border plants and are very effective when planted against walls. After flowering is over, the leaves become lax and floppy. Shear them back, almost to the ground, and a new crop of leaves and flowers will appear.

Unless taken directly from the wild, the plants usually sold today are a series of hybrids (*Tradescantia × andersoniana*), produced with *T. virginiana* and a number of other wild species, and registered in 1954. The flowers are larger and the colors are brighter. *Index Hortensis* lists over 30 such cultivars.

Today's nurseries stock a number of choices, including 'Snow Cap', with pure white flowers on 20-inch stems; 'Valor', bearing deep reddish purple flowers, also on 20-inch stems; and 'Pauline', having pink flowers on 12-inch stems. 'Double-Up Mixed' is a collection of semidouble flowers of violet, white, and bicolored forms with centers of pink or lilac on pastel backgrounds, easily grown from seed.

Tradescantia ohiensis, is a native species to 3 feet high with blue, rose, or white flowers. The stems bear a whitish bloom.

Botanical name: *Viola* spp.
Common name: Violet.
Habitat: Ordinary well-drained but moist garden soil with added humus; full sun to partial shade.
Description: Perennial American wildflowers with basal leaves; single-stalked, 5-petaled flowers in blues, purples, yellow, or white; to 8 inches.
Period of bloom: Early spring into summer.
Propagation: By division or runners; seed.

Before the First World War, violets were the most popular flower that one could give his ladylove; Eliza Doolittle in *My Fair Lady* started out by selling the sweet-smelling *Viola odorata* in London's Covent Garden. And over 80 common names listed in *Hortus Third* attest to their wide-ranging habits. Included in the genus are the pansies (*Viola × Wittrockiana*) and the Johnny-jump-ups, often called the European wild pansy (*V. tricolor*). The botanical name of *Viola* comes from the Greek *ion* for violet, the Latin *viola,* and the French *violette.*

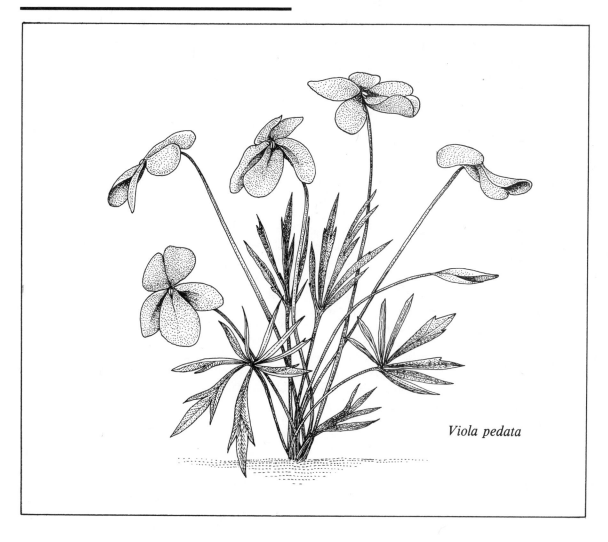

Viola pedata

Violets have been used in medicine for thousands of years, for treating everything from sleeplessness to heart trouble. The leaves have a high concentration of vitamins A and C and are frequently used in salads, but take care—they act as laxatives with some people. The flowers are candied as cake decorations and can even be made into violet jelly.

Although the flowers are welcome signs of spring and the leaves are attractive both in the wild garden and as groundcovers or edging in the more formal perennial bed, violets are, for the most part, weedy. They are cleistogamous, producing two sets of flowers. The first blooms normally. But the second batch, which lies close to the ground, have no petals; they are self-pollinating and bear plenty of fertile seed.

There are a number of wild violets that are useful in the formal and the wild garden. The following three are favorites in our gardens.

Viola pubescens var. *eriocarpa* (also sold as *V. pensylvanica*), the smooth yellow violet, wants partial shade and a good soil, and if so provided will produce stems as high as 1 foot.

Viola pedata, the bird-foot violet, is often called the most beautiful of these wildflowers. They prefer well-drained, acid, sandy soil, and, unlike other violets, full sun. Although harder to grow than the other plants in this book, bird-foot violets are worth the effort. After planting, mulch well with pine needles. Unlike other violets, they do not produce cleistogamous seeds, so if you want more, don't pick the flowers.

Viola rotundifolia, the southern downy violet or the round-leafed violet, will take more shade, especially in the South. While the yellow flowers are pretty, the leaves make a lovely addition to the wild garden or the edge of a border.

Botanical name: *Yucca filamentosa*.
Common name: Yucca.
Habitat: Ordinary well-drained garden soil; full sun in the North, but partial shade in the South.
Description: Perennial American wildflowers with stout clumps of stiff, sword-shaped leaves; tall stalks of nodding, bell-shaped, waxy white flowers, usually blooming at night; to 12 feet.
Period of bloom: Summer.
Propagation: By offsets; seeds.
Zone: 5.

Winter can be bleak but is often especially so in the North: barren fields, barren gardens, barren trees, and for weeks on end, gray and lifeless skies. The view from my old studio window featured many of the aforementioned trees and fields, but thankfully in addition to the green of the white pines and the hemlocks there were the fans of sharp-pointed leaves, dark green and strong, growing on plants that looked to be more at home in the deserts of Arizona. Such were the yuccas (*Yucca filamentosa*), the hardiest of the species able to endure the northern winter without injury. Their popular name is Adam's-needle, since the leaves come to a sharp point and the edges throw off numerous fine white hairs that are the consistency of buttonhole thread. *Yucca* is based on the Spanish *yuca,* a name derived from the Indian name for the plant. The species name refers to the loose fibers on the leaf margins, fibers used by the Southwest Indians as thread and in weaving cloth.

In the middle of the summer, a strong flower stem appears, shooting up higher than the surrounding leaves—often to 6 feet or more—and bearing numerous cream-colored, bell-like, pendant flowers. As darkness falls, the individual flowers lift up and point to the night sky, exuding perfumes to attract pollinating moths.

Since a well-grown plant will often be over 3 feet in diameter, these are not for the small garden. But the plant form plus the interesting seedpods make yuccas valuable additions to the landscape that has space to hold them. Use these plants with plenty of rocks or in groups of three or more. Gravel mulch is more in keeping with the plants than a leaf mulch or peat moss.

Once established, yuccas will perform every year regardless of the amount of rain that falls; they have a very deep taproot. In order to ensure such performance, give them a good start, then let them be.

The following two cultivars of *Yucca filamentosa* are offered by nurseries: 'Bright Edge' has variegated foliage, with the leaves edged in yellow-gold; 'Variegata' has leaves with various sized stripes of creamy white.

Yucca flaccida from North Carolina is a smaller plant but usually not hardy north of New Jersey.

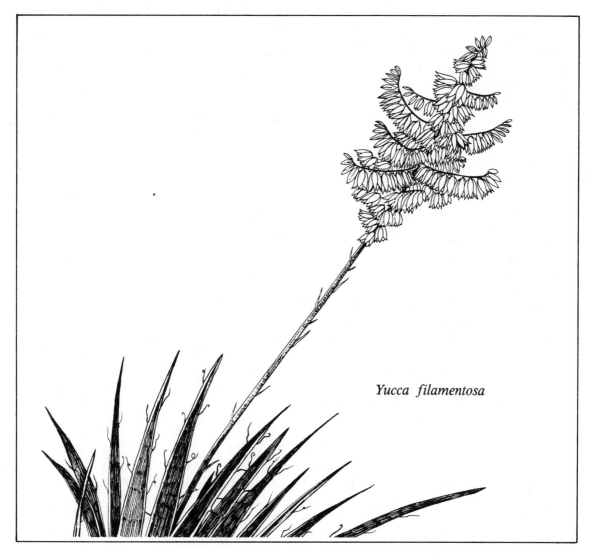

Yucca filamentosa

Ornamental Grasses

Botanical name: *Chasmanthium, Festuca, Hakonechlora, Imperata, Miscanthus, Molinia, Pennisetum,* and *Spartina.*
Common name: Ornamental grasses.
Habitat: Ordinary garden soil in full sun or some light shade.
Description: Perennial grasses; form clumps of narrow, grassy but attractive leaves; often very showy feathery or plumelike flowers; to 8 feet.
Period of bloom: Summer into fall.
Propagation: By division in spring or fall; seed.
Zone: 5.

In the fall of 1975, I knew nothing of grasses. I struggled (as did many other gardeners) to make an English garden border in the heavy clay and shale soil in the Catskill Mountains of New York State and not always to the best effect. Then a publisher asked me to do a book on grasses, and I knew in order to take on the job I had to try them in the garden.

At that time there were about 20 perennial grasses to consider for the garden (today there are well over 100). And only one major supplier of grasses was found in the United States, plus a few smaller nurseries that handled one or two species. In England, there were four or five that would ship plants to the States. Today, it's rare to find a nursery or garden center that does not carry a large selection of these magnificent plants.

Soil need not be fancy for ornamental grasses, just reasonably worked and provided with adequate drainage. And strangely enough, many can grow quite happily in damp or ever-wet spots. Sunlight is necessary for most, but it need not spotlight their leaves from dawn to dusk. Six to eight hours of sun is enough for general health and later bloom. Grasses will tolerate dryness better than many plants, but they do need to be watered if the rains escape your garden for weeks on end. And every spring, the gardener must cut the now-tattered leaves and stems to the ground, so the new growth is not hampered in its rise to meet the coming seasons.

When considering the addition of the grasses to any garden, think first of size. Some members of the *Miscanthus* species will reach a 12-foot height in one season, and that is formidable indeed. But few nursery-grown plants are that large upon receipt: They are usually immature, small, and, unfortunately for the unwary gardener, easily positioned in a spot hardly large enough to hold a miniature rose. And in the passion of planting, not only is it easy to forget about ultimate height, but just as easy to overlook eventual girth.

The next consideration should be form. An entire garden devoted to grasses is interesting to the specialist, who is usually more of a plant collector than a gardener. But for most of us, the grasses work to better advantage when the linear look of the leaves is played against plants exhibiting different forms and textures.

Some thought should also be given to flowers for winter bouquets. I personally hate to cut flowers in a formal garden, so I always keep a few species of ornamental grass in the cutting garden where blossoms can be cut without harming the overall look of the garden.

Chasmanthium latifolium, northern sea oats, is still known as *Uniola latifolia* in some parts of the nursery trade. The genus name means gaping flower in Greek. This is a native American grass found from the woods of Pennsylvania west to Montana and then south to New Mexico and back to northern Florida. Height is up to 4 feet when found in the woods, but usually no more than 3 feet in the garden. Plants are hardy in Zone 5.

Sea oats is a beautiful grass both in form, with its arching leaves of a very light green, and

Hystrix patula

Molinia caerulea
'Variegata'

in flower. The spikelets are extremely attractive and, when dried, will stay whatever color they were when picked, whether fresh green or golden brown. A clump of these grasses will slowly increase in size, reaching a diameter of some 3 feet. I have them planted underneath a white ash tree, *Fraxinus americana,* next to a large clump of fragrant plantain lily, *Hosta plantaginea,* and backed by variegated cord grass (*Spartina pectinata* 'Aureomarginata').

Hakonechlora macra 'Aureola', golden hakonechlora, is a variegated form of a grass originally from the mountains of Japan, where it grew on wet, rocky cliffs overlooking the sea west of Mt. Fuji. *Hakone* is a place on the Japanese island of Honshu, and *chlora* is from the Greek for grass. It is considered to be rather rare. In Japan, the variegated forms are cultivated as pot plants. The leaf color of this particular cultivar is a warm yellow with both green and off-white stripes; though beautiful in the summer, it is absolutely striking in the fall, when touches of magenta appear. Plants reach about 2 feet in height and spread very slowly, so if you are interested in a real statement, it's a good idea to buy at least three plants and space them about 6 to 8 inches apart.

Although hardy in Zone 5, the hakonechloras are never quite as splendid in that climate as they are where winters are a bit warmer. My specimen is at home in front of my scree-bed wall, where it is offered some protection from bitter winds in winter. In milder climates, it is excellent as a border along a stone path and will even take a small bit of shade and still produce the fine coloration.

Hystrix patula, the bottlebrush grass, is a native American found in damp spots in the open woods and along stream beds. The genus name means porcupine-like. The grass ranges throughout the Northeast and makes an effective addition to a woodland or wildflower garden. The spikes of blossoms, which are aptly named, begin to bloom from late summer into early fall. The blossoms persist for some time.

Plants turn a light brown in the autumn. This grass should be planted against a darkened background so the seed heads show up to good effect. In our garden, they grow between sumac trees and a large clump of *Ligularia.*

Imperata cylindrica 'Rubra', Japanese blood grass, is a comparatively recent addition to our garden. The genus is named in honor of Ferrante Imperato, an apothecary in Naples in the late 1500s. Originally from Japan, and considered somewhat tropical in habits, this grass is listed by most growers as hardy only to Zone 7, so the first few years I applied a very heavy mulch in early winter. Then, at a meeting of the American Rock Garden Society, I found from a number of gardeners that it is quite happy down to Zone 5 if given a spot with just a bit of protection from fierce winter winds, or provided with a light mulch after the ground freezes. The leaves vary between 1 and 2 feet in height and will adapt to partial shade if given good drainage. Plants also do well in pots. As the summer days get warmer, the individual blades of grass begin to turn blood red: A mass planting of this grass is quite startling in its effect, but you will need at least six individual plants to get off to a good start.

Festuca ovina var. *glauca,* blue fescue, is a shorter ornamental grass, best used for edging or creating a sense of pattern over a small area. The genus name is Latin for a grass stem. This grass grows about 1 1/2 feet high and has a bluish bloom, which is actually a powder that covers the leaf-blade surfaces and that will easily rub off. Plant these grasses in clusters or use them to edge the bed or border, where their steely blue becomes a happy combination with any pink-flowered annuals or perennials. While the fescue flowers are not too impressive on their own, when seen on top of many plants, they are quite lovely. There are over 20 different cultivars of the fescues stocked by ornamental grass suppliers, including the 4-inch 'Tom Thumb' and the 2-foot-high giant fescue (*F. gigantea*).

Eulalia grass, sometimes called Amur silver grass, is a giant among giants. *Miscanthus sacchariflorus* is the botanical name in *Hortus Third,* and *M. sacchariflorus* 'Robustus' is the name used by the trade. The genus name is Greek for flower on a stalk. Eulalia grass is a stout and coarse perennial that can reach a height of 10 feet or more—not including the inflorescence—in one good summer season. As the summer passes, the lower leaves die back. By removing them, you will reveal more of the handsome stems, stems that darken with age to assume a maroon tint, and which take a beautiful polish. We use them in the garden for pea stakes.

These grasses are hardy in Zone 5 but in areas with a growing season of less than 90 days, there is a chance they will not flower unless the gardener throws giant sheets of plastic over the top to protect from frost. Those that perform this act of mercy are rewarded by foot-long silvery plumes at the top of each stem, strongly resembling the fans that cooled Cleopatra on her journeys down the Nile. Each plume is made up of hundreds of individual flowers that lack petals. In this species, the flowers also lack a major structure of the grass flower: the awn, a long, hairlike projection usually found on the back of each individual floral part.

The following grasses are three of a number of cultivars derived from Japanese silver grass, *Miscanthus sinensis,* a shorter and more graceful species than eulalia, its plumes more of a light tan than silver and having floral parts that bear an awn.

Miscanthus sinensis 'Gracillimus', maiden grass, as its namesake suggests, is one of the most graceful grasses in cultivation. Stiff culms can reach a height of 7 feet and a mature clump has both stately beauty and great architectural quality. The leaf is fine in texture and has a conspicuous white midrib. Like many grasses plants do well in spots with moist or wet soil.

Miscanthus sinensis 'Variegatus', variegated maiden grass, rarely grows taller than 7 feet and bears leaves edged with white. This grass will adapt to partial shade and is quite happy (as are the others of the genus) growing at the water's edge or, if potted, directly in the pool or pond. In our garden, this grass sits nearby a Japanese maple that provides shade for half the day.

Miscanthus sinensis 'Zebrinus', zebra grass, belongs in every garden. It's difficult to believe that any grass with such an obvious tropical look would succeed in the Northeast, but it's hardy in Zone 5. The individual leaves are not striped but dashed with horizontal bands of a light golden-brown, an effect that does not appear until the days of summer descend and temperatures reach the upper seventies.

Massive clumps are formed over the years reaching a height between 6 and 8 feet. To save time, start with three plants about 1 foot apart, and in three years, visitors to your garden will be properly impressed. A specimen planting in the midst of a lawn is quite beautiful and never quite as blatant a show as the popular pampas grasses (*Cortaderia* spp.). The flowers are large and showy with purple-silver tints, eventually opening to a tan rather than a silver hue. Full sun is preferred.

Molinia caerulea 'Variegata', variegated purple moor grass, is another of the grasses that should be found in even the smallest garden. The genus is named in honor of Juan Ignacio Molina (1740–1829), a Chilean writer on natural history. We started ours in 1976. Every year the fountain of rather rigid leaves, each banded with white stripes and gently curling towards the ground, appears in early spring and often reaches a height of 3 feet by the end of May. The diameter increases less than 1 inch a year. The flowering stems are striped like the leaves, but tinged with violet and light green highlights.

Perfectly hardy in Zone 5, this particular plant is striking throughout the garden year. After the first frosts of fall, the leaves turn a light tan and the plants resemble a bursting skyrocket that is tied to the ground rather than lighting up the sky. *Molinia* will accept some partial shade

Continued on page 164

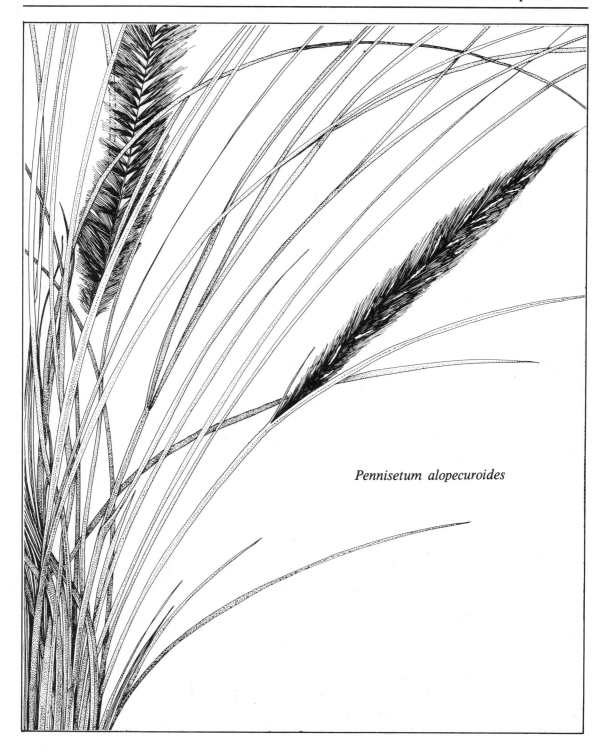

Pennisetum alopecuroides

Festuca ovina var. *glauca*

Spartina pectinata
'Aureomarginata'

and, because of its ancestry as a grass of the wet moorlands of northern Europe, prefers an acid soil. The root system is tough and fibrous, making it an excellent choice for planting steep banks and hillsides.

Pennisetum alopecuroides, fountain grass, existed quite happily on top of the bank overlooking our back border. There it was buffeted by the bitter west winds of winter, yet held its fountainlike form until finally torn asunder by the gales of March. The botanical name is from *penna,* feather, and *seta,* bristle, in allusion to the long, feathery bristles of the inflorescence. The grass is especially beautiful as the arching leaves sparkle in the rays of the setting sun after a summer afternoon thunderstorm. The plumelike flowers are a light tan, and a mature plant will bear dozens of blossoms. The height of the plant varies between 3 to 4 feet, and a spot in full sun is preferred.

Spartina pectinata 'Aureomarginata', variegated prairie cord grass, is a cultivar of an American native that at one time was one of the dominant plants found on the tall grass prairies that covered the north-central part of the United States. The name is from the Greek *spartine* for rope or cord, as the leaves are fibrous. In fact, the pioneers of America used this grass to thatch roofs and protect haystacks against the winter. As proof of the popularity of this plant, its common names include: bullgrass, tall marsh-grass, slough grass (*slough* is an old Anglo-Saxon word meaning a wet or marshy place), freshwater cord grass, and Upland Creek grass. Today it is popular in the construction of archery targets.

The graceful clumps stay about 5 feet tall. Our original plant now covers a rectangle of 4 by 2 feet, the stems arching in the slightest wind. The saw-edged leaves of this cultivar have a yellow margin. Plants prefer full sun. In 10 years, this particular cultivar never flowered in our garden, but it is so beautiful that it hardly matters.

We planted the variegated cord grass on a bank that rises up behind the scree bed, where the leaves are silhouetted against a background of either cut lawn grass or snow, depending on the season.

Bulbs

Botanical name: *Allium* spp.
Common name: Flowering onion.
Habitat: Ordinary garden soil in full sun.
Description: Bulbous plants with an onion scent and long straplike leaves; flowers of purple, pink, yellow, or white in ball-shaped umbels; to 4 feet.
Period of bloom: Late spring into fall.
Propagation: By division of clumps; bulbils; seed.
Zone: 4 and 5, depending on species.

If you are thinking that onions could hardly be valuable additions to the floral border, read on. These bulbous plants bloom with clusters of star-shaped blossoms of great charm starting in late spring and providing color accents well into September. A mild oniony smell when leaves and stems are crushed is the only clue to their heritage. Many seed heads dry with great effect to make stunning additions to dried flower arrangements.

There are over 50 species of alliums available from nurseries and seed lists in the U.S. and Canada (there are over 400 species in the genus). *Allium* is taken from the ancient Latin name for garlic. Cultivation demands are few: a reasonable soil that is loose enough to allow bulbs to expand and as much sun as possible. When planting flowering onions, use at least five bulbs to form a small grouping. After a few years, when fewer flowers are produced, divide the bulbs and replant.

Allium cernuum, the nodding onion, blooms in the summer with pendulous heads of some 40 rose to purple flowers (the species name is from the Latin *cernuum* for drooping). The flower clusters resemble bursting skyrockets tied to earth. Look for variations in color; the white form 'Alba' is especially beautiful. The stems (really scapes) are about 18 inches high. In the fall, the seed heads dry and split, revealing shiny black seeds that look like Victorian jet jewelry.

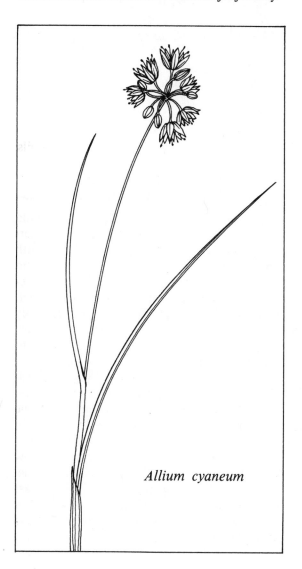

Allium cyaneum

Allium cyaneum has no common name, but the species name means having a blue color. The flowering scapes are small, usually no higher than 8 inches, but the bell-shaped, nodding flowers that bloom in early summer are of such a perfect shade they brighten any corner.

Allium moly, the lily leek, has been a garden favorite for many years. The bright yellow flowers bloom in early to midsummer, the heads some 3 inches across on 12-inch scapes. They are more vigorous than most alliums, and with a good spot in the border, the gardener will soon have a sizable clump of flowers.

Chives, or *Allium schoenoprasum,* have always had bad press as garden flowers. Many gardeners accuse them of having a too-violent shade of rose or rose-violet that clashes with everything else in the border. I say: Let them clash. We have a proverbial clump in front of a gas plant (*Dictamnus albus*), where the colors complement perfectly. The species name is Greek for rush-leek, referring to the narrow leaves. The common name came to English from the French *cive,* which came from the Latin *cepa,* or onion. After they have finished blooming, cut the plants back for a second crop of leaves for soup and flowers for the soul.

Chinese chives (*Allium tuberosum*) are called *gow choy* by the Chinese. We grow them like regular chives, starting new plants indoors from seed and setting them out in May. By July, the foot-high leaves wind about scapes topped with flat clusters of tiny white flowers. These blossoms can be picked and added to salads where they depart a gentle hint of garlic and a touch of the exotic, too. The leaves taste more like onions.

Botanical name: *Colchicum* spp.
Common name: Autumn crocus.
Habitat: Ordinary well-drained garden soil with added humus.
Description: Bulbous plants that bloom in fall; crocuslike blossoms of mauve, pink, or white; large pleated leaves that usually appear the following spring; to 1 foot.
Period of bloom: Late August through November.
Propagation: By division of clumps; seed.
Zone: 5.

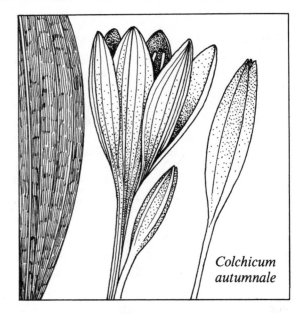

Colchicum autumnale

Colchicums are usually called autumn crocus, but they are a distinct genus of cormous plants. The genus is named for Colchis, an ancient province in Asia, east of the Black Sea. These plants belong to the lily family and are the source of colchicine, a narcotic and poison. Colchicine has been used in the treatment of gout and in plant breeding. It causes plant cells to multiply, producing tetraploids with flowers larger than normal. It has also been featured in a number of mystery stories where the poison has been used to dispatch victims.

Chalice-shaped flowers appear anytime from the end of August into late November; white stemlike funnels are divided into 6 petal-like segments. The leaves appear the following spring and vary in height between 6 to 18 inches depending on the species, so be sure to keep this in mind when choosing a spot for planting. Unlike crocuses, colchicum leaves are not too attractive, but they must be left to brown and fade on their own in order to produce flowers for the next autumn.

Plant colchicums 3 to 4 inches deep (from the top of the corm), and space them 6 inches apart on center. Leave them alone until flowers start to diminish from overcrowding, a condition that develops when conditions are favorable to the corm. I've found them to be quite beautiful when naturalized beneath trees or in clumps at the edge of a wild garden.

Colchicum autumnale, known as the autumn crocus, meadow saffron, mysteria, naked ladies, or the wonder bulb, usually flowers in September and October with blossoms 3 to 4 inches high. Corms are hardy in Zone 4. 'Album' is white; 'Roseum' is rose-pink; and 'Plenum' has double flowers of a lilac hue. The spring leaves are up to 1 foot long.

Colchicum cilicicum (from Cilicia in Asia Minor), has flowers of a deep shade of rosy lilac standing 5 inches high. These spring leaves are also up to 1 foot long.

Colchicum speciosum has rose to purple flowers 5 inches high and often 4 inches across. The leaves are often 16 inches long. They are hardy in Zone 4. 'Album' has white flowers; 'Atrorubens' is dark red; and the variety *bornmuelleri* has larger and earlier flowers. The leaves are shorter, usually only 6 inches long.

Colchicum 'Waterlily' is a hybrid registered before 1927, and nothing better has appeared on the market since then. Mauve-colored double blossoms that really look like their namesakes appear in early October. The spring leaves are 6 inches long. If you have room for only one, choose this. It's hardy in Zone 4.

Botanical name: *Crocus* spp.
Common name: Crocus.
Habitat: Ordinary well-drained garden soil with added humus.
Description: Bulbous plants with narrow grass-like leaves; silky-petaled blossoms, usually purple, lilac, yellow, or white; to 10 inches.
Period of bloom: Early spring or fall, according to species.
Propagation: By division of clumps; seed.
Zone: 3; most crocuses will not survive where cooler winter temperatures are not available.

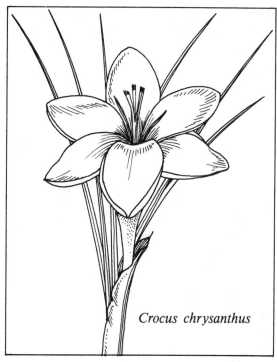

Crocus chrysanthus

Because of their ability to be among the first or the last to bloom in the garden year, crocuses should be used in every garden, whether wild or proper. Unlike many spring or fall bulbs, crocuses have attractive and unobtrusive leaves; most gardeners are unaware as they age and fade away. As for being tough, I've seen beds of crocuses that have persisted year after year until they finally gave in from overcrowding.

Crocus is from the Greek word for thread and refers to the three threadlike stigmas on each flower. The flowers close at night to protect the nectar and pollen for visiting bees. The derivation is also from *krokos,* saffron, in reference to the true saffron crocus, *C. sativus,* the chief source of saffron for cooking and coloring.

Crocuses are corms, not bulbs, producing new corms on top of the old. Plant the initial corms 4 inches deep. After three or four years, you will note that the corms have come close to the surface. This is because the new corms form on top of the old, just like bricks added to a wall, eventually reaching the surface.

They should be planted in the fall and are best when naturalized. Roll a handful of corms like dice and plant where they fall, or poke a finger in the dirt, using an abstract pattern for the holes. Use them under deciduous trees, at the edge of walkways, beneath shrubbery, on banks, and in the rock garden.

Crocus angustifolius (the species name means narrow-leaved), or the cloth-of-gold crocus, has bright yellow flowers, the outer petals feathered with bronze. They are hardy in Zones 4 to 8.

Crocus chrysanthus (the species name means golden-flowered), are hardy in Zone 4 and will bloom at a height of 3 inches as the snow begins to melt. They, and all the following crocuses, should be planted at about 180 corms per square yard for the maximum amount of show. Corms are usually found in a number of cultivars: 'E. A. Bowles' has lemon yellow flowers with a bronzy base; 'Ladykiller' bears purple-violet blossoms edged with white; and 'Princess Beatrix' is a clear lobelia-blue with a golden base.

Crocus imperati (the species name means commanding), the Italian crocus, has flowers that are buff-yellow in bud but open to a violet interior tinged with rose. The height is 4 inches. They are hardy in Zone 6 south to Zone 9.

Crocus korolkowii, the celandine crocus, is named for a Russian general who found the flowers in Turkestan. Flowers are a bright golden yellow with a hint of green, opening flat instead of like a chalice or cup. Height is 2 1/2 inches, and they are hardy in Zones 5 to 8.

Crocus sativus is the saffron crocus, which has been in cultivation since the times of the ancient Hebrews for its value as a spice and coloring agent. Flowers are a rich purple, grow 4 inches high, and appear in October. If you are interested in going into the business of gathering saffron, it takes 35,000 flowers to yield 8 ounces of commercial saffron. Corms are hardy in Zone 6.

Botanical name: *Endymion hispanicus* (sometimes listed as *Scilla hispanica*).
Common name: Spanish bluebells.
Habitat: Ordinary well-drained garden soil with added humus; partial to full shade.
Description: Bulbous plants with straplike leaves that bend to the ground; tall stalks of many hyacinth-like flowers in blue, pink, or white; 12 to 15 inches high.
Period of bloom: Spring.
Propagation: By division of clumps; seed.
Zone: 3.

Many years ago, some friends bought an old farm in upstate New York. It was a small house along with a ruined barn and two other outbuildings. The driveway was a dirt road that ran through the woods and along the edge of a field in the same serpentine shape that ancient river valleys assume. Every spring when the snows were melting, the absolute blue and sapphire brilliance of the Siberian squills sparkled against the receding white. Their botanical name is *Scilla siberica.* Originally native to Asia Minor, they are among the earliest of spring flowers. After we had a home of our own, we planted batches of these squills and never tired of their charm.

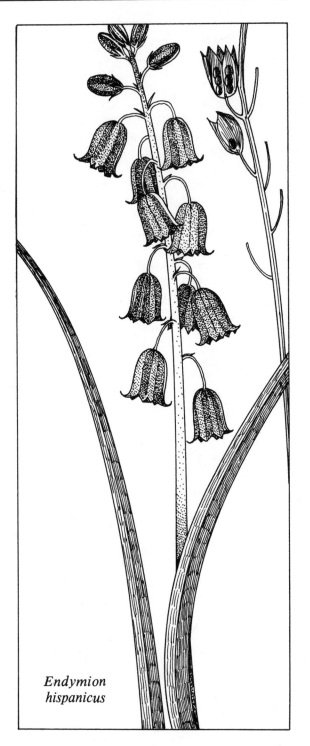

Endymion hispanicus

But some years later I read of another squill, described by many of the older garden authors as being a most beautiful flower that resembled the English bluebell, but even bigger and better. The name was *Scilla hispanica,* or the Spanish bluebell. *Scilla,* a Greek word meaning to injure or harm, refers to toxic properties of some species.

"It is a plant for almost universal use," wrote Louise Beebe Wilder. "Beautiful planted in broad masses in light woodland, or naturalized in grassy places, lovely in half-shaded borders among ferns, particularly the white kinds, along woodland walks, or used freely in the borders."

Some years ago the name changed to *Endymion hispanicus.* Endymion was a beautiful Greek youth who fits right into the majority of psychodramas on today's TV shows. He was loved by Selene, the moon goddess, and was thrown into a perpetual sleep so that he would not be aware of her nightly embraces. Since the bulbs awaken every spring, I can't fathom the name.

Cultivars are available in blue, pink, or white. The large bulbs should be planted from 4 to 6 inches deep in garden or woodland soil, well-drained, never sitting at any time in water. Once in place, they get better every year.

Botanical name: *Lilium* spp.
Common name: Garden lily.
Habitat: Ordinary well-drained garden soil with added humus; full sun to partial shade.
Description: Bulbous plants with tall, erect stems and narrow, shiny leaves; showy funnel-shaped flowers, usually fragrant, in most colors except blue; to 9 feet.
Period of bloom: Late spring into early fall.
Propagation: By division of clumps; seed.
Zone: 4.

True lilies are a gigantic genus with perhaps over 90 species and, like dahlias or gladiolus or daylilies, hybridized to such an extent that choices are quite overwhelming. The Persian word *laleh* and the Greek *leiron* both mean lily and are thought to have been used to describe *Lilium candidum,* the pure white Madonna lily.

The most important thing to remember about lilies is that, unlike other bulbs, they are never dormant. The scales that surround the bulb have no protective covering and are easily broken. Handle with care is the rule.

A few lilies, like the Madonna lily, want shallow planting with the top of the bulb only 1 inch below the soil. But most of the other species and cultivars have flowering stems that produce roots as they grow up to the surface, and depth must be allowed for this growth habit. This means setting them 4 to 8 inches deep and 10 to 18 inches apart, depending on the ultimate height and type of lily. On the average, position the bulbs two or three times deeper than their diameter and between 12 and 18 inches apart. Today's lily merchants provide all the necessary planting information when you buy the bulbs.

Plant out the bulbs as soon as you receive them. If your soil is heavy, dig the hole an inch or so deep, and put in a layer of sand, then scumble a teaspoon of bonemeal in the bottom of each hole. After inserting the bulb, add some more sand before covering it up.

Over the years of gardening, I've worked with and had success with the following lilies, all hardy in Zone 4. The soil we started with was pure clay over a base of red shale. The soil was improved with cow manure, leaf litter, and sand added as suggested above. The lilies did beautifully.

Lilies called Asiatic hybrids in most American catalogs are hybrids obtained from *Lilium cernuum, L. davidii,* and other species. They flourish in full sun to partial shade with a well-drained soil, producing a number of blossoms on 2- to 4-foot stems, in colors of white, cream, orange, pink, and yellow. Look for 'Sinai', bearing speckled orange blossoms in late spring, or

Lilium auratum

'Red Night', with cherry red blossoms dotted with many black spots, heaviest at the throat.

The de Graf hybrids were produced by a Dutch breeder, Jan de Graf, who changed the world of lily hybrids forever. These flowers begin to bloom in late June and carry on into September. The careful gardener can mix various de Graf hybrids to obtain all-season bloom. Many more spectacular hybirds were developed by the Oregon Bulb Farm. Dozens are available, but 'Enchantment', created in 1947 by de Graf, is still one of the most beautiful, bearing up to 16 nasturtium-red, 6-inch-wide flowers on 3-foot stems. 'Firecracker' has blossoms of a vivid scarlet, 5 inches across, on 3-foot stems; it was developed in 1975 by the Oregon Bulb Farm.

The Chinese trumpet lilies bloom in midsummer with a heavy fragrance. Back in 1983 I set out three bulbs of 'Black Dragon', another creation of de Graf's from 1950. The lily trumpets have ivory interiors and deep maroon on the outside, edged in white. Each 6-foot stem will support up to a dozen 6-inch flowers. A number of cultivars are now available, but 'Black Dragon' is, to me, still the best. They bloom in late July and early August.

Lilium auratum, the gold-banded lily, is from Japan, where the bulbs are still used for food. As food for the soul, these lilies are my favorite. The blossoms can be up to 10 inches across, with intensely fragrant, white, waxy blossoms banded with gold. Up to 20 flowers can arch a 6-foot stem into a gentle curve, without breaking. They bloom in September.

Lilium candidum, the Madonna lily, has been in cultivation since the Minoan culture, 1500 years before the birth of Christ. The pure white, fragrant flowers perch on top of stems up to 6 feet tall, with up to 15 flowers per stem. Unlike the other lilies mentioned, these should be planted with only an inch or two of soil over the top of the bulb. And they should be mulched in areas of cold winters that lack snow cover.

For bloom in mid-to late September, use the fine *Lilium formosanum,* with its elegant, 6-inch-long, white blossoms on top of 4- to 6-foot stems. 'Little Snow White' is a cultivar from Taiwan with large solitary, paired, or multiple flowers on a 9-inch stem. If grown from seed sown in September, this lily will bloom the following summer. It also makes an excellent pot plant.

If you have the room, try one of the numerous lily naturalizing mixtures offered by many nurseries. For a very reasonable amount of money, you can purchase unnamed cultivars of blooming-sized bulbs, in colors of red, orange, yellow, pink, cream, or white.

Botanical name: *Lycorus squamigera.*
Common name: Surprise lily, hardy amaryllis.
Habitat: Ordinary garden soil with added humus; full sun.
Description: Bulbous plants with long strap-shaped leaves; showy red, rose-lilac, or white lily-like flowers; to 2 feet.
Period of bloom: Summer into fall.
Propagation: By division of clumps.
Zone: 5.

My first introduction to this lily surprise came in a brown paper bag of bulbs carried by Janet Gracey on a flight from Indianapolis to New York City. Janet was a garden friend from up North who never missed a chance to bring me plants from her mother's rural Indiana garden without the airlines knowing exactly why her bags were always so heavy. Out there these lilies grew under the hot Midwest sun with some years wet and some years dry, so I knew they would do well in our mountain garden. Their common name is naked-lady, surprise lily, or the resurrection lily: The straplike leaves that appear in spring disappear by midsummer, and naked scapes topped with trumpetlike blossoms follow in August.

The genus *Lycoris* is named in honor of a beautiful Roman actress and one-time mistress

Lycorus squamigera

of Marc Antony; *squamigera* means with scales and refers to small scales found in the flower's throat. The flowers are rose-pink and tinged with amethyst-blue, having a slight glisten to the petals. Usually eight to ten blossoms appear on top of a 2-foot stem. Use about 16 bulbs per square yard of display.

In our garden, the slope behind the scree bed is heavily planted with variegated cordgrass (*Spartina pectinata* 'Aureomarginata'), its long, ribbonlike blades curling about like graceful tresses of green-gold hair. I planted dozens of surprise lilies right in front of the grass clumps, and in late summer, the flowers stick up through the wavy grasses for a spectacular effect.

In another part of the garden, they are used in combination with spring columbines and a large clump of yarrows (*Achillea* spp.). The lily blossoms appear, their stalks encirled with yarrow leaves, against a backdrop of columbine leaves.

Lycorus sprengeri (in honor of Carl Sprenger), comes from central China and closely resembles *L. squamigera,* but the flowers are a bit smaller and the color is purple-pink. They bloom in late summer on 15-inch stems.

There are two other species of *Lycorus,* but they are only hardy in frost-free climates. *L. radiata,* the spider lily, has crimson blossoms with long spidery anthers. It has been in cultivation since the early 1700s. *L. aurea,* the golden spider lily, bears golden-yellow flowers that resemble nerine lilies in having long curving stamens and petals that have a sparkle in the sunlight. Both species produce their flowers on 20-inch scapes.

Botanical name: *Narcissus* spp.
Common name: Daffodils and narcissus.
Habitat: Ordinary well-drained garden soil with added humus; full sun to partial shade.
Description: Bulbous plants with strap-shaped leaves; white or yellow flowers with a petaled collar; flowers with a short trumpet are called narcissus and those with long trumpets are daffodils; to 18 inches.
Period of bloom: Early to late spring.
Propagation: By division of clumps; seed.
Zone: 4.

I wandered lonely as a cloud
That floats on high o'er vales and hills,
When all at once I saw a crowd,
A host of golden daffodils;
Beside the lake, beneath the trees,
Fluttering and dancing in the breeze.

The words of William Wordsworth are best read as you look out of your window toward the garden—or, if in the country, out upon the fields and forest edges—and spy the daffodils and narcissus that you planted the previous fall.

Narcissus is a genus of about 30 species of spring and fall-flowering bulbs, named either in honor of the Greek god Narcissus, who was transformed into a flower by Nemesis, the god of vengeance, or from the Greek word *narkeo,* to be stupefied, since a number of the bulbs contain narcotic alkaloids. *Daffodil* comes from the medieval Latin *affodilus* which goes back to the Greek *asphodelus,* a name for a plant that grew in the meadows of Hell.

Fledgling gardeners are sometimes confused about daffodil and narcissus and which is which—although the differences are more of a concern to gardeners than to botanists. Daffodils have a large, long trumpet while flowers with a small, short cup are known as narcissus.

Daffodils naturalize with ease and spread over almost any terrain except waterlogged soil (although they will take quite a bit before giving

*Narcissus
poeticus*

out), or solid rock or clay. They need a sunny spot in spring but do not object to some shade as leaves develop on deciduous trees. Even the midst of a lawn is a good spot as long as you don't cut the grass where the bulbs lie until the leaves have withered and browned, allowing the bulbs to store food for next year's blossoms.

Since these plants prefer acid soil, the edge of woodlands is an excellent place to plant the bulbs. Although wild animals do not eat these bulbs, deer will sometimes nip off the flower buds, then toss them away.

Many of the smaller species are at home in the rock garden, and a few like *Narcissus bulbocodium* and *N. calcicola* will do well in pots of well-drained soil if given very cool growing conditions in a greenhouse.

There are many cultivars available from bulb dealers and nurseries across the country. Each year finds new refinements of the old favorites; there are over 1500 registered cultivars in *Index Hortensis*. But of the old favorites, there are three that in my experience are still the best for viewing, for cutting, and for naturalizing.

The first is *Narcissus* 'King Alfred', a hybrid created in 1899 by one John Kendall. This is a mid-season bloomer on 15-inch stems with large, bold, golden yellow flowers, especially valuable for cutting. It's a very tough plant.

The second is *Narcissus* 'Mrs. R. O. Backhouse', registered by Mrs. Backhouse in 1923. It was the first pink daffodil of any consequence. The petals are ivory white and surround a trumpet of clear apricot pink. This is also a mid-season bloomer, with flowers on 14-inch stems.

The third is the poet's narcissus, *Narcissus poeticus*. "The Poets Narcissus," said Louise Beebe Wilder, "is perfect for dampish locations, or lovely . . . beneath Apple trees, for they flower at the same time, and a canopy of pink blossoms over the gleaming white Narcissus would cause the most hard-boiled to catch his breath." We took Mrs. Wilder at her word and naturalized the poet's flower beneath and

Narcissus 'King Alfred'

around three ancient apple trees in our upper field. A fading color 8-by-10 from 1979 still sits in our living room, quiet testimony to the beauty of that planting. These glorious flowers are sweetly scented, with snow-white petals surrounding a small flattened eye of yellow edged with scarlet. The most popular cultivar is 'Actaea', registered in 1927.

When naturalizing daffodils and narcissus, plant the bulbs as soon as you receive them. Never let them lie about in paper bags and be forgotten; before you know it, they will sprout and it will be too late in the season for planting.

Go outside and scatter the bulbs at random, planting them where they fall, thus achieving a completely natural look. Use a special bulb planter (either in shovel or trowel form) to remove a round clump of soil. Put a dash of bonemeal in the hole's bottom, scumble it up a bit, pop in the bulb, replace the divot, and go on to the next bulb.

Tulipa sylvestris

Botanical name: *Tulipa* spp.
Common name: Species tulips.
Habitat: Ordinary well-drained garden soil in full sun.
Description: Bulbous plants of dainty habit with attractive leaves and tulip-shaped flowers of red, yellow, violet, or white; to 1 foot.
Period of bloom: Early to late spring.
Propagation: By division of clumps; seed.
Zone: 4; many tulips, like crocuses, need a period of cold to flower so Zones vary according to species and are listed below.

I've never liked hybrid, cottage, or Darwin tulips except when the blooming bulbs were taken from the soil, washed carefully, and displayed roots and all in a glass-brick vase from the 1950s. There's something about the polished, waxy petals that reminds me of the worst of carpet bedding and the unimaginative approach that most public parks take when planting spring bulbs. In fact, the most exciting thing to me about tulips is their history and the fact that gardeners in the 1600s would gladly pay as much for tulip bulbs as pork futures bring today, one Dutch farmer in the 1700s giving a new carriage and twelve horses for a single bulb. Fortunes were made and lost in search of the fantastic black tulip—Alexander Dumas even wrote a novel about it. And it's quite possible that the word *bourse* for stock exchange came from that period because tulip speculators held their market meetings in the house belonging to one Herr Van Bourse. The genus *Tulipa* is testimony to the similarity of an upended tulip flower to the Turkish turban, the *tulband,* eventually abbreviated to tulip.

Finally, I've never found tulips to perform year after year, regardless of how well the beds were prepared. It's probably a failing on my part, but the result has never been worth the effort.

Not so, though, with the one group of tulips that I truly admire: the wild or species tulips. Here are flowers of restrained charm and lovely, artful colors, not braggadocios of the border. They are perfect for edges of the wild garden, for the rock garden, along walls and walkways, and between paving stones. In their native haunts, these tulips grow in a heavy clay soil that is subjected to being completely dry in the summer; the bulbs must have a bake to prepare for the next spring display.

Plant them in groups of one color and kind. They want full sun and well-drained soil. Remove spent blossoms to save the bulb's energy unless you specifically want seed. Always let the foliage die back naturally before you remove it. If you remember, top-dress the area where the bulbs are planted with some composted cow or sheep manure or composted humus, but this is not necessary for continued flowering. Make sure that any nurseries that you use as wild tulip suppliers post the notice in their catalogs that all their wild tulips (and other bulbs) are commercially propagated and not taken from the wild.

Tulipa acuminata

Tulipa acuminata, the fireflame tulip, bears flowers of scarlet and yellow twisted petals up to 3 inches long that look like living flame. They sit on foot-high stems, blooming in May. The species name means long and pointed. The species are not really wild at all but thought to be of garden origin. They are hardy from Zones 3 to 8.

Tulipa eichleri is from southern Russia and Turkestan. This species has large, 4-inch-wide flowers with intensely scarlet petals on 15-inch stems. The center of the flower is black and yellow with black anthers. The leaves are broad and gray-blue in color. The species is in honor of discoverer August Wilhelm Eichler (1839–1887). They are hardy from Zones 3 to 8.

Tulipa kaufmanniana, the waterlily tulip, originally came from Turkestan. The slightly reflexed petals open wide in the spring sun and do, indeed, resemble waterlilies. Plant height is low, usually under 6 inches. Bulbs come in a number of cultivars including 'Alfred Cortot', a deep scarlet blossom with white-striped leaves, and 'Heart's Delight', having carmine red petals, edged in pale rose. The species name is again an honorarium, but I don't know who Kaufmann was. They are hardy from Zones 3 to 8.

Tulipa sylvestris has many small sweetly scented flowers that are yellow with just a touch of green and red on the outer petals. References say these tulips multiply nicely with stoloniferous roots that come from the mother bulb. The height is 6 inches. They are originally from West Africa and Asia Minor. The species name means from the woods. They are hardy from Zones 4 to 10.

Tulipa tarda were first found in central Asia and bear white-petaled flowers with hints of bronzy green with a yellow base. The basal leaves form a rosette but a number of bulbs act like a groundcover; flower height is 4 inches. *Tarda* means they bloom late. They are hardy from Zones 4 to 8.

Groundcovers

Botanical name: *Aegopodium podagraria* 'Variegatum'.
Common name: Bishop's weed, goutweed.
Habitat: Ordinary garden soil in partial shade, but will grow in full shade or adjust to full sun, although the leaves often burn at the edges.
Description: Perennial with toothed leaves variegated with green and white; small white flowers on tall stems; to 1 foot.
Period of bloom: Early summer.
Propagation: By division in spring or fall; seeds.
Zone: 4.

When our first country garden was being assembled, a call went out for plant donations, and because beggars should not be choosy, we took anything that came along. A lady in the nearby village gave us a clump of bishop's weed, and since the slope behind the new perennial border needed a groundcover of some sort, we took the gift and planted it. A few years later, the entire slope was covered with this pernicious plant. The only way we kept it in check was to never let it form seed and to promptly axe any seedling found. Eventually I planted some carpet junipers on the bank, and the goutweed grew between their branches, making an effective combination.

The genus name is from *aix,* for goat, and *podion,* from little foot, because the leaflets are supposed to look like a goat's hoof. The species name is from the Latin, *podagric,* meaning afflicted with gout, and refers to goutweed's use as a cure for gout and sciatica. Folklore maintains that just carrying cuttings in the pocket will stave off an attack.

I take exception with nursery ads that describe this plant as "carefree and vigorous," but must admit that, in the right place, nothing is tougher or does a better job as a groundcover.

*Aegopodium
podagraria
'Variegatum'*

At one point I threw a clump into the nearby woods. There the soil was the poorest in our garden, and the area was in continual shade from the surrounding white pines, now some 30 years old. The goutweed took and, in a few year's time, formed a lovely circle of the variegated foliage that makes it a perfect plant for the right spot.

Under no circumstances should you plant the species, a plant known in England as ground elder and described as a persistent weed, deep-rooted, and difficult to remove once introduced. The leaves are not variegated like the cultivar.

Botanical name: *Ajuga reptans.*
Common name: Bugleweed.
Habitat: Ordinary well-drained but moist garden soil in full sun to partial shade.
Description: Perennial with creeping stems; basal rosettes of smooth, oval leaves, often tinged with bronze; spikes of blue flowers; to 6 inches.
Period of bloom: Early summer.
Propagation: By division and rooting stems.
Zone: 3.

Bugleweed, like goutweed, is another plant that is tough and invasive. Use should be dictated by need. As a groundcover, this is a great plant, but it doesn't quite know when to stop. Care should be exercised when setting it out. Rosettes of leaves send out surface runners like spokes from the hub of a wheel. These root and send out more. The genus name is from the Latin *a,* not, and *jugum,* yoke or ridge, meaning the flowers have a nonbilabiate calyx, a fancy way of describing the upper flower lip as lacking a division. *Reptans* means the stems creep and root.

Aside from spreading, the other drawback with bugleweed is the need for somewhat moist soil sites. The roots are shallow, giving plants little or no drought resistance, and in full sun without moisture, the leaves quickly burn. In areas of Zone 6 and south, the leaves are

Ajuga reptans
'Burgundy Glow'

evergreen. In colder areas, especially without snowcover, the leaves die over winter, but they quickly reappear the following spring.

There is also a problem with crown rot on plants grown in the warm parts of the South but planting in well-ventilated areas and dividing every few years helps to control this disease.

Spring brings 6- to 10-inch flower spikes that bear little snapdragon-like flowers, usually blue but also found in various shades of pink or white. A carpet of these blossoms is indeed a beautiful sight, and the honey- and bumblebees delight in their presence. But for a year-round effect, the leaves are the thing. Set out plants 10 inches apart for a quick-growing cover.

There are a number of cultivars available. 'Alba' has creamy white flowers; 'Atropurpurea' has bronzed leaves; 'Burgundy Glow' bears tricolored leaves that begin growth as bright burgundy but, as they age, turn creamy white and pink; 'Rosea' has pink flowers; and 'Variegata' has dark green leaves mottled with creamy white blotches.

Ajuga pyramidalis does not spread with runners but forms 8- to 10-inch clumps of deep green leaves and the typical flower spikes. 'Metallica Crispa' has blue flowers with purplish brown leaves that are crisped at the edges.

Botanical name: *Epimedium* spp.
Common name: Barrenwort, bishop's-hat.
Habitat: Ordinary moist garden soil but will adapt to dry; full sun but prefers partial shade.
Description: Perennials with woody roots and very attractive compound leaves; unusual nodding flowers with tiny spurs, in pink, yellow, orange, red, or white, depending on the species; to 1 foot.
Propagation: By division in spring or fall.
Zone: 5.

There are few plants so tough that they can be moved at most any time in the garden year and continue to bloom immediately after the journey. Hostas and daylilies come to mind, and so do barrenworts.

These flowers entered European gardens at the end of the sixteenth century. Supposedly the genus was so named by Linnaeus because many of these plants grew wild in the ancient Asian country of Medea. A number have also come to our gardens from Japan. The common name of barrenwort (remember that *wort* is an old English word for plant) comes from a remark made in 1597, in Gerard's *Herbal*: "I have thought good to call it barren woort in English . . . bicuase . . . being drunke it is an enimie to conception." Obviously it didn't work. *Bishop's-hat* refers to the flowers; their 4-spurred form resembles a bishop's biretta.

Both the leaves and flowers sit on strong, wiry stems. The leaves, while not truly evergreen, have a papery texture that lasts well into winter, especially south of Philadelphia.

Barrenworts are excellent along walkways, the edges of wild gardens, edging in general, and as effective groundcovers. Use them under and between shrubbery or under trees. They are also excellent on slopes. Try them in the rock garden, too. They transplant easily and should be divided every few years.

Epimedium alpinum 'Rubrum' produces flowers of red and yellow on 8-inch stems.

Epimedium grandiflorum grows about 12 inches tall, with heart-shaped leaves that are bronzy when young, then turn green. The flowers are yellow and bloom in spring. 'Album' has white flowers, and 'Rose Queen' bears rose-colored flowers on 10-inch stems.

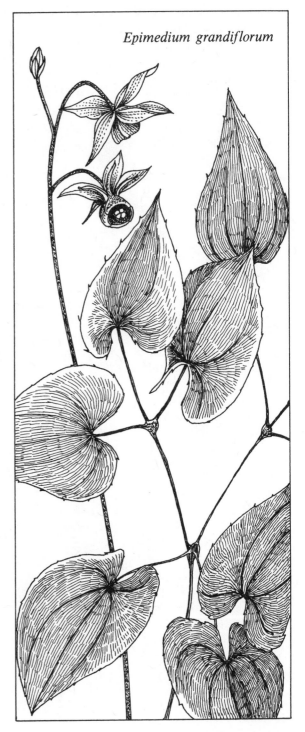

Epimedium grandiflorum

Botanical name: *Equisetum* spp.
Common name: Horsetails.
Habitat: Ordinary garden soil but prefer moist spot; full sun to partial shade.
Description: Perennials that resemble an ancient group of fossil plants; tall, hollow stems with minuscule leaves and no flowers; to 4 feet.
Propagation: By division anytime.
Zone: 5.

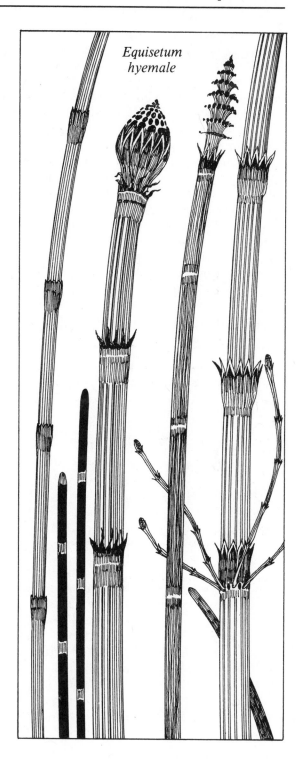

Equisetum
hyemale

Horsetails are represented by one genus, *Equisetum,* and are found throughout North America. The name comes from the Latin for *equus,* horse, and *seta,* tail. Known as the common scouring-rush, the stems have a very high silica content and in pioneer days were used to scour cabin floors and clean cooking utensils. If you're ever caught on a camping trip without a Brillo pad, look for a bunch of these odd plants and there will be no excuse for having a dirty frying pan. *Equisetum hyemale,* the common horsetail, grows along streams, lakes, swamps, in roadside ditches, and often on the edge of railroad beds.

The evergreen shoots grow from a perennial rhizome, or thickened root. Since they are not fussy as to drainage, I keep a large clump in a 9-inch pot without a drainage hole. All summer the pot sits in the full sun; in early fall, it is brought inside to the sun porch. Another 8-inch pot holds a clump set out in the middle of a small pool. When a dragonfly alights, it's a small throwback to a million years or so ago and the Carboniferous period of geologic time.

The tiny pennants circling the rings that connect the hollow stems are primitive scalelike leaves, but the major part of photosynthesis occurs in the stem. The individual stem sections can be pulled apart like pop-it beads and temporarily stuck back together.

Admittedly, this plant is not for everyone. Some visitors to our garden, upon spying a large clump of *Equisetum hyemale* 'Robustum' growing in the midst of a colony of hardy begonias (*Begonia grandis*), always find time to ask about that unusual begonia that blooms and survives where temperatures fall below freezing, but they completely ignore comment on the half-inch dowels of green sticking up from the middle.

A few years ago, I grew a bunch of horsetails close to a hefty planting of wild sweet peas; it's a combination that works well together. Just remember they are rampant once begun and should be contained with a shield to prevent uncontrolled spreading.

Equisetum hyemale 'Robustum' is best contained—as are they all—by a plastic or metal ring so it stays confined to the proper area, but once settled in, it makes a sure statement. *E. scirpoides,* or the dwarf scouring rush, forms a tangled mat of tiny, wiry stalks and is perfect in the rock garden—but be careful, because it spreads.

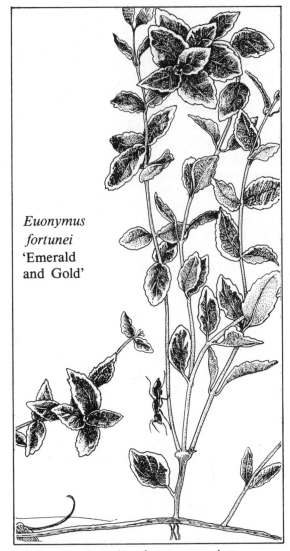

Euonymus fortunei 'Emerald and Gold'

Botanical name: *Euonymus fortunei.*
Common name: Evergreen wintercreeper.
Habitat: Ordinary well-drained garden soil in full sun to partial shade.
Description: Low shrub with branches that spread almost horizontally, or climb a wall if allowed; leathery, oval evergreen leaves; insignificant flowers, followed by pink fruit; to 3 feet.
Period of bloom: Spring.
Propagation: By layering; seed.
Zone: 5.

Trailing or climbing by rootlets, these creeping stems will cover the ground, climb a wall, or move up a trunk. They make one of the best groundcovers for flat or sloped areas. The genus name is from the Greek and literally means of a good name, possibly referring to a onetime medicinal use. Originally from China, they were brought back by Robert Fortune.

They are not fussy as to soil but perform well in rich or poor alike. They will cover rocky areas and cover unsightly stumps. In fact, the only drawback to the wintercreeper is a susceptibility to a scale that encrusts the branch and leaf undersides with gray or white insects. By looking at all the plants in your garden, you can be warned of any infestations and take proper care, in this case, insecticidal soaps.

In old books, wintercreeper was called *Euonymus radicans.* If given a wall, the species will cling to it with tiny rootlets. Four cultivars are generally available: 'Minima' is a creeper with tiny, dark green leaves that clamber over the ground forming a mat 2 to 3 inches high; 'Argenteo-marginata' either climbs or crawls, depending on the location. For over five years, it was reliably winter-hardy in our northern garden in upstate New York, where it rambled along the side of a bank beneath a very large white pine, making a most effective ground-cover. The leaves are variegated with green, white, and shades of pink, some having a combination of all three; 'Colorata' has leaves that start as green but become a deep purple for winter; and 'Emerald and Gold' bears small green leaves with a gold margin.

Hedera 'Buttercup'

Botanical name: *Hedera helix.*
Common name: English ivy.
Habitat: Ordinary moist garden soil but likes added humus; full sun or partial shade according to type.
Description: Perennial creeper to 10 inches tall, with aerial rootlets that cling to stone or masonry; leaves usually lobed and with many colors and shapes; flowers are greenish and inconspicuous, followed by tiny black berries that only appear on adult specimens.
Propagation: By cuttings.
Zone: 6.

For many years, our northern garden in upstate New York had one small patch of English ivy that required constant ministrations but never really took to the climate, being barely able only to survive our harsh winters. In New York City and other spots in Zone 6, ivy is evergreen, and once you get to the areas south of Philadelphia, it can easily become a weed.

The lobed, glossy, deep green leaves are evergreen and come in various sizes and variegations, especially with yellow or white. *Hortus Third* lists over 80 cultivars and that list is ten years out of date. *Hedera* is the ancient Latin name for ivy, while *helix* refers to the spiral climb of the vine.

These are tough plants. Dr. Robert E. Atkinson, in his excellent book, *The Complete Book of Groundcovers* (1970), writes about the selections made by T. H. Everett of the New York Botanical Garden, including the cultivar called '238th Street', with its "exceptional ability to withstand urban smog and adverse winter conditions in New York City." Atkinson also mentions the cultivar 'Bulgaria', an ivy that does well in the hot, dry regions of Bulgaria and, after introduction by the Missouri Botanical Gardens, in the gardens of St. Louis. 'Baltica', from Latvia, is a fairly hardy strain.

Where the climate allows, there is no better groundcover. A shaded garden of tall trees, with one of the variegated forms of ivy allowed to grow up to flagstone walkways, around a stone bench or two, and circling a small garden sculpture, is a treasured place to sit and think about the garden chores ahead. Ivy covers the rear wall of our stone house, and each spring we go out and shear it back, thus forcing new and crowded growth. Unfortunately, the ivy has also overtaken a shaded bed of ferns and wildflowers, leaving us with a great deal of ivy eradication ahead of us.

When ivy becomes mature, especially when climbing trees above 15 feet, small greenish flowers appear. You'll see them first because of the bees that swarm to the blooms. In the autumn, blue-black berries appear.

Ivy, especially when grown in pots or on topiary forms, is susceptible to spider mites. If tiny webs appear on the undersides of leaves and the foliage begins to brown, use heavy sprays of water and insecticidal soap immediately.

Ivy roots easily from cuttings struck in either moist sand or water. Or put cuttings directly in the ground where you want the plants to be, and cover them with individual plastic, ventilated tops. Plant cuttings on 18-inch centers. When a planting is old, it can be rejuvenated by cutting the stems back in spring and allowing new growth to begin.

Of the myriad cultivars of ivy, look for 'Anne Marie', with variegated medium gray-green leaves with yellow margins; 'Buttercup', with bright gold, shiny leaves about 2 inches wide that turn green in the shade and with age; 'Manda's Crested', with light green, 3-inch, fluted leaves, which curl inward, turn a copper color in winter, and bear light green veins; '238th Street', that very hardy cultivar with gray-green, heart-shaped leaves and white veining; and the most hardy of all, 'Thorndale', having matte green 3-inch leaves with white veining and said to be hardy in Zone 4 with some protection.

Botanical name: *Houttuynia cordata.*
Common name: Houttuynia.
Habitat: Ordinary moist garden soil or shallow water; full sun or partial shade.
Description: Perennial with heart-shaped leaves and small white flowers resembling begonias; to 9 inches.
Period of bloom: Late spring.
Propagation: By division in spring.
Zone: 5.

Over seven years ago, my friend Budd Myers gave me some houttuynia plants that he grew from seed obtained from a member of the American Rock Garden Society. We planted them down at the edge of our pond, in the shade of a very old red maple tree. They soon formed a spectacular groundcover, and while their invasive qualities were noted, the water depth and various rocks in the area kept them in check.

Now every nursery is offering this plant along with the veiled caveats, ". . . it grows extremely vigorously," and ". . . rapid growing groundcover," so be warned that it can get out of bounds. The spreading is due to two facts: First, the seeds develop parthenogenetically, from an unfertilized egg cell, and the

Houttuynia cordata
'Chameleon'

creeping rootstock can produce new plants from very small pieces. But kept in check, it's a beautiful plant. And note: There is a very strong citrus smell when leaves are crushed that some people find offensive (but then I've never found geraniums or marigolds to be bothersome as many people do).

Houttuynia was discovered in 1784, so this one took a long time to market. It was named in honor of Martin Houttuyn, a Dutch naturalist (1720–1794); the species name means heart-shaped. The original plant has been largely replaced by the cultivar 'Chameleon' (sometimes called 'Variegata'), bearing its heart-shaped leaves with variegations of yellow, pink, and red.

Botanical name: *Iberis sempervirens.*
Common name: Perennial candytuft.
Habitat: Ordinary well-drained garden soil in full sun.
Description: Perennial with woody stems bearing thin, glossy evergreen leaves; clusters of white, 4-petaled, fragrant flowers; to 1 foot.
Period of bloom: Spring.
Propagation: By division and cuttings; seed.
Zone: 5.

Even in our northern garden in upstate New York, the perennial candytuft—a kind of miniature shrub that bore shiny, dark green leaves attached to a brown, knobby stem—remained evergreen in the winter. Then with spring, each tightly packed disk of buds became a mass of small white flowers, blooming in racemes that lengthened with age. These blossoms, with two petals longer than the others, turned pink with age. Candytuft graced not only the edge of the scree bed, but also nestled between some large rocks at the base of that slope at the back of the garden. The genus is named for Iberia, the ancient name of Spain, since many wild species are found there. The species name means ever green.

Iberis sempervirens

Use candytufts for edging, along rock walls, in rock garden clefts and crevices, and, if you will remember to water them, in clay pots artfully placed throughout the garden. They are excellent tumbling over walls and stones. Once established, as long as there is full sun and good drainage, candytufts are extremely drought resistant.

Start seeds in early spring, and take cuttings after flowering is finished. Our original start of candytuft was an unnamed cultiver with more flowers than found on usual plants. It came from seeds provided by the Royal Horticultural Society, planted out in the spring of 1981. To keep flowers coming, continually deadhead old flowers.

Botanical name: *Juniperus* spp.
Common name: Juniper.
Habitat: Ordinary garden soil in full sun.
Description: Prostrate conifers with long spreading branches with either scaly or needle-like leaves; blue fruit; to 1 foot.
Propagation: By cuttings and layering; seeds.
Zone: 3.

Though bona fide members of the pine family, junipers produce a berrylike fruit. But on close examination, this berry turns out to be a modified cone, covered with resin and dusted with a bloom. Its pungent perfume can readily be identified as a flavoring agent of gin. The genus is from the old Latin name used by Virgil and Pliny. Leaves have two forms: when young they are awl-like or needle-shaped, while the adult forms are scalelike, clasping the shoot and overlapping.

The demands of junipers are minimal—just lightly acid to neutral soil and water during prolonged dry spells. Prune in spring to remove any winter damage.

Juniperus communis var. *depressa,* the ground juniper, is a low evergreen shrub with sharp needles of blue-green and thin bark that shreds with ease. Usually about 3 feet high, it will tumble over walls and rocks. 'Depressa Aurea' starts out the year with a vivid gold-yellow foliage that slowly turns to a bronze-yellow and then bronze as the summer passes. It will reach 2½ feet in ten years and is hardy in Zone 4.

Juniperus horizontalis, the creeping juniper, grows about 1½ feet high, but the form is prostrate. This is an evergreen conifer with low, spreading or creeping habit, which varies from cultivar to cultivar. The foliage is needle- or scalelike, of medium green, blue-green, or gray-green, often purple in winter. These plants tolerate a range of soils, as well as hot, dry, or city conditions. Best as groundcovers, they can be pruned back to promote bushy growth.

There are several cultivars of *Juniperus horizontalis.* 'Douglasii' originated 135 years ago in Waukegan, Illinois, and is known also as the Waukegan juniper. Main branches hug the ground and side shoots swerve upward; the color is blue-green in summer and purple-blue in winter. 'Bar Harbor' is a popular form that follows the contours of the land and weaves between rocks, and 'Glauca' will completely cover the chosen site with a living carpet of blue-green foliage. Both are beautiful when hanging over the edge of a wall and are good for seaside gardens. The average growth rate is 15 inches a year.

Juniperus procumbens is an ornamental conifer discovered in the mountains of Japan some 100 years ago. It is usually available as the cultivar 'Nana', the dwarf Japanese juniper. Foliage is a fresh green in spring, turning to a blue-green with summer's advance, and ending as bronzed for the winter. It was introduced to America by the Hill Nursery of Dundee, Illinois, in 1904 as *J. japonica* var. *nana* until receiving its new name in 1942.

This conifer will eventually cover an area of 10 to 12 feet in diameter. Of all the ground huggers, this particular plant is my favorite. The needles are sharp, so sharp that it came as a surprise to me when I found that deer—when pressed by hunger—will devour this creeper, patiently removing needle after needle.

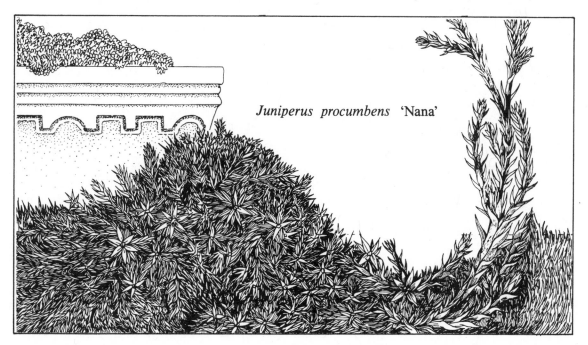

Juniperus procumbens 'Nana'

Botanical name: *Microbiota decussata.*
Common name: Siberian cypress, Siberian carpet cypress.
Habitat: Ordinary garden soil in full sun or partial shade; drought resistant when established.
Description: Evergreen conifer with arching branches of small, scaly leaves resembling feathers, turning bronzy in winter; to 20 inches.
Propagation: By hardwood cuttings or layering of older branches.
Zone: 3.

Believe it or not, there are new plants out there waiting to be discovered. Then once found, years can go by before the plant in question is readily available at the nursery center—that is, unless the discovery is shrouded in mystery, steeped in tragedy, or fraught with drama. Three or four tragic accidents, the likes of Cher and Madonna as team cosponsors, and tons of money at stake from the start, might generate enough publicity to get a new plant noticed.

The Siberian cypress was originally discovered on a mountain in southeastern Siberia near Vladivostock back in 1921, yet 70-some years later, it's still not very common. *Microbiota* is from *micro,* meaning small, and *biota,* meaning sphere of life, and can refer either to the limiting climate where it was found or to the fact that each of the round yellow-brown cones contains only one seed. The species name, *decussata,* means cross-shaped, and here refers to the leaf habit of growth.

This conifer forms a wide-spreading, flat-topped plant that resembles a juniper, with an ultimate spread of 15 feet. The flat sprays of scalelike leaves are yellow-green in partial shade. But if grown in the open, the leaves turn a beautiful bronze overlaid with purple when the cold of winter strikes, a color habit exhibited by many conifers. There is one cultivar, called 'Siberian Carpet'.

Once established, the Siberian cypress is extremely drought resistant. It is one of those rare plants that, once settled in, can be ignored except for appreciative glances. We only had one plant in our northern garden in upstate New York, but it easily withstood temperatures of −25°F in a stiff wind without snow cover. It has been used as a very effective groundcover in the conifer collection of the Brooklyn Botanic Garden.

Microbiota decussata

Botanical name: *Pachysandra* spp.
Common name: Pachysandra, Japanese spurge.
Habitat: Ordinary moist, but acid, garden soil in partial shade.
Description: Perennial with fleshy stems and whorls of rounded leaves; spikes of off-white flowers; to 10 inches.
Period of bloom: Spring.
Propagation: By cuttings taken in summer.
Zone: 5.

Just as there are clichés in the world of words and of fashion, there are popular trends in plants. It all starts innocently enough: A

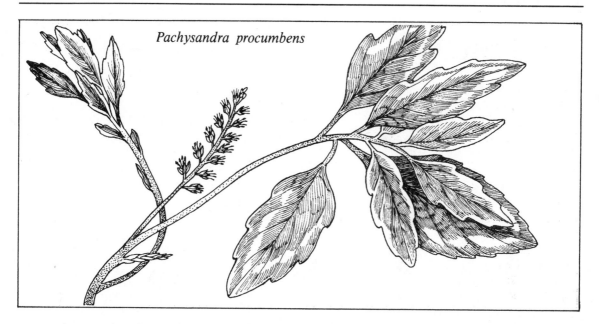

Pachysandra procumbens

new variety reaches the market, and gardeners, after seeing advertisements and articles in various magazines from *Ellé Decor* to *Flower & Garden,* begin to want it. Soon the nurseries produce more and more, and production becomes easier and easier. When fledgling gardeners arrive on the scene, it's easier to sell them the now-timeworn stalwart, rather than to interest them in a plant that is less well known. Such is *Pachysandra terminalis*: Once it was unusual and interesting and now it's everywhere you look.

Here is a plant, by-the-by, that is better known by its botanical name than by the common name of Japanese spurge. The genus name is from the Greek *pachus,* thick, and *aner,* man, referring to the stout filaments in the flowers.

Now, don't get me wrong. In certain places there is nothing better than covering ground with pachysandra. In the 1950s, over 150 different plants were tested at the Arnold Arboretum for their ability to grow in shade. Pachysandra came out tops, being able to grow in 50 percent shade. But it has been overdone.

There are limitations to this plant, and they deal with too much light. In ignorance, we planted a number of cuttings on our back bank in the full sun; the result is that the deep rich green turns the color of chartreuse liqueur, admirable on the cocktail table but definitely not *de rigueur* in the garden.

So for that shady bank, or that open area beneath tall trees, or about and under the rhododendrons, or next to that old stone wall, nothing beats pachysandra. Set out the plants at 1-foot intervals.

A number of cultivars have appeared over the years. 'Green Carpet' is hardier than the species, with glossy, deep green, slightly larger foliage; 'Silveredge' is a variegated type but best for areas of full shade.

There is also a native pachysandra called Alleghany spurge (*Pachysandra procumbens*), growing about 1 foot high. The leaves are oval and gently toothed, with lighter areas of green touched with silver marking the regular dark green surface of each leaf. The flowers have a purplish cast and consist mostly of stamens. This is a more beautiful plant than the Japanese, especially the flowers, but since it isn't evergreen in truly cold areas, it is not as popular.

Parthenocissus quinquefolia

Botanical name: *Parthenocissus quinquefolia.*
Common name: Virginia creeper.
Habitat: Ordinary well-drained garden soil in full sun or light shade.
Description: Perennial creeping deciduous vine that climbs with tendrils; large palmate leaves divided into 5 leaflets; inconspicuous white flowers, followed by small blue-black berries; brilliant scarlet foliage in autumn.
Period of bloom: Unimportant.
Propagation: By division or layering where stems touch the ground.
Zone: 5.

By all definition, Virginia creeper should be included in the vine section of this book. But—and it's a big but—although this native American plant will quickly climb a tree or trellis, where no support is available or where support has been denied, this vine turns into a magnificent groundcover, wandering about the allotted area, holding the foot-wide cluster of leaves on foot-high stems. The genus name is Greek for virgin ivy, and the species name means with five leaves or leaflets.

We found out by accident about this groundcover ability when I happened to cut down a poorly placed white pine at the edge of the woods that was acting as host to a Virginia creeper. Not wanting to lose the vine, I carefully pulled the tendrils away from the tree's bark and laid it on the ground, intending to eventually transplant it to another spot. Later I returned to find the vine wandering over the ground and taking root.

So let me introduce you to the creeper as a groundcover, not a climbing vine. And the glory of it all is in the autumn when the creeper's leaves turn a brilliant scarlet-red, quite unrivaled by anything else except perhaps the sour gum (*Nyssa sylvatica*) or sumac (*Rhus* spp.). This vine is also resistant to salt spray, making it a natural for the seaside garden, and birds love the berries. Once established, it is quite drought resistant.

Two cultivars, 'Engelmannii' and 'Saint-Paulii', have smaller leaflets on a smaller scale and are well-suited to city gardens. The second is especially good at climbing low stone walls.

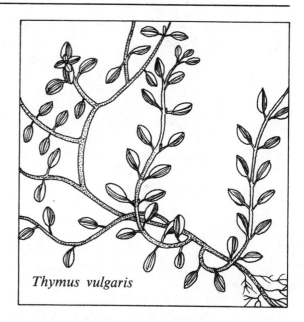

Thymus vulgaris

Botanical name: *Thymus* spp.
Common name: Creeping thyme.
Habitat: Ordinary well-drained garden soil in full sun.
Description: Perennial woody-stemmed sub-shrubs with tiny aromatic leaves and small flowers of purple, lilac, or white.
Period of bloom: Summer into fall.
Propagation: By division or cuttings.
Zone: 4.

Here's a little creeper, perfect for the dirt between paving stones or for filling small cracks in artful walls, providing a fascinating variety of scents, subtle colors, and textures. As a plant, its history is very long. The genus name is from the Greek *thymon,* meaning to make a burnt offering or sacrifice, in reference to the ancient religious role of this little herb.

Just don't violate the meager wants of thyme: full sun and well-drained, even dry, soil. You will be amazed at the progress of growth as the tiny green fingers work their way into and between every nook and cranny. In fact, if the spot is to their liking, they have a tendency to become weedy, albeit charming weeds.

Even though these plants are tough, break up the soil when planting, especially if it's rock-hard. And keep them watered if rainfall is sparse until they have settled in.

Thymus × citriodorus is a low evergreen subshrub up to 1 foot high with lemon-scented wood and leaves.

Thymus praecox, or mother-of-thyme, is the traditional groundcover, growing about 2 inches

high, and evergreen in mild areas. *T. praecox* subsp. *arcticus* forms a fuzzy gray-green mat to 8 inches high with the appealing scent of lemon. Its lovely leaf color makes a beautiful color complement both to flagstone walks and to the green plants in the garden.

Lemon or wild thyme is often listed as *Thymus serpyllum* in nursery catalogs. There are many cultivars but 'Pink Chintz' has a longer than average blooming period and tolerates dry conditions even better than the others.

Thymus vulgaris is the common garden thyme and the most powerful spreader of the lot. Be careful about using it in rock gardens, since garden thyme can crowd out weaker plants. It's a very variable species and four different varieties and cultivars are usually available. English thyme is the species and grows to 12 inches with small oval, gray-green leaves; miniature English narrow-leaf thyme is a cultivar that reaches a height of 6 inches, with narrower, more delicate leaves; French thyme is a shorter variety that grows to 10 inches and has narrower and more delicate leaves; German winter thyme is another variety, and is a more compact version of the previous two.

Botanical name: *Vinca minor.*
Common name: Myrtle, common periwinkle.
Habitat: Ordinary garden soil with added humus; tolerates full sun but appreciates partial shade.
Description: Perennial trailing evergreen subshrub with shiny leaves; funnel-like, 5-petaled flowers of violet, blue, or white; under 2 inches.
Period of bloom: Spring and fall.
Propagation: By division or cuttings.
Zone: 5.

Myrtle, or periwinkle, is an evergreen groundcover that does well in either sun or shade—though too much sun in the South can burn the leaves. It was originally brought over from Europe with the colonists but has since escaped from cultivation. It is found in fields, old lots, and old gardens, and especially in old cemeteries, where it was often planted in lieu of grass. It covers ground in all but the worst soils, the stems rooting whenever a node touches the ground. The flowers are, of course, periwinkle blue. *Vinca* is the classic Latin name and is a contraction of an old Slavic word, *pervinca,* which comes from the word *pervi,* or first, since it is one of the first flowers of spring.

On a more morbid note, wreaths of myrtle were hung about the necks of people condemned to death in medieval England and Italy. The Italians placed it on the biers of dead children as a symbol of immortality and called it *Fiore di Morte.*

In 1939, Liberty Hyde Bailey wrote in *The Standard Cyclopedia of Horticulture:* ". . . a hardy, trailing plant with shining evergreen foliage . . . it forms a dense carpet to the exclusion of other herbs [and] is a capital plant for clothing steep banks, covering rocks, and carpeting groves." Myrtle also makes a capital plant for hanging baskets; the stems will hang in the open air to great lengths.

In our northern garden in upstate New York, myrtle grew in an area of open shade, under a very tall white pine tree. In early spring, the first flowers would appear, lasting for weeks. Then again in autumn, a few blossoms appeared, usually at the end of September.

When planting myrtle, buy it by the flat and set out the individual plants from 12 to 14 inches apart. If you buy property with an established grove of myrtle, crowded and neglected plants can be improved by severe thinning. It is very important to water well while myrtle is becoming established. Once rooted, it is remarkably drought resistant.

There are a number of cultivars, including 'Alba', with white flowers, and 'Atropurpurea', having blossoms of dusty rose. 'Bowles Variety', now known as 'La Grave', has 1-inch-wide flowers of a deep lavender blue, and 'Multiplex' has double flowers of purple-blue.

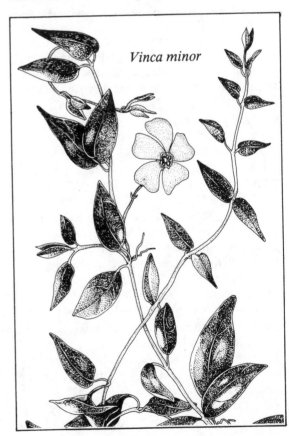

Vinca minor

Ferns

Botanical name: *Adiantum pedatum, Asplenium platyneuron, Athyrium filix-femina, Dennstaedtia punctilobula, Matteuccia pensylvanica, Onoclea sensibilis, Osmunda* spp., and *Polystichum acrostichoides.*
Common name: Ferns
Habitat: Ordinary to moist garden soil in full sun or partial shade.
Description: Perennial fern with sweet-smelling fronds that turn a beautiful golden yellow in fall; to 2 ½ feet.
Propagation: By division in spring; spores.
Zone: 4.

In our original country garden there was a slope behind our perennial border, about 6 feet high, originally part of a landfill to protect the house from winter winds out of the northwest. The slope's middle was marked at the bottom by a giant clump of eulalia grass (*Miscanthus sacchariflorus* 'Robustus'). The soil content was rubble and clay. To the right of the grass, we planted goutweed (*Aegopodium podagraria*); at the left, the slope angled down, and here I planted hay-scented fern gathered from the edge of the woods. Unlike the goutweed, I never once considered this fern a mistake. It was named in honor of August Wilhelm Dennstedt, a German botanist circa 1818. *Punctilobula* means the lobes are dotted with spores.

Some gardeners accuse this fern of being invasive and aggressive—and it is; I would never plant it in a formal perennial border or a rock garden. But for carpeting a bank or an area at the edge of a woodland lot, especially where little else will grow, it's a perfect choice.

The fronds are sweet-scented when crushed or when drying. Thoreau said of this, his favorite fern: ". . . Nature perfumes her garments with this [plant]. She gives it to those who go

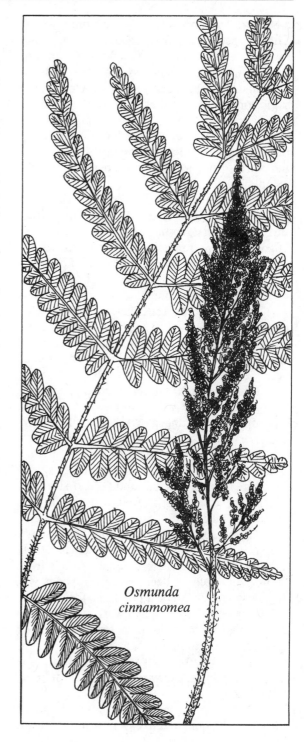

Osmunda cinnamomea

a-barberrying and on dark autumnal walks. The very scent of it, if you have a decayed frond in your chamber, will take you far up country in a twinkling." Hairlike glands on the fronds release an ester that smells of new-mown hay, the same compound found in many of the grasses.

This is the most adaptive garden fern there is. It will tolerate wet, dry, or damp, adapting to full shade, dappled shade, open shade, and, in the North, full sun. It does its best job in acid woodland soil.

During the summer months, fronds are light green and quickly crowd their immediate area. But after the first frosts, they turn a lovely shade of golden tan and persist until either buried by snow or blown apart by winter winds. To propagate, plant egg-cup sized sections of the matted rhizomes, spacing about a foot apart.

There are other ferns that are valuable for gardening in the shade. The following will tolerate temperatures to −20°F. and will thrive in areas of filtered sunlight, the kind of light found near the forest floor.

Adiantum pedatum, the maidenhair fern, is a great beauty. The genus name is from *adiantos,* meaning dry; if plunged in water, the fronds remain dry. The fan-shaped, light green leaflets are set on top of shiny, near-black stalks, and the grace of this plant is evident to all. Fronds grow between 1 and 2 feet tall and spread slowly in partial shade. Every so often, a dwarf form is offered by nurseries.

Aspleniums, or the spleenworts, are usually evergreen. Their leaves may be simple or deeply cut or compound. The botanical name is from *a,* not, and *splen,* spleen, since the genus was formerly thought to be a medicine for ailments of the spleen. Ebony spleenwort, *A. platyneuron,* is a good choice for a spot in a shady rock garden. Although many of these ferns grow best in the more alkaline soils found near limestone rock, the ebony spleenwort is also quite at home in acid soil.

Athyrium filix-femina, the lady fern, grows about 2 ½ feet tall and likes a position in moist,

Onoclea sensibilis.

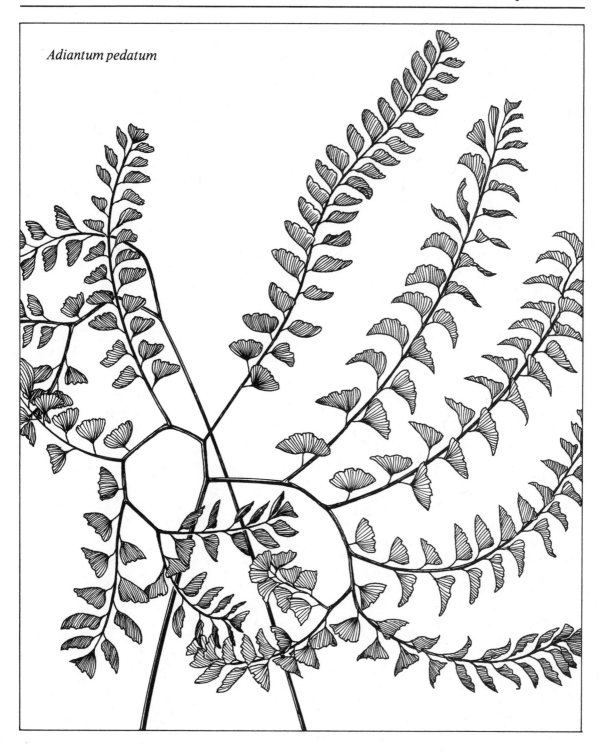

Adiantum pedatum

partial shade, though it will live—but not well—in full sun up North (never in the South). The name comes from the delicate structure of the leaflets, which are very finely cut. The genus name is from *athyro,* to sport or mutate, and refers to the many different shapes found among the sori, or spore cases; *filix* means fern. The ostrich ferns, *Matteuccia* spp., reach heights of 3 feet and are great for backgrounds, taking more sun than most ferns. They were named in honor of C. Matteucci (1800–1868), an Italian physicist. You'll often find *M. pensylvanica* at the edge of a woods or lining an old country road, especially if it has a wet ditch for a rhizome-or root-run. New plants appear at the ends of runners.

Onoclea sensibilis, the sensitive or bead fern, is grown both for its leaves, which are decidedly unfernlike, and for its spore-bearing fertile spikes, which look like beaded feathers. The genus name is from the Greek *onos,* a vessel, and *kleio,* to close, referring to the closely rolled fertile fronds. These ferns are called sensitive because the leaves die quickly when first touched by frost. But for most of the year, they are a good contrast to the typically ferny look of the others. They do become invasive when environmental conditions include great soil and plenty of water, but have never been a problem in our garden. They will grow in partial sun or shade.

Osmunda regalis var. *spectabilis* is a variety of the royal fern. *Osmunda* is derived from a name for Thor, the Scandinavian deity. In native haunts, royal ferns can reach 10 feet in height, but this particular type settles for 6 feet in the garden. If given adequate moisture, it can tolerate some sun, but it does better in light shade. The manner of growth is a crown rather than runners, so the plant spreads slowly. Leaflets turn golden brown in autumn.

Two other osmundas are the cinnamon fern, *O. cinnamomea,* and the interrupted fern, *O. claytonia.* The cinnamon fern is noted for its fertile "cinnamon stick" of fertile fronds and its vigorous sterile leaves. It thrives in moist, acid

soil. The interrupted fern has two or more fertile leaves that interrupt the normal leaves on a stem.

As its name implies, *Polystichum acrostichoides,* the Christmas fern, is green for Christmas, and cut fronds make excellent holiday dec-

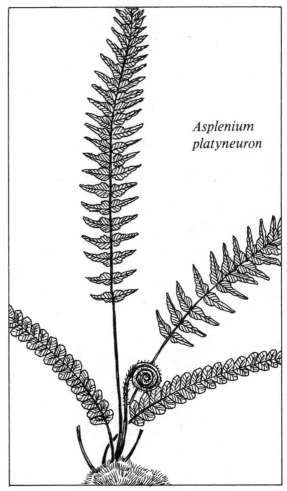

Asplenium platyneuron

orations. The genus name is from *poly,* for many, and *stichos,* for row, referring to the spore cases being in several rows. The species name suggests a resemblance between this particular fern and members of the swamp fern genus, or *Acrostichum.* Plants grow about 3 feet high. Sterile leaves—those without sori—remain evergreen through the winter, although leaflets are often burned with frost; the fertile leaves wither.

Polystichum acrostichoides

Vines

Botanical name: *Clematis* spp.
Common name: Wild clematis.
Habitat: Ordinary moist garden soil with added humus; roots need shade while vine likes full sun.
Description: Perennial vines with heart-shaped leaves; small white flowers, followed by fluffy seed heads; climbs to 30 feet.
Period of bloom: Late summer into fall.
Propagation: Softwood cuttings; seeds.
Zone: 5.

There are many garden clematises, so many, in fact, that entire collections could be built around this vine. There are even some shrubby forms. With over 200 species, not to mention the hundreds of cultivars produced over the last 100 years, the total is large and still growing.

I've tried a number of the clematis cultivars over my years in the garden, but the conventional admonitions "keep the vines in the sun but provide a cool root run," and "don't forget these vines like lime" always caused problems. Wherever we've gardened, the soil has been decidedly acid and the cool place for roots has been lacking. The plants did okay but were never as spectacular as the color photos in books, magazines, and catalogs. That is, until I tried the sweet autumn clematis in the garden proper and virgin's bower (*Clematis virginiana*) in the wild garden.

Some botanical name changes are not always for the best. In the case of the sweet autumn clematis, *paniculata* rolled off the tongue (it means the flowers are carried in panicles), while the new species appellation names the plant for C. J. Maximowicz (1827–1891), a man credited with the introduction of over 200 new or little-known species to the St. Petersburg Gardens and who could have done without this

Clematis virginiana

particular honor. *Clematis* is derived from the Greek *klema,* meaning vine branch. The correct pronunciation, by the way, is clem'-a-tis not cle-mat'-is.

To further complicate matters, according to my reference books, *Clematis paniculata* was discovered in 1760 by Carl Peter Thunberg in Japan. But *Hortus Third* claims it's from New Zealand and could be *C. dioscoreifolia.* Henry A. Gleason's *New Britton and Brown Illustrated Flora* describes *C. dioscoreifolia* as a native Japanese vine that was commonly cultivated but has now escaped.

Anyhow, Pizzetti and Cocker, in *Flowers: A Guide for Your Garden,* write that this clematis is "a particularly successful species in the eastern part of the United States, where the climate is much to its liking. The masses of feathery silver-gray seeds are also very ornamental." And when it blooms in the fall, the masses of 4-petaled white blossoms that cover the vines are truly spectacular.

This vine can reach a height of 30 feet and is quite at home twining about the branches of any tree in sight. It's very valuable for covering old stumps or a fence that is unsightly but necessary. Or grow the vine on a trellis or allow it to ramble over shrubs in the wild garden. Older stems should be trimmed to the ground to stimulate new growth, since flowers bloom on the current season's growth. For those with seaside gardens, the foliage is moderately resistant to salt spray.

In the pest department, watch out for spider mites during prolonged weeks of hot weather and little rain. Blister beetles have a particular fondness for clematis foliage—watch out for blister beetles yourself, too, since they can discharge a very disagreeable fluid that can burn skin. For the mites, use the hose and blasts of water; for the beetles, try insecticidal soaps and pyrethrums.

Clematis virginiana, the mountain clematis or virgin's bower, has white flowers, too, but they are smaller than *C. maximowicziana*

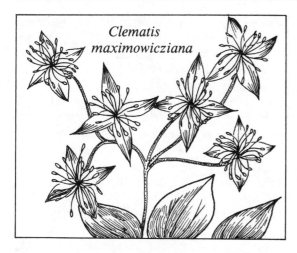

Clematis maximowicziana

and flower on and off throughout the summer. The entire vine is somewhat coarse and more suited to naturalized plantings than to the formal garden.

Virgin's bower will tolerate some shade, especially in the South. This vine has a more moderate growth rate, eventually stopping at about 15 feet. It's especially beautiful in the fall when the seeds, called achenes, display long, twisting plumes adorned with shiny hairs.

Botanical name: *Hydrangea anomala* subsp. *petiolaris.*
Common name: Climbing hydrangea.
Habitat: Ordinary moist garden soil with added humus; partial shade but will take full sun in the North; will not bloom well in dense shade.
Description: Perennial woody vine with aerial rootlets; shiny green leaves, turning yellow in fall; flat-topped clusters of fragrant white flowers in spring; to 70 feet.
Period of bloom: Summer.
Propagation: Heel cuttings; seed.
Zone: 5.

Most people think of hydrangeas as those bushes or small trees of autumn bearing huge snowball mounds of flowers, often found in old gardens or planted on the hillsides of country cemeteries. This particular hydrangea is not a tree or a bush but a beautiful vine. *Hydrangea* is from two Greek words meaning water vessel, and refers to the cuplike form of the seed vessel. *Anomala* means unusual or out of the ordinary, and a hydrangea that climbs certainly is. *Petiolaris* refers to the stalk of the leaf.

This is a deciduous climber, clinging to any vertical surface using aerial roots. Its yellow-orange bark peels much like a birch tree. The dark green leaves are 2 to 4 inches wide on long slender petioles. The flowers are flat-topped clusters 6 to 10 inches wide, looking like typical hydrangea blooms. This vine looks best when set against a stone wall.

My first introduction to this plant was at the garden of Harold Epstein, the prominent plantsman in Larchmont, New York. There the soaring trunks of two oaks (one black and one red) stand to either side of his front door and serve as poles for climbing hydrangeas. The hydrangea on the right is the typical form, but on the left is the cultivar 'Skyland' (recognized by the well-known horticulturist Tom Everett some 30 years ago), a stronger plant with larger flowers.

Now, that isn't all. The climbing hydrangea will not only climb, it will ramble. Years ago I found the following in Pizzetti and Cocker's *Flowers: A Guide for Your Garden*: "[It] will thrive in shade as well as in a partially sunny position, and really beautiful effects can be created by allowing the plants to cover large rocks, old walls, or dead tree trunks with a huge rounded mass of spreading vegetation." So I planted one not on a tree or wall but halfway up a 6-foot-high sloping bank. The first year it settled in; the second year it began to stretch; the third year it took off. Since this plant resents disturbance, make sure you buy only container-grown plants.

In our new garden, I planted a well-rooted container-grown plant in July. By the end of September, it had taken hold and one searching

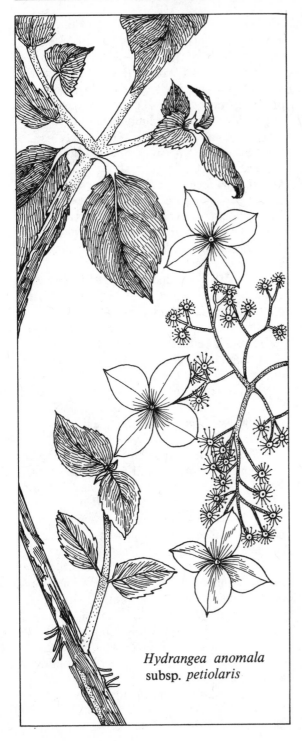

Hydrangea anomala
subsp. *petiolaris*

branch had already wormed its way between large mortared stones on the front of our house. Be patient with the climbing hydrangea. You will be rewarded by a fantastic addition to your home and garden.

Botanical name: *Lathyrus latifolius.*
Common name: Wild sweet pea, everlasting pea, perennial sweet pea.
Habitat: Ordinary well-drained garden soil in full sun.
Description: Perennial vine with compound leaves, climbing with tendrils; long-stalked clusters of red, pink, or white pea flowers; to 10 feet.
Period of bloom: Summer into fall.
Propagation: By division; seeds.
Zone: 5.

I knew that the wild sweet pea was a tough plant when I saw it grow with such abandon in the fields around our old farmhouse and along the banks of streams and ditches. It is one of over 100 species of the genus *Lathyrus,* which features a number of very popular garden plants including the annual sweet pea, one of the most beloved flowers in a cottage garden. *Lathyrus* is the ancient Greek name for pea and comes from *la,* addition, and *thouros,* irritant, referring to the medicinal uses of the plant. The genus is also important in the world of genetics. *L. odoratus,* the annual climbing sweet pea, was the plant used by Father Gregor Mendel in his experiments that revolutionized the science of heredity.

Native to southern Europe, this is a vigorous, vining perennial that holds by means of quick-growing tendrils. Its original home helps to explain the plant's ability to withstand hot and dry conditions; it's even at home planted between paving stones. If given half a chance, perennial sweet peas will scramble over bushes, up and over old tree trunks, and in and out of field grasses. Although they can be staked, any attempt to civilize them detracts from their healthy scampering.

Since these sweet peas rarely grow higher than 8 feet, a number of older books on growing vines suggest planting them along the bottom of clematis and rose vines, allowing their climbing stems to cover over the sparse bottom branches of the others. Try this vine along the base of an old wall or to cover the ugliness of cyclone fencing.

The gray-green winged stems have narrow paired leaves and are hosts to many upright stalks, each holding 12 or more sweet-pea-like flowers that appear in many shades of pink.

Lathyrus latifolius

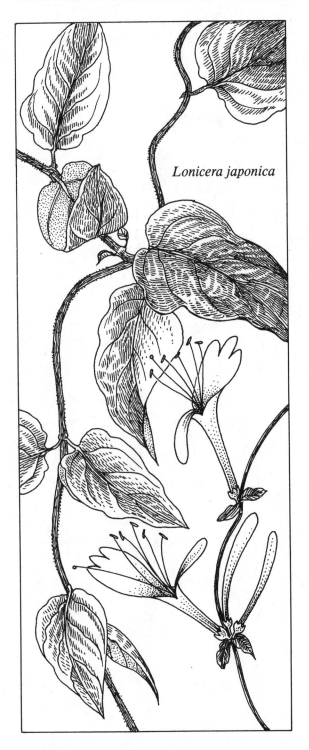

Lonicera japonica

There are a number of cultivars, including 'Snow Queen' and 'White Pearl', each with flowers of dazzling white; 'Red Pearl', with red flowers; 'Roseus', bearing rich pink flowers; 'Pink Pearl', with light pink flowers; and 'Splendens', having flowers of dark purple and red.

Botanical name: *Lonicera japonica.*
Common name: Japanese honeysuckle.
Habitat: Ordinary moist garden soil with added humus; full sun to partial shade, but flowering ceases as shade increases.
Description: Perennial semi-evergreen climber; long pointed leaves; fragrant tubular flowers of white, fading to yellow; black fruit; to 30 feet.
Period of bloom: Late spring into summer.
Propagation: Cuttings of ripe wood in June and July; seeds.
Zone: 5.

Having spent the better part of a year fighting the up-to-now uncontrolled ravages of Japanese honeysuckle, I write the following with the warning that this beautiful but tough vine can be a problem if left to its own resources—and that includes abandonment.

This graceful woody climber belongs to a genus of over 100 species, usually deciduous, sometimes evergreen. Every child of the suburbs or country has, at one time or another, pulled the trumpetlike flowers from the vine to taste sweet nectar at the base of the tube. The genus honors Adam Lonitzer (1528–1586), a German botanist and physician who was pensioned as a naturalist by the city of Frankfurt for 32 years.

The Japanese honeysuckle can reach 30 feet and is an evergreen or partly evergreen vine, depending on the climate. The 1½-inch fragrant white flowers, often tinged with purple, turn yellow with age. They appear from summer and on into fall. Honeysuckle is very easy to grow but, as noted above, can become a nuisance if not kept under control. In fact, in various woodland areas of the North and Southeast, this particular honeysuckle runs second only to kudzu and unless you have the time and strength to cut it back, choose another vine.

But if you have the space (and the strength) for this vine, it should be planted by itself, allowed to scamper up a dead tree trunk or twine around a stout trellis. Unlike the other honeysuckles, the vine does not need pruning to survive but merely to keep it in check. Nothing is better to carpet a difficult bank or bare slope, and honeysuckles do their bit to control soil erosion. Once established, they are very drought tolerant.

One of the more colorful trellises that have been mentioned to hold honeysuckles was described by William Robinson in *The English Flower Garden:* "A good plan is to plant some in good soil against wooden posts at distances of 12 feet apart, and when they have reached the top of the posts to connect them by festooning a chain from post to post, as roses and clematises are often done."

Lonicera japonica 'Halliana', or Hall's honeysuckle, bears 2-inch white flowers that turn creamy yellow on the second day. It is not quite as invasive as Japanese honeysuckle.

Botanical name: *Polygonum aubertii.*
Common name: Silver lace vine, silver fleece vine.
Habitat: Ordinary moist but well-drained garden soil; full sun or partial shade.
Description: Perennial deciduous vine with stems that climb to a height of 20 feet or more; dark green heart-shaped or arrowhead leaves; in autumn, long panicles of fragrant white or greenish white flowers, followed—but rarely—by small pink fruits.
Period of bloom: Late summer to early fall.
Propagation: Softwood cuttings in late spring; division; seeds.
Zone: 4.

If you have a wall, fence, or trellis that begs to be covered with a fast growth of leaves and flowers to boot, the silver lace vine is the perfect answer. The small flowers that cover twining stems with great abundance become a white haze from a distance, completely hiding the leaves from view. Also called the China fleece vine and the mile-a-minute plant, this vine is billed as one of the fastest growing vines in existence, reaching 20 feet of its ultimate 30-foot length in the first season.

The genus name is from the Greek *polys,* many, and *gonu,* a small joint, referring to the many joints on the stems. The species is named in honor of the discoverer, Père Georges Aubert, who found the vine in western China in 1899.

Make sure that you buy container-grown plants for faster growth; bare-root vines often take a month or more to settle in before they snap out of a self-imposed lethargy. Give them a reasonably good soil for a start, since once this vine is established, you will never get it out of that spot. They must be pruned back severely, especially when loose in small gardens. Even when drastically cut back in early spring, the vines will usually bloom by fall. They tolerate bad air and do well in city gardens.

Unlike many ivies and the like, silver lace vines are harmless to foundations, walls, and brick mortar, because they cling by twining about and not by utilizing suckers. Give them a warm and sunny spot.

Instead of using plastic strips to weave in and out of chain-link fences, people with something to hide should take advantage of silver lace vine, using its rampant growth to cover multitudes of sins. In our northern garden in upstate New York, this vine first covered, then covered over, a green plastic trellis. I have no doubt that as the plastic deteriorates the vine will continue to hold.

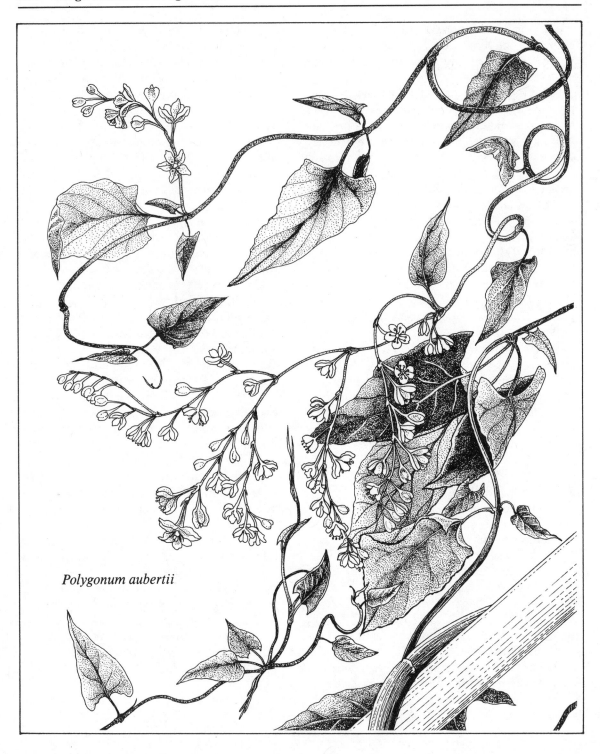

Polygonum aubertii

Shrubs and Small Trees

Botanical name: *Abeliophyllum distichum.*
Common name: White forsythia, Korean abelia-leaf.
Habitat: Ordinary garden soil in full sun.
Description: Deciduous shrub with square branches and light greenish-blue oval leaves; white, heavily fragrant, forsythia-like flowers; to 6 feet.
Period of bloom: Early spring.
Propagation: By softwood and hardwood cuttings; seed.
Zone: 5.

No other shrub has the place in my heart that the white forthysia has, since no other has done such a great job in brightening up late mountain springs—and those springs are always late. Even though winters could plunge to −25°F, this shrub bloomed every April in my upstate New York garden, long before the yellow forsythias were even thinking about opening up. Although it resembles a forsythia, this plant has a genus all to its own; *A. distichum* is the only species. *Abeliophyllum* means resembling the leaves of Abelia, another genus of some 20 ornamental shrubs. *Distichum* means arranged in two rows, referring to the flowers.

In late winter of 1987, as I interviewed the renowned plantsman Harold Epstein for my book *American Gardens,* we paused in front of a bush with a very old-looking trunk and tiny buds, dark purple against the brown of the bark.

"Know what this is?" he asked.

"I do. It's an *Abeliophyllum distichum,* but surely the oldest I've ever seen."

"It's about 35 years old. Some 20 years ago, I tried to get a local nurseryman interested in

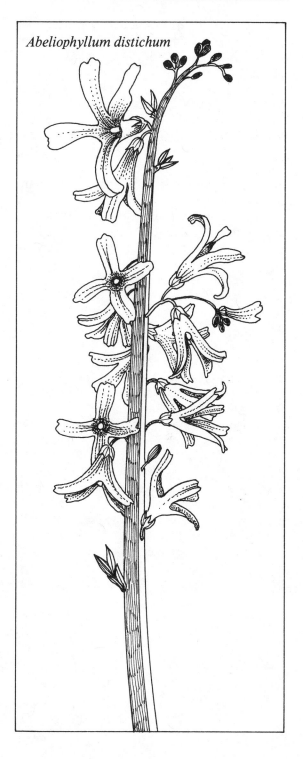

Abeliophyllum distichum

that shrub. Told him he could take cuttings. He didn't think it would be worth the effort. Now he carries this shrub every season. Suddenly it's popular."

And deservedly so. A native of central Korea, *Abeliophyllum* has been growing in American gardens since 1924, but it still doesn't have the popularity it deserves.

Although the nurseryman who gave it its common name has been criticized by the cognoscenti, white forsythia is a far better name than Korean abelia-leaf.

The flower buds appear in late summer, so always do any pruning in the spring after blossoming is over for the year. Although hardy in our cold country garden, the shrub had protection from the worst of the winter winds, a necessity since the flower buds remain on the stems all winter and can be damaged by severe weather.

Not only is this shrub valuable for the early spring flowers, but it makes an excellent shrubbery backdrop for small gardens. The arching branches and attractive leaves become excellent foils for all sorts of other perennials, especially those with white flowers. The branches are easily forced to provide flowers for the winter table.

If you start with a good-sized container-grown plant, it should reach 6 by 4 feet in about three years. If your garden is small, it can be easily pruned if it becomes too large. Root the severed cuttings for your garden friends.

A new cultivar called 'Rosea' is now on the market. It bears light pink flowers and should be especially beautiful in early spring gardens.

Botanical name: *Amelanchier canadensis.*
Common name: Serviceberry, juneberry, shadblow.
Habitat: Ordinary garden soil in full sun.
Description: Deciduous small American tree with gray bark; 5-petaled white flowers that appear before the simple leaves; small red fruits; beautiful yellow to red leaves in fall; to 45 feet.
Period of bloom: Early spring.
Propagation: Softwood cuttings; seed.
Zone: 4.

"To see the real beauty of the juneberry is to see its frail blossoms intermixed with snowflakes on a stormy day in early spring—youth daring the tempest," Jens Jensen, one of America's pioneer landscape architects, wrote in his book *Siftings.*

And here again we have an American tree perfect for the small garden, but ignored by many landscapers and gardeners because, like most Americans, it has a common background. Since much of my familiarity with landscape trees began with those found on our country property, I haven't always been forced by popular taste to garden with horse blinders on. One of the stars of our early spring was the shadblow, so-called locally because the clusters of white flowers opened within a day of the arrival of the shad. *Blow* is an old English word for flower, and shad are a fish of the herring family that swim up the Delaware River to spawn. Other common names are the serviceberry and the juneberry.

Amelanchier is adapted from the French name of a European species, *A. ovalis.* The plant was brought back to England by John Tradescant, and the common name serviceberry is derived from the resemblance of the American plant to the English service tree (*Sorbus domestica*). Serviceberry is a variation of the Latin *sorbus,* a name used by Pliny for the fruit of *Sorbus domestica,* a Mediterranean relative of the mountain ash.

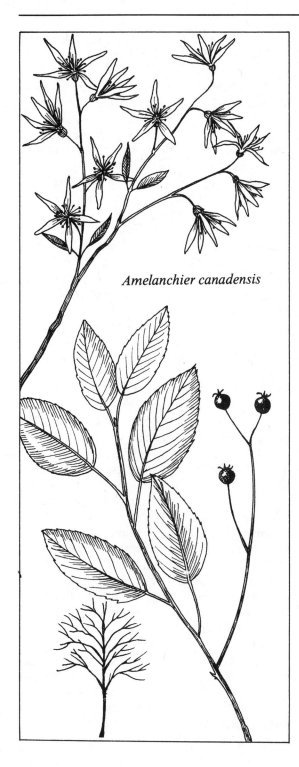

Amelanchier canadensis

While at its best in well-drained loam, this is a tree that is at home almost anywhere except solid rock or clay. The purple fruit makes a serviceable jelly, but since the berries are attractive to birds, there are rarely enough left to cook. The bark is smooth and purplish brown with pale markings. The wood is heavy and was once used to make handles for tools.

Amelanchier alnifolia, the western serviceberry, has a thicker and rounder leaf, broad and toothed, and is a finer foliage tree than its eastern brother. The berry is larger and of finer flavor. It is thought that *A. canadensis* and *A. alnifolia* were the offspring of a single species that originally came from the North and spread east and west on the slopes of the Rocky Mountains.

Amelanchier laevis has larger flowers and is usually found in nurseries as the cultivar 'Rosea', having flowers flushed with pink.

Amelanchier × grandiflora (a hybrid of *A. arborea × A. laevis*), often called *A. lamarckii,* is offered as the cultivar 'Autumn Brilliance'. It has better than usual autumn foliage of orange and red, and reaches 25 feet at maturity.

Botanical name: *Betula populifolia.*
Common name: Gray birch.
Habitat: Ordinary garden soil in full sun.
Description: Deciduous small American tree with chalky gray-white bark and black marks where branches have been; small triangular leaves; drooping catkins; to 30 feet.
Period of bloom: Early spring.
Propagation: By seed.
Zone: 4.

The gray birch is an underestimated tree. Large numbers of them grew in the abandoned fields between our New York garden and the woods proper. Instead of being papery white like the canoe birch, they have a chalky white bark with triangular black marks below the

Betula populifolia

mal height is about 35 feet, with a trunk diameter of 1 foot. The natural range is from Nova Scotia to Delaware.

Gray birches have the ability to bend without breaking, almost to the ground, under the weight of heavy snow. Critics call attention to the birches' difficulty in straightening up again. But we found that if we removed the snow, they quickly returned to their original shape.

Some writers have said the gray birch is a weedy and poor relation of the paper birch, its only merit being an ability to withstand city soot and smoke. It seems to me that is enough to merit inclusion in any hall of fame.

In 1914, Julia Ellen Rogers wrote in *The Tree Book:* "Graceful and hardy ornamental tree; thrives in any soil, but rarely planted. Wood used for spools, shoe pegs, wood pulp, and fuel. Valuable nurse trees to hardwoods and conifers on land Nature is reforesting."

Obviously something went wrong with the garden tastemakers between then and now, but this is not the first time that high culture has replaced high drama in the garden. Whether for the small city garden or the wild garden, this is an excellent and inexpensive choice when compared to some of the popular *Betula* cultivars.

In a New Jersey garden belonging to Florence and Robert Zuck, botanists at Drew University, several old gray birch volunteers were left to form an allée of great charm. I say "left" because, as mentioned before, these trees are usually doomed by landscapers who wish to recommend the white birch (*Betula papyrifera*). In one place in the Zuck garden, a gray birch is surrounded by rings of creeping blue phlox (*Phlox divaricata*) and primroses (*Primula vulgaris*), while English ivy grows up the multiple trunks.

Catkins are produced on the branches in autumn but bloom the following spring. The eventual seeds provide excellent food for wildlife, including ruffed grouse and songbirds. Deer leave these trees alone unless there is absolutely nothing else to eat.

branches. They are graceful in habit until well into old age, which is about 30 years. *Betula* is the ancient name for this genus, and *populifolia* means having leaves like a poplar—simple and triangular in shape. Often multiple trunks will arise, but the unwanted can be cut off. The nor-

Botanical name: *Caragana arborescens.*
Common name: Siberian pea tree.
Habitat: Ordinary garden soil in full sun, but will tolerate light shade.
Description: Deciduous small tree or large shrub, usually with spines; compound leaves; showy yellow pealike flowers singly or in small clusters, followed by stalked seedpods; to 20 feet.
Period of bloom: Late spring.
Propagation: Softwood and hardwood cuttings; seed.
Zone: 2.

Few shrubs are as beautiful in spring as the Siberian pea tree or shrub. Its common name should signify to all that this species is, if nothing else, hardy as can be. The genus name is derived from *Karaghan,* the Mongolian name for this shrub. The species name means of treelike growth.

Many reference books talk of using Siberian pea trees as windbreaks on the windswept Canadian plains of Alberta, Manitoba, and Saskatchewan, but I've seen it used to great effect in small gardens and rock gardens around the Northeast. My garden friend Budd Myers has used *Caragana arborescens* forma *lorbergii* as a spring focal point at the edge of his Pennsylvania rock garden, and nothing is more beautiful than seeing its bright yellow blossoms against a clear blue sky in May.

The Siberian pea tree is fast-growing when young. Its soft, oval leaves grow in pairs, then in groups of four to six, giving a cloud effect from a distance. The main branches have thorns with smaller spines at the leaf axils. In May, clusters of yellow pealike flowers cover all the branches. The seedpods that follow remain on the plant after opening, making artistic shapes against the autumn sky. The leaves turn yellow in autumn, and during the winter months, the greenish stems make an interesting

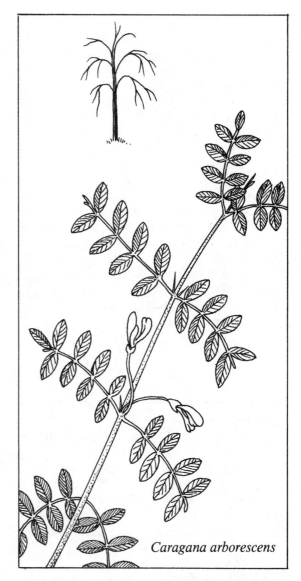

Caragana arborescens

addition to the landscape (especially if the red-stemmed Siberian dogwood, *Cornus alba* 'Sibirica', is planted nearby for contrast). It's a very effective plant for small gardens or in rock gardens. Earlier writers have often spoken of this shrub with disdain, remarking that there are other shrubs of greater ornamental value; as someone who lived for years where the winters were bleak and frigid, I say: Pshaw!

Since this species is a very fast grower, seed becomes a very practical way to acquire plants. Seed soaked in hot or cold water for 24 hours will usually germinate within five days. In five years, you will have a blooming plant.

If you want to grow the species itself, you will probably need to acquire seed from the various seed exchanges. Usually only the form *lorbergii* and the cultivars are found at nurseries and through mail-order.

Caragana arborescens forma *lorbergii* has been called a gem among small trees and is not only useful planted out in the garden, but also does well in containers. It can either be left to grow as it will or pruned to encourage new growth.

Caragana arborescens 'Pendula' is an exceptionally beautiful weeping cultivar of the pea tree introduced into the Imperial Botanical Gardens of St. Petersburg back in 1730. Usually grafted to a 3-foot trunk of *C. arborescens,* it is perfect as an addition to the small garden or as a border centerpiece.

Cotinus coggygria

Botanical name: *Cotinus coggygria.*
Common name: Smoke tree, wig tree, Venetian sumac.
Habitat: Ordinary garden soil in full sun.
Description: Deciduous small tree or shrub with simple leaves; small, yellowish nondescript flowers with hairy pedicels that produce a beautiful effect like pinkish-gray smoke; yellow-orange leaves in autumn; to 15 feet.
Period of bloom: Summer.
Propagation: Softwood cuttings taken in July, overwintering with protection; by seed.
Zone: 5.

Our gardens have always been hosts to smoke trees. The first was the cultivar 'Pink Champagne', raised from seed collected by Kew Garden in London, and in our present garden is a very old 'Royal Purple' that has been in place over 20 years. These plants are considered either small trees or bushy shrubs according to their habit of growth. Their claim to fame is not the insignificant flowers themselves, but the pedicels, or stems, of the non-fertile flowers, which are long and covered with silky hairs, giving the look of puffs of smoke. In addition, a number of cultivars have been developed that have leaves in very beautiful shades of purple and red.

Like the sumacs and the poison oaks, smoke trees belong to the cashew family. The genus and species names are a Latin and Greek name for this shrub.

In our northern garden in upstate New York, we grew the common smoke tree (*Cotinus coggygria*) at the edge of a slope with mugo pines in front and the rising fields behind. Around these shrubs was a wide bed of cordgrass (*Spartina* spp.). The effect of the green needles, the waving grasses, and the gray smoke of the *Cotinus* blossoms was truly beautiful to see.

If growing these shrubs from seed, remember that they are polygamous, and a few seedlings will have male flowers alone and lack the smoky panicles. Either raise a number of seedlings until flowering or buy a labeled tree from a nursery.

When planting out new shrubs, keep them well-watered until established. After that, they are reliably independent and will require no ministrations from you, the gardener.

There are a number of cultivars available. They include 'Flame', which bears flower heads of purplish pink and green leaves that turn a brilliant orange-red in autumn; 'Notcutt's Variety' (once called *Cotinus rubrifolium*), with leaves of a light purple; 'Pink Champagne', with flower heads that produce vast billows of light pink smoke; 'Purple Supreme', a cultivar with foliage that turns deep purple in the spring, keeping the color all summer, then turning bright red in autumn; and 'Royal Purple', with deep pink plumes and deep purple leaves that usually do not fade with the advancing heat of summer.

Cotinus obovatus is the American smoke tree, once common but now rare because of the vast numbers cut down for an orange-colored dye produced by the wood. It's a larger tree, to 30 feet, and while the female trees do not have as many bundles of feathery flowers, the leaves turn a marvelous yellow-orange to red in autumn. The species name refers to the shape of the leaves.

Botanical name: *Elaeagnus* spp.
Common name: Russian olive, thorny elaeagnus, cherry elaeagnus.
Habitat: Ordinary garden soil but light sandy soil preferred; in full sun.
Description: Deciduous small tree or shrub, bearing spines; simple narrow but attractive leaves, silvery beneath; small but very fragrant off-white flowers, followed by small silvery-scaled fruits; to 20 feet.
Period of bloom: Late spring.
Propagation: Softwood and hardwood cuttings; seed.
Zone: 2.

When we first began our country garden, we planted a bare-root Russian olives (*Elaeagnus angustifolia*) in a long row, about 25 feet long and 6 to 8 feet wide, the width depending on the growth of the individual shrubs. The line was initially used as a windbreak, both for the house some 50 feet away and for a bed of what I hoped would be unusual, but not always hardy, wildflowers.

The shrubs began to bloom by mid-June of the second year, their small flowers giving off a delightful—but heavy—odor that was evident for a very wide range. Visitors to the garden would stand for minutes, enjoying the perfume. Their joy was nothing compared to the ravenous appetites of flocks of birds that turned up in late summer to devour the berries produced by those fragrant flowers.

Elaeagnus angustifolia

In the winter when the leaves had fallen, the gray bark of the Russian olives provides more interest to the garden. These shrubs age quickly, and before ten years have passed, their trunks are gnarled and wrinkled with the look that others fight for decades to have. The genus is named after the Greek word for the sacred olive tree, because of the resemblance between the leaves of this shrub to those trees of Greece and Italy; the species name means narrow-leaved.

This is an especially good tree for the small lawn or as a backdrop for other shrubs. Some authorities have called it a dirty tree because of shedding bark, but this was never evident to our sensibilities. It's also a popular shrub for seaside gardens.

Russian olives are very easy to start from seed and grow quickly, reaching 6 feet in four or five years. They often seed about the garden.

Elaeagnus multiflora, the cherry elaeagnus, is hardy in the southern range of Zone 4. It is grown for the red cherrylike berries that appear in summer. The dark green leaves are silvery underneath, about 2 ½ inches long, and flowers are, once again, extremely fragrant. Some authorities credit Commodore Perry with the introduction of this plant from Japan in 1862.

Elaeagnus pungens, the thorny elaeagnus, is not reliably hardy below Zone 7, but in the South it's used to plant median strips along highways. The gardenia-like fragrance of the flowers—which bloom in October—can confound the motorist driving with windows open on a lovely autumn day. Introduced from Japan in 1830, this shrub with evergreen leaves grows about 12 feet high and can be sheared to make an effective hedge. 'Variegatus' has leaf margins of yellowish white.

Botanical name: *Forsythia* spp.
Common name: Forsythia.
Habitat: Ordinary but well-drained garden soil including those that are strongly alkaline; in full sun or partial shade.
Description: Deciduous shrubs with gracefully arching stems; slightly toothed, oval leaves; many 4-petaled, yellow, bell-like flowers before leaves appear; to 10 feet.
Period of bloom: Early spring.
Propagation: Softwood and hardwood cuttings; layering; seeds.
Zone: 5.

Forsythia suspensa

Forsythias have been around for so long that their bright yellow spring flowers have almost become garden clichés. Notice I said almost, for no matter how common they become, who within the gardening world would wish to be without them? After the barrenness of winter, the sight of those myriad golden yellow flowers of early April, whether from one bush or many, bring cheer to the most hardened heart.

In the world of plants, forsythias have not been around too long. The first plants brought to gardens were *Forsythia viridissima,* arriving from China in 1846, imported by the great plant collector, Robert Fortune. The genus is named in honor of William Forsyth (1737–1804), the superintendent of the Royal Gardens at Kensington and author of an important book on fruit cultivation. The species name in this case means very green.

Mr. Forsyth was the inventor and distributor of Forsyth's Plaister, a so-called miracle compound that was a mixture of soap, wood ash, sand, lime, dung, and urine, not necessarily in that order. He claimed that his concoction would cure all the problems suffered by trees. The British Government was so impressed they gave him £1500 to produce perfect oak for use in building warships. Needless to say, the mix didn't work, and Forsyth ceased selling it.

Forsythias as a group may grow at best 15 feet tall but usually under 10. Bright yellow flowers appear before the leaves in early spring. They are excellent for use as an informal hedge or as specimen plants or integrated in a shrubbery border. Unlike many other shrubs, they can be planted among the roots of larger trees. Use plenty of water when establishing these shrubs, especially during dry summers.

Forsythia branches are easily forced by cutting them in February and bringing indoors to a warm room. In fact, you can thin out old bushes by cutting branches for forcing. Do any pruning necessary to remove weak shoots after flowering. The shape of these shrubs is usually so attractive when left to their own devices that such pruning should be kept to a minimum.

Forsythia × intermedia is a hybrid of *F. suspensa* and *F. viridissima,* the result of the two species being planted close to each other at Germany's Göttigen Botanic Garden in 1885. The stems are sometimes hollow but layered with pith at nodes, and the leaves are sharply toothed. This forsythia can reach 15 feet of upright growth, bearing many blossoms. There are a number of cultivars with larger flowers in varying shades of yellow.

Forsythia suspensa reaches 10 feet, with a weeping form. Many bright yellow fragrant flowers are produced on well-ripened wood of the previous season's growth; *suspensa* means hanging and refers to the dangling blossoms. This species is easily recognized by the stems, which are perfectly hollow except at the nodes; in fact, the brown and bumpy stems look exactly like pretzel sticks. Many cultivars are available including 'Variegata', with leaves edged with yellow.

Forsythia viridissima reaches a height of 10 feet, bearing greenish yellow flowers. In this case, the pith at the nodes grows in layers.

Botanical name: *Hibiscus syriacus.*
Common name: Rose-of-Sharon.
Habitat: Ordinary garden soil in full sun in the North and partial shade in the South.
Description: Deciduous small tree or shrub with upright branches bearing 3-lobed leaves; large, funnel-shaped, 5-petaled flowers of purple, red, or white; to 15 feet.
Period of bloom: Late summer.
Propagation: Softwood and hardwood cuttings; seeds.
Zone: 6; Zone 5 with protection.

The Royal Horticultural Dictionary of Gardening lists the introduction of the rose-of-Sharon into English gardens as 1596, a date that is ten years before the birth of Rembrandt, so this shrub has been around for a long time. It arrived in American gardens about 1790. The common name pays homage to the Biblical rose-of-Sharon, but things got out of kilter over the intervening years because that flower of legend is now thought to be either a narcissus or the autumn crocus (*Colchicum autumnale*). *Hibiscus* is Latin for a marsh mallow to which this shrub is related. The species name credits the plant with origins in Syria, but it originally came from China and India.

Because the rose-of-Sharon is often planted as a lonely specimen tree out in the middle of the lawn, alone and in the hot sun, many gardeners believe that's the perfect place for this shrub. On the contrary, it will do better when the soil is not too dry and, aesthetically, it looks better in company with other plants. Although I have seen these shrubs do quite well in extremely acidic soil, if you live in an area where pH is in the low 4's, add a bit of lime to the soil when planting, to ease its transition to those extremes.

The rose-of-Sharon is easy to grow. Just remember to give enough water for the first year of planting and, in the colder parts of Zone 5,

Hibiscus syriacus

also do well in containers on the deck or patio, as long as you provide plenty of water.

The original species has bluish purple flowers with crimson centers, but today's cultivars have 2- to 4-inch-wide, single, semidouble, or fully double flowers that run the gamut of colors from pure white to pale pink to reddish purple. They usually bloom for most of the summer.

Of the current cultivars, the following are very attractive in the garden: 'Blue Bird' has large azure blue flowers; 'Diana', a triploid introduction from the U.S. National Arboretum, bears pure white flowers often up to 6 inches across and opens at night when most roses-of-Sharon are closed. But to produce these large flowers, prune severely in the spring before the leaves emerge, leaving 2 or 3 buds per branch. 'Helene' has large white flowers with a red eye and is usually seedless; and 'Paeoniflora' bears double blossoms of pale pink.

Botanical name: *Hydrangea* spp.
Common name: Hydrangea.
Habitat: Ordinary, well-drained garden soil; in full sun or slight shade, except in hot and dry areas; some shade is preferred in the South.
Description: Mostly deciduous American and Asian shrubs that form loose mounds of many branches; simple but large oval leaves; rounded or flat-topped heads of many small, infertile white flowers.
Period of bloom: Summer into fall.
Propagation: Softwood and hardwood cuttings; seed.
Zone: 5.

provide some winter protection for the first few years. These shrubs will self-sow, and seedlings can become something of a nuisance. Few will have the qualities of the parents. Since flowers bloom on new growth, shrubs can be pruned to shape in March and grown as a hedge. If larger flowers are wanted, prune back the previous year's shoots, leaving 3 or 4 buds on each shoot. Here is a candidate for seaside gardens. They

Hydrangeas are many plants to many people: Some think only of the pink and blue large-flowered bushes of the garden (*Hydrangea macrophylla*), while others picture the beautiful American native, the oak-leaved hydrangea (*H. quercifolia*), and still others picture the snowball shrubs found in old cemeteries,

Hydrangea quercifolia

the tree form of the peegee Hydrangea (*H. paniculata* 'Grandiflora').

The first hydrangea introduced into Europe was the white-flowered *Hydrangea arborescens,* an American plant that grows wild from southern New York south to Georgia and west to Ohio and Missouri. One Peter Collinson, a Quaker linendraper of London, imported seeds sent over the Atlantic by America's first botanist, John Bartram (1699–1777), but it literally did not flower in English gardens for ten years. But by the early 1800s, this was the flower of choice for decorating window boxes and filling pots on patios, until it was superseded by *H. paniculata,* arriving from Asia in 1861. *Hydrangea* refers to the shape of the seed, which resembles a tiny water pitcher.

These resilient shrubs will survive with the minimum of attention, as evidenced by their presence in many old city, suburban, and country gardens. They can be used as specimen plantings, as large hedges, or as backgrounds for perennial beds and borders. Many do well in seaside gardens. The flowers dry beautifully for winter bouquets.

Our first introduction to hydrangeas was a very old and very undernourished peegee hydrangea (*Hydrangea paniculata* 'Grandiflora') planted many years before we acquired our country property and living in the shade of a very old and very high white pine. This species can reach a height of 18 feet and is often just too large for the average garden; peegee, by-the-by, stands for P.G., an abbreviation of the species and cultivar names. This deciduous shrub bears terminal panicles of large creamy white flowers aging to copper-pink and often lasting well into winter. This is the one hydrangea that can be severely pruned in early spring to produce larger flower clusters. The other hydrangeas want only the dead wood removed in early spring, including what's left of last year's flowers, leaving a few inches of stem above the present year's dormant buds.

Hydrangea quercifolia, the oak-leaved hydrangea, will reach a height of 8 feet with very attractive leaves that resemble those of an oak. Upright panicles of beautiful and fragrant white flowers appear from July to September, followed by leaves that turn scarlet to burgundy for autumn. These bushes are beautiful as backdrops for a bed of flowers or simply as hedge borders. Although catalogs list them as being hardy in Zone 5, that really includes only the southern precincts, and then they need protection from bitter winter winds. If you have room in your garden for only one shrub, consider this in the top ten choices.

A new cultivar of *Hydrangea quercifolia* called 'Snow Queen' is remarkable for the number of blossoms and the magnificent autumn color. Its compact growth reaches a height of 7 feet and the same spread in about six years.

Hydrangea macrophylla reaches a height of 6 feet. These are deciduous shrubs (evergreen in mild climates) that, in acid soil, bloom in various shades of blue; in neutral soil, both pinks and blues can be present. To make flowers blue, add to the soil about one tablespoon of aluminum sulfate per plant. These are hardy in Zone 6.

Botanical name: *Ilex verticillata.*
Common name: Winterberry.
Habitat: Ordinary moist, even wet, garden soil in full sun.
Description: Deciduous dioecious American shrub or small tree with many twigs bearing small elliptic leaves; small, inconspicuous flowers followed by brilliant red berries; to 12 feet.
Period of bloom: Spring.
Propagation: Softwood cuttings; seed.
Zone: 5.

Every year in late autumn, the carmine berries of *Ilex verticillata,* the winterberry, dot the landscape with their insistent color. But

Ilex verticillata

many gardeners wonder why berries so plentiful in fall are usually gone by midwinter. The answer is the birds. As other food supplies dwindle, our resident chickadees, blue jays, and such zero in on these tasty—at least for birds—tidbits.

These deciduous shrubs—sometimes small trees—are members of the holly clan. *Ilex* is the ancient name of the Holm oak, *Quercus ilex,* an evergreen oak with dark, shining, toothed leaves, resembling holly. *Verticillata* means whorled and refers to the leaves.

Winterberries grow to a height of between 6 and 20 feet. The smooth bark is a warm, dull gray. They are quite fond of a wettish or swampy site but will surprise all collectors of plant lore by occasionally appearing on the steepest of dry hillsides. Another name is black alder.

Most of the year, the branches are hidden by tall field grasses, other shrubs like the sweet bush (*Clethra alnifolia*), or larger and bushier neighbors. The flowers are small and white, blooming in late June and early July, escaping the notice of all but the most careful observer. Not until late autumn, when most leaves have fallen, do the beautiful and brilliant red berries begin to be seen.

Winterberries—in fact, all the hollies—are dioecious, meaning they have male and female flowers on separate plants. Make sure you have both kinds. Male plants bear only staminate flowers having many anthers; flowers cluster where the leaf stems meet. Female plants bear fewer flowers, each displaying a prominent stigma.

This is the only species of holly that is fully winter-hardy in the colder parts of Zone 3. They do well in poor soil and even partial shade. Plant them out in spring or fall. Protect them from the local deer herd until they gain a bit of stature.

If you wish to cut a few branches for indoor decoration over Christmas, cover the bushes with bird netting until you start collecting in early December. Keep the branches in water or the berries will shrivel and fall off.

Plant breeders have been at work, and there is a cultivar 'Winter Red', with darker and greener foliage than the species and more fruit. Just remember that you must have a male in the area to pollinate the female flowers.

Magnolia tomentosa

Botanical name: *Magnolia tomentosa* (formerly *M. stellata*).
Common name: Star magnolia.
Habitat: Ordinary well-drained but moist garden soil with added humus.
Description: Deciduous small tree or shrub with deep green foliage; flower buds like pussy willows, opening to fragrant, many-petaled white flowers tinged with pink; to 25 feet.
Period of bloom: Early spring.
Propagation: Softwood cuttings; seed.
Zone: 6; most of Zone 5 with protection.

It was a wet day in late December of 1990, just two days before Christmas, and most of the United States was suffering with an advancing cold front with windchill temperatures of way below 0°F. Only the East Coast had been spared, but predictions were that it, too, would suffer in a day or two. I took advantage of the last bit of warmth to walk out into the garden and look at the buds of the star magnolia.

Garden dirt was soft underfoot and the fallen leaves were soaked through: The garden was, in fact, a dismal place to be, especially when you knew that the temperature would plummet in a day or two. But the buds of the star magnolia would be perfectly comfortable, for they are covered with a coat of fur exactly like that furry fuzz that protects the pussy willow.

This is another tree originally from the Orient. After Commodore Perry opened Japan to foreign trade in 1854, a number of enterprising botanical collectors descended upon that country in search of the new. Among those eager botanists were John Gould Veitch of England,

Carl Maximowicz collecting for Alexander II of Russia, and Dr. George Roger Hall of Rhode Island. In 1875, Hall's plant was named *Magnolia halleana,* but in 1872 Maximowicz called his specimen *M. stellata* (for star-shaped), and according to botanical convention, since it was first, that name applied. Recently, for reasons I don't know, *tomentosa* entered the scene.

The genus is named in honor of Pierre Magnol (1638–1751) the director of the botanical garden at Montpellier, a city in southern France and an institution founded by Henry IV in 1593. The old species name referred to a star while the new name is from the Latin *tomentose,* meaning a stuffing of wool, hair, or feathers, and refers to the buds' wooly coats.

The star magnolia is called a shrub or small tree. It is especially valuable for the northern garden, since it's the only magnolia that is reliably hardy in Zone 5 if given protection from the worst of winter winds. From the buds of late fall and winter, to the spring flowers and attractive summer foliage, to the attractive compact growth habit, this is one of the best plants for the small garden. The double, star-shaped white blossoms have floppy petals tinged with pink and fill the garden with fragrance.

When planting a star magnolia—or any magnolia for that fact—be sure to buy a plant that is container-grown. Transplanting is best accomplished in early spring when the thick and fleshy roots become active. Although roots are always easily broken and prone to injury, at that time of the year they will usually heal.

Recently a new hybrid between the star magnolia and *Magnolia kobus,* a tree from Japan, has produced *M. × loebneri,* and in particular the cultivar 'Merrill', a rapid grower to 25 feet with larger than usual blossoms, and reportedly hardy in Zone 4.

Botanical name: *Potentilla fruticosa.*
Common name: Potentilla, shrubby cinquefoil, hardhack.
Habitat: Ordinary garden soil in full sun; partial shade in the South.
Description: Deciduous North American shrubs with compound leaves, medium green above and whitish beneath, usually with 5 leaflets; many yellow, 5-petaled flowers; to 4 feet.
Period of bloom: Summer into fall.
Propagation: Softwood and hardwood cuttings; seed (male and female flowers on separate plants).
Zone: 2.

The potentillas, or cinquefoils, are members of the rose family, with a homeland that spreads from Greenland to Alaska, south to New Jersey, and over northern Europe and Asia. In many localities potentilla is looked upon as a weed; being a weed means it does well where others perish. The genus name is from the Latin *potens,* for powerful, and refers to the plant's use as a medicine in the Middle Ages; *fruticosa* means shrubby. The common name of *cinquefoil* is French, from *cinque,* five, and *feuilles,* leaves, because each of the featherlike leaves bears 5 leaflets.

We first used this particular species of potentilla as a low hedge along the top of the bank of soil behind our perennial border. Three plants of the cultivar 'Goldfinger' circled around the front of a very attractive dwarf conifer, the golden thread Sawara cypress (*Chamaecyparis pisifera* 'Filifera Aurea'), and were bounded on the other side by a carpet juniper (*Juniperus horizontalis* 'Gray Owl'), in a combination that gave color interest throughout the season. And no matter how hot the sun or how dry the summer, once established, the potentillas thrived, often blooming until the blossoms were cut down by the frosts of late September.

While they prefer full sun, potentillas will adjust to partial shade but will produce fewer flowers. Remove any seedcases in the fall; if pruning is necessary, remove older wood in early spring. They are excellent as groundcovers or edging plants, or just to brighten up the perennial border. These shrubs will also do well in containers—just don't forget to water, especially during hot weather.

My only complaint is common to all members of the rose family: the Japanese beetle. They delight in these leaves. Well-placed beetle traps keep most away. It's easy to pick off these shiny-backed pests with your fingers, tossing them into a can of soapy water.

Potentilla fruticosa

Dozens of potentilla cultivars have been developed over the years. They usually grow to a height between 2 and 3 feet, blooming from May until September. Some currently available choices are 'Abbotswood', the best white so far, with large white flowers that hover above dark blue-green foliage; 'Day Dawn', having peachy pink flowers suffused with cream; 'Dakota Surprise', with light yellow flowers on dense growth; 'Goldfinger', having 2-inch-wide bright yellow flowers on deep green foliage; 'Katherine Dykes', bearing light yellow blossoms on 36-inch-high rounded plants; 'Klondike', with large, deep yellow flowers; 'Pink Queen', bearing pink flowers; and 'Sunset', with small dark green leaves and red-orange flowers in summer that deepen to red in the fall, all on a low-growing, 16-inch-high plant.

Botanical name: *Rhododendron* spp.
Common name: Rhododendron and azalea.
Habitat: Ordinary moist, but acid, garden soil with added humus in shade.
Description: Evergreen shrubs or small trees with large or small leathery leaves, usually oval; clusters of flowers in many colors; to 20 feet.
Period of bloom: Spring or fall.
Propagation: Softwood or hardwood cuttings; seed.
Zone: 6; 5 with protection.

When dealing with rhododendrons, one must be prepared for a world complete unto itself. Many gardeners have started with one or two plants and wound up abandoning all else and making these shrubs the object of lifelong pursuits.

The genus *Rhododendron* represents some 800 species of usually evergreen, sometimes semi-evergreen, and often deciduous shrubs—rarely small trees—found in the Northern Hemisphere, chiefly in the Himalayas, southeast Asia, and the mountains of Malaysia, but, in fact, almost everywhere except the continents of Africa and South America. The genus name is taken from the Greek *rhodon,* rose, and *dendron,* tree.

There are two major divisions in the genus: rhododendrons and azaleas. Both belong to the same genus, but azaleas are either evergreen or deciduous and have flowers shaped like funnels, whereas rhododendrons are usually evergreen and have bell-shaped flowers.

Cultural requirements for rhododendrons and azaleas are the same: a well-drained acidic soil composed of leaf mold combined with sphagnum peat moss well mixed in. Except for the native species, heavy clay soil, even with added humus, and alkaline soils are slow death to the whole group. May is the best month for

rhododendron displays, but a lot of the dwarfs bloom in April.

Both prefer a location that protects them from the continuous heat of a summer sun and from harsh winds both in summer and winter. Their root systems are shallow and thinly branched, so both plants need a soil that remains continually moist. Care should be taken in cultivation since the roots are so close to the surface. Though some species are quite hardy (to −25°F), even when exposed to bitter winter winds in the northern part of the country, most prefer winter temperatures above 0°F.

Generally, rhododendrons should be planted out in the early spring. Dig a hole that

Rhododendron catawbiense

is large enough for the roots to spread out, and set the root ball so that the crown is at the same depth it was in the container. Take the excavated soil and cut it in half with a mix of peat moss and compost (half and half). Keep the soil moist and follow a careful watering schedule for the remainder of the growing season.

When rhododendrons are planted next to a masonry wall of brick or stone, they will eventually suffer. Lime is leached out of the wall over the years by the action of rain, and eventually the soil becomes alkaline. Adding ferrous sulfate should rectify the situation for a time, but consult your local extension agent for a correct reading of the soil pH and the right amount of chemical to add. Do not be tempted to use aluminum sulfate—it can have an adverse effect on rhododendrons.

Rhododendrons can be moved with relative ease, since their root systems are shallow and so close to the stems. Just remember to take enough soil and use enough water to settle in the new plants.

Remove the spent blossoms to prevent seed formation and channel the plant's effort into next year's crop of blooms. Prune rhododendrons in early spring, so that new growth has a chance to harden before winter sets in. Cut back the new leaf shoots to a small bud, sometimes so small as to be easily missed. Do not cut off branches without leaving a bud below the cut, or you will not get any new growth. If there is a dead branch on a plant, cut it off back to live wood; new shoots will then emerge. In general, branches should be cut back to 1 foot to encourage compact growth on old, overgrown plants. I have often seen rhododendrons slaughtered by the knife and saw, yet they put forth new growth, and in a few years, you would never know they had been attacked.

Rhododendron catawbiense, the mountain rhododendron, grows to 20 feet. This is an evergreen shrub (often with age a small tree), bearing 6-inch-long oval leaves, glossy above. Clusters of lilac-purple bell-shaped flowers appear in late spring. An American native rhododendron, the parent of many Catawba hybrids, it is valuable because of its hardiness, surviving in Zone 5.

Rhododendron fortunei, the cloud brocade rhododendron, grows to 12 feet tall. The broad leaves are glossy deep green above and smoky blue beneath. Clusters of fragrant pink funnel-shaped flowers appear in spring. It is not hardy north of Zone 6.

Rhododendron obtusum, the Hiryu azalea, grows to 4 feet and is semi-evergreen but often deciduous. It is a dimorphic shrub, meaning it has two sets of leaves: 1-inch-long, elliptical, dark green leaves in spring, followed by more oval-shaped summer leaves, with a few leaves persisting to the following spring. Flowers come in various shades of rose, magenta, red, or red-violet, depending on the cultivar, and bloom in spring. It is not hardy north of Zone 6.

Botanical name: *Rosa* spp.
Common name: Rose.
Habitat: Ordinary garden soil in full sun.
Description: Deciduous shrubs with thorns or prickles; compound leaves; fragrant flowers with 5 or more petals, followed by fruit called hips; to 8 feet.
Period of bloom: Summer into fall.
Propagation: Softwood and hardwood cuttings; seed.
Zone: 4 and 5, depending on species.

"A large rose-tree stood near the entrance of the garden: the roses growing on it were white, but there were three gardeners at it, busily painting them red. Alice thought this a very curious thing, and she went nearer to watch them, and, just as she came up to them she heard one of them say 'Look out now, five! Don't go splashing paint over me like that!' "

Everyone knows what happened next in *Alice's Adventures in Wonderland,* and all about the playing-card gardeners painting the white roses red so that the Queen of Hearts would not behead them. Standing at the entrance of almost any rose garden, especially if it has white lattice fences, it's easy to imagine not only Alice and the playing-card gardeners, but the whole population of Wonderland enjoying an afternoon with the roses.

Rosa is an ancient Latin name for this flower, and it is an ancient flower, beloved through the ages, the subject of poetry and song, anecdote, fable, perfume, and even medicine.

My wife's grandfather grew roses—in Buffalo, no less. He spent hours in his rose garden, taking infinite pains and that included heavy mulching for winter. His roses were hybrid teas, the type that most people think of when they think of roses. People came from miles around to see his flowers. I tried these beauties in our northern garden in upstate New York but never had much success, since the winters were too cold and I often forgot to mulch properly. But we did have roses in the garden. And none of those roses were fussy in the least. They were given full sun and ordinary garden soil that had originally been part of a field of hay, wild grasses, and goldenrod.

The first plants we grew were multiflora roses (*Rosa multiflora*), consisting of a number of plants that previous owners had set out as a living fence. *R. multiflora,* whose species name means many-flowered, were originally natives of Japan. These bushes made fountains of long, curving green branches, liberally spiked with small thorns, and covered with many leaves made of 5 to 9 individual leaflets. In May, those branches were covered with hundreds of clusters of small and fragrant, 5-petaled flowers. Then, by fall, the bushes were covered with quarter-inch red hips, beloved by the birds.

The growth rate is rapid: In a period of a few years, a seedling will make a bush 4 to 6 feet high, eventually spreading up to 15 feet. By planting these roses on 3-foot centers, an impenetrable hedge is formed, which nothing outside of Godzilla will be able to maneuver. Pruning is

Rosa
'White Meidiland'

limited to removing old and weak canes, and they are quickly replaced by new.

The problem is that *Rosa multiflora* will seed about—with a vengeance! Since this particular tough plant is tough to control and really tough to get rid of, it should only be used in situations where neighboring farmers won't mind the invasion of their fields.

The multiflora variety *cathayensis* has pale pink flowers. Two cultivars are available: 'Inermis' has thornless branches, and 'Platyphylla' bears deep pink flowers.

Rosa rugosa, the Japanese or rugose rose, is a sturdy shrub with upright and prickly stems (the species name means rough) covered with leaves much like those of the multiflora rose. it grows to a height of 4 to 6 feet and has a 5-foot spread. The lovely flowers appear in spring but, if deadheaded, will continue to bloom on and off until fall. Depending on the cultivar, the flowers are 3 1/2 inches wide, of purplish rose through white, and are followed in fall by large orange-red hips and foliage that turns orange with the coming of frost. Pruning is limited to removing old dead branches and suckers.

Try a rugosa rose as a specimen in the flower border or as a dependable hedge or naturalized at the edge of a field or meadow. These roses are one of the best bets for a seaside garden. 'Alba' has flowers of white, and 'Rubra' has blooms of magenta-red. 'Sir Thomas Lipton' bears fragrant, snow-white double flowers.

The new Meidiland (pronounced MAY-de-land) or landscape roses, originally came from France. They are perfect as groundcovers and for hedging in a small garden. Since they are reproduced by cuttings and grow on their own roots—unlike many specialized roses—they are hardy throughout most of the contiguous United States, surviving in Zone 4.

I can't say enough about the Meidilands. For the gardener who wants roses without the fuss, these are the answer. Any ground that grows grass can grow these roses. They require little if any pruning. Some have attractive fruits, and

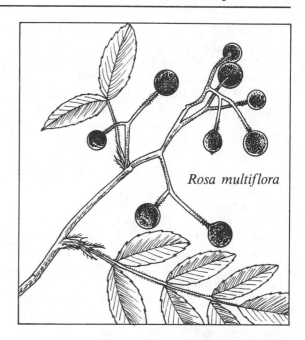

Rosa multiflora

most bloom from spring through to fall. Unless noted otherwise below, plant on 3-foot centers.

My first experience with Meidilands came with three bareroot plants, shipped early in May of 1990 to our northern address. UPS noted the change from New York to North Carolina and the box of roses was forwarded. Twelve days after leaving the nursery, the bareroot roses arrived. I soaked the roots in a pail of water for 24 hours, then planted them out in the front yard. They all bloomed in June.

'Alba Meidiland' is a white everblooming groundcover rose bearing clusters of small white blossoms on plants that reach 2 feet in height with about a 4-foot spread. This is a great plant for carpeting a difficult bank or slope. For a hedge, plant on 4-foot centers.

I noticed a heavy infestation of aphids on all the buds of the 'White Meidiland' in mid-April of this year. There was no insecticidal soap in the potting shed and I was afraid these insects were really doing a deal on the roses. So I grabbed a bottle of Fantastik spray cleaner and doused the aphids. Ten minutes later, I hosed the plants with water.

Every aphid was dead and the buds were not damaged at all.

'White Meidiland' bears up to 3-inch-wide, pure white double flowers that begin to open in June and repeat throughout the summer. The plants grow about 2 feet high and spread to 5 feet. Leaves are a glossy dark green. The only chore is deadheading to prolong bloom.

'Pink Meidiland' is everblooming, with 2-inch single flowers of bright pink with a white center. The height is 3 to 4 feet, and the width, 2 to 3 feet.

'Bonica' has 3-inch double pink flowers on plants eventually reaching 5 feet in height with a 5-foot spread (they can be trimmed to a desired height). This particular Meidiland produces bright red fruit.

'Scarlet Meidiland' flowers with vivid scarlet blooms up to 1½ inches across, lasting up to two weeks on the bush and one week as cut flowers. The shrubs grow to a height of 3 feet with a 5-foot spread and will adapt to some shade. Plant on 4-foot centers.

Botanical name: *Rhus typhina.*
Common name: Staghorn sumac.
Habitat: Ordinary garden soil in full sun.
Description: Deciduous small American tree or shrub with tropical appearance; brown and hairy stems, and compound leaves that turn a glorious orange-red in fall; inconspicuous flowers form clusters of small red fruits that persist after the leaves have fallen; to 30 feet.
Propagation: By suckers; seed.
Zone: 4.

First cultivated in the early 1600s, the staghorn sumac is a tree that has few demands. It grows so quickly that gratification gets a good turn and, though short-lived, is quite beautiful throughout the garden year. *Rhus* is an old Latin name for the genus. *Typhina* pertains to fever, referring to a tea made from the densely hairy berries (really drupes) or leaves to treat fevers and sore throats. The natural range is throughout temperate eastern North America. The staghorn sumac is called a shrub or a tree, with an ultimate height of about 30 feet. The leaves are pinnate, with between 11 and 31 leaflets each. The look is decidedly tropical.

American nurserymen and gardeners usually think poorly of this tree, calling it a trash tree, and suggesting that it be put in only the poorest of soils and relegated to hillsides and then only when erosion seems to be a problem. But our old friends, the English gardeners, say it offers tropical-type leaves for shade in the summer, glorious and brilliant orange and scarlet foliage in the fall, unusual felted stems when the leaves have gone—like the antlers of a stag "in velvet"—and terminal cones of dark crimson fruits that persist throughout the winter. The hair on the branches changes from pink to green the first year and is shed by the time the bark is about three years old.

The most imaginative use of this tree that I have seen is in the Wild Garden at Wave Hill, a public garden located in the community of Riverdale in the Bronx, New York. There a 50-year-old tree has generated a multitude of smaller trunks, and all have been allowed to twist and turn either naturally or by shaping and pruning so they have become a bower with a look more likely to appear in Brazil than overlooking the Hudson River just above Manhattan.

We, too, started such a bower at the side of our northern garden in upstate New York. The largest tree—a chance seedling from the nearby field—harbored hanging houseplants in the summer, giving them the filtered sunlight they prefer. Underneath was a cool and pleasant place to sit on a hot summer's day. By selective cutting of the suckers that arose throughout May, June, and July, I was able to plan the direction that my living house of shade would pursue.

Staghorn sumac can also be used as a living hedge by cutting its tropical foliage to the ground

Rhus typhina

in early spring and only allowing it a year of growth before cutting again.

There is a very attractive cultivar available called 'Laciniata', with individual leaflets that are finely cut. It also deserves a place in the garden.

Botanical name: *Rubus odoratus.*
Common name: Flowering raspberry, Virginia raspberry, thimbleberry.
Habitat: Ordinary garden soil in full sun to light shade.
Description: Deciduous American shrub with upright canes with shredding bark; 5-lobed leaves; fragrant purple flowers followed by dry drupes; to 8 feet.
Period of bloom: Summer.
Propagation: By division; softwood and hardwood cuttings; seed.
Zone: 4.

Many years ago, while driving between the towns of Claryville and Woodstock in New York State, I took a winding and somewhat decrepit road that alternated between paving and ruts, and ruts and gravel, as it wound its way around Slide Mountain. On one side of that road, the mountain fell many feet below; on the other side, it rose some thousands of feet over me. It had been a good summer, and the ferns and bushes were green and full. Suddenly I saw a tumbling waterfall bursting spray and glistening the rocks around its plunge into a sparkling mountain pool. And all around that pool were flowering raspberries, full of flowers, light purple against the maplelike leaves.

"But where the bright blossoms of the Virginia raspberry," wrote Neltje Blanchan in *Nature's Garden,* "burst forth above the roadside tangle and shady woodland dells, even those who despise magenta see beauty in them where abundant green tones all discordant notes into harmony."

Rubus odoratus

That very summer, I asked a garden friend for one of the suckers these shrubs so freely produce and planted it along the slope behind the perennial border, to the right of a Japanese maple, so the leaves and flowers would overhang an old concrete birdbath. In fact, the shrub soon grew large enough that leaves touched the water's surface, and the birds that visited splashed between those leaves as though they were strutting on a watered stage.

The flowers are fragrant, up to 2 inches across, and bloom most of the summer, often producing into fall. There are many yellow stamens, but when fertilized, the flowers become dry and tasteless berries completely unlike that delicious fruit produced by many other members of the genus. The generic name is taken from the Latin *ruber,* for red, referring to those same berries. Even the bark is attractive, since it shreds, coloring the branches with many shades of reddish brown. If left to their own devices, flowering raspberries will form large colonies, using their proclivity to spread by suckers. But if unwanted, they are easily removed.

Don't look for this plant at fancy nurseries; like many of our American natives, the management considers these shrubs too coarse for the gardening public. But those firms devoted to furthering the cause of our native flora usually carry the flowering raspberry.

Here is yet another plant that our English gardeners have introduced into their own gardens. "One of the handsomest species—," says the *Royal Horticultural Dictionary of Gardening,* and William Robinson, the famous English garden writer, mentions in *The English Flower Garden:* "There is no finer shrub for planting under the shade of large trees and in rough places."

Botanical name: *Salix* spp.
Common name: Willow.
Habitat: Ordinary moist, even wet, garden soil in full sun.
Description: Deciduous trees and shrubs with narrow leaves on gracefully bending branches; some with colored twigs; often furry catkins; to 30 feet.
Period of bloom: Early spring.
Propagation: Softwood and hardwood cuttings.
Zone: 3–5, depending on species.

Nothing in my mind is more beautiful than the waving branches of a willow tree (*Salix babylonica*) in early spring when the bark turns a light golden brown, overlaid with the faint flush of bright green, a sure sign that spring is on the way. The first tree we planted when the pond was finished at our country garden was a weeping willow. There is no finer tree for the water's edge; its reflection just doubles the beauty.

The various willows have long been part of our natural world, used for medicine, basketmaking, and decoration. A bit of bark from the white willow (*Salix alba*) is chewed to treat a headache (the bark contains salicin, a precursor to aspirin). The pliable twigs and branches of the osier willow (*S. viminalis*) are bound together to make baskets or wreaths for the celebration of spring. While snow is still falling, pussy willows (*S. discolor*) are brought indoors to open their delightful catkins. In fact, the word *willow* reaches far back into the roots of old English, Dutch, German, and Anglo-Saxon, while the genus name *Salix* is the ancient Latin name for willows.

The species name *babylonica* was a mistake on the part of Linnaeus, who thought it was the same tree as mentioned in Psalm 137: "By the waters of Babylon we sat down; yea, we wept when we remembered Zion. We hanged our harps upon the Willows in the midst thereof." But that area of the world is too warm for this particular willow.

Although the nativity of this willow is uncertain, it's thought to be China. And if the old china pattern known as willowware is any indi-

Salix babylonica

cation, that would certainly seem to be the correct homeland.

All the following members of the willow family have had a part in our garden at one time or another. My only cautionary remark is: Never plant them close to a sewer system or drainage pipes of any kind. Their roots have an uncanny ability to ferret out any nearby sources of water and will travel many feet for just a hint of permanent moisture. The first is hardy in Zone 5; the others in Zone 4.

Salix babylonica, the weeping willow, has an ultimate height of 30 to 50 feet, so it's obviously not for the small garden. But where there is room, this ultimately magnificent tree is far better than its shortcomings would have it. True, it's somewhat untidy, dropping branches and requiring twig cleanups after major windstorms and usually when winter is over. But when the siting is well chosen, nothing is more beautiful—at any season of the year.

Salix matsudana 'Tortuosa', the dragon-claw or corkscrew willow, is a flower arranger's delight. In summer, it's just another pretty tree, but in the winter, the tortuous route of the branches is clearly revealed, their shape echoing a corkscrew used for opening wine bottles. The ultimate height is 25 to 30 feet, and a good specimen will reach between 12 and 15 feet in eight years.

Salix melanostachys, the black pussy willow, is far more interesting than the wild pussy willow. The catkins are so dark that they appear to be black, in stark contrast to the reddish stems that bear them. Then, as they mature, the red stamens that surround bright yellow stigmas are again in sharp contrast to the "fur." They eventually reach a height of 10 feet with a 12-foot spread.

Salix sachalinensis 'Sekka', the Japanese fan-tail willow, is another unusual tree, this one with flattened branches that assume twisted and contorted designs. It, too, is best appreciated in flower arrangements and in the winter garden. The eventual height is 30 feet.

Botanical name: *Syringa* spp.
Common name: Lilac.
Habitat: Ordinary garden soil in full sun.
Description: Deciduous shrubs or small trees with upright branches bearing heart-shaped leaves; clusters of fragrant, small, 4-petaled tubular flowers; to 15 feet.
Period of bloom: Spring.
Propagation: Softwood cuttings.
Zone: 4.

By 1960, there were about 600 known cultivars of lilac in seven distinct colors—white (including cream), violet, lilac, blue, pink, purple, and red. Included in these numbers were single and double flowers, plus 23 distinct species, including the common lilac (*Syringa vulgaris*). Today there are about 2,000 named cultivars, still in the same original seven colors and the same number of species. Obviously, lilacs are popular!

"When lilacs last in the dooryard bloomed," wrote Walt Whitman in the mid-1800s. But there have been lilacs in the dooryards of America since the middle 1600s, when the first common lilac arrived on our shores. Lilac is an old English word, taken from the Arabic *laylak* and the Persian *nilak,* this last from *nil,* meaning blue. The genus *Syringa* is Greek for pipe, referring to hollow stems, and *vulgaris* means common. The most important thing to remember is that lilacs need full sun. Those in partial shade will bloom but not to their best advantage. They also need a period of winter cold, so lilacs do not do well south of Zone 7. The cut-leaf lilac (*Syringa laciniata*), is fairly adaptable to warm weather areas, but southern lilacs never bloom with the beauty of those in the North.

Lilacs need a reasonably fertile, well-drained garden soil, preferably with a good organic content. A second layer of organic mulch will conserve soil moisture, reduce weeds, and protect the plants from mechanical injury usually associated with lawn mowers.

As far as pruning is concerned, many lilacs left to their own devices in abandoned gardens bloom year after year. But diseased canes plus the suckers that grow around the base should be cut out, with the process beginning after flowering is over. Lilacs should be deadheaded to save on energy for the shrub and for cosmetic reasons as well. Be careful not to remove next year's flower buds, which are located on the two branches below the dead flower heads.

Pests that affect lilacs can usually be controlled by good cultural practices, pruning, choosing the proper plant for the climate, and, if necessary, applications of horticultural oils and soaps. Powdery mildew often occurs in areas with high summer humidity but usually does no harm to the shrub itself.

Among the more attractive *Syringa vulgaris* cultivars are 'Ellen Willmott', bearing double white flowers, and 'Mont Blanc', with single whites; 'President Lincoln', having single blues; 'Belle de Nancy', with double pink flowers; 'Firmament', a particularly beautiful single blue; and 'Sensation', a beautiful single flower of purple with white picotee edges.

Syringa patula 'Miss Kim' is a Korean lilac that is dwarf in size, being 5 by 5 feet when mature, and in perfect scale for a very small garden.

Syringa vulgaris

Appendixes

Appendix A: Sources for Seeds

The following list consists of catalogs issued by seed companies mostly involved with flowers, although a few also stock vegetables. Because of fluctuating costs, I've not included any charges incurred with receiving these publications, so write first. The list is in no way complete since there are now hundreds in business in the United States and Canada.

Abundant Life Seed Foundation, P.O. Box 772, Port Townsend, WA 98368. Dedicated to keeping species from disappearing from the garden scene.

The Banana Tree, 715 Northampton Street, Easton, PA 18042. Exotic seeds: bananas, trees, flowers.

Bio-Quest International, P.O. Box 5752, Santa Barbara, CA 93150. Many interesting South African seeds and bulbs.

W. T. Atlee Burpee Company, Warminster, PA 18974. One of the oldest seed companies around today.

John Chambers, 15 Westleigh Road, Barton Seagrave, Kettering, Northants, England NN15 5AJ. A large collection of wildflower and grass seeds.

Chiltern Seeds, Bortree Stile, Ulverston, Cumbria LA12 7PB, England. One of the largest collections of annual and perennial seeds for the garden.

The Country Garden, Route 2, Box 455A, Crivitz, WI 54114. A very large collection of annuals and perennials both for cutting and the border.

William Dam Seeds, P.O. Box 8400, 279 Highway 8, Dundas, Ontario, Canada L9H 6M1. An old and established Canadian firm.

The Fragrant Path, P.O. Box 328, Ft. Calhoun, NE 68023. A wonderful collection of fragrant plants, both annuals and perennials.

Garden City Seeds, P.O. Box 297, Victor, MT 59875. All kinds of seeds for a short growing season.

Gurney Seed & Nursery Co., 2nd & Capital, Yankton, SD 57078. An old-fashioned catalog with old-fashioned pictures and many interesting varieties.

Harris Seeds, 961 Lyell Avenue, Rochester, NY 14606. Another old and established American seed company.

Hastings, P.O. Box 115535, Atlanta, GA 30310. Seeds and garden supplies for the Southeast.

High Altitude Gardens, P.O. Box 4619, 620 Sun Valley Road, Ketchum, ID 83340. Flowers and native grasses adapted for a high-altitude, short-season climate.

J. L. Hudson, Seedsman, P.O. Box 1058, Redwood City, CA 94064. A giant selection of interesting seeds from all over the world.

J. W. Jung Seed Co., 335 S. High Street, Randolph, WI 53957. Roses, perennials, and seeds.

Earl May Seed & Nursery Company, 208 N. Elm Street, Shenandoah, IA 51603. Another famous American nursery with a large selection of seeds.

Moon Mountain Wildflowers, P.O. Box 34, 864 Napa Avenue, Morro Bay, CA 93442. Annual and perennial wildflowers including a number of mixes.

Nichol's Herb and Rare Seeds, 1190 N. Pacific Highway, Albany, OR 97321. Herbs, flowers, and bulbs.

Geo. W. Park Seed Company, Greenwood, SC 29647. One of the most famous seedhouses in the country.

Plants of the Southwest, 930 Baca Street, Sante Fe, NM 87501. A marvelous collection of seeds for native American wildflowers, trees, and shrubs.

Clyde Robin Seed Company, P.O. Box 2855, Castro Valley, CA 94546. One of the biggest sources of wildflower seeds.

Seeds Blum, Idaho City Stage, Boise, ID 83706. A chatty catalog with many seeds for perennial and annuals.

The Seed Source, Balsam Grove, NC 28708. An extensive collection of unusual seeds plus many perennials, gathered from all over the world.

R. H. Shumway Seedsman, P.O. Box 1, Rte. 1, Whaley Pond Road, Graniteville, SC 29829. Marvelous old-fashioned catalog with a large selection of seeds.

Thompson & Morgan, P.O. Box 100, Jackson, NJ 08527.

Appendix B: Sources for Plants

The following suppliers grow and sell live plants to be shipped—usually by United Parcel—throughout the country. Over the years I've ordered hundreds of plants by mail and almost everything has arrived in fine shape; when it hasn't the nursery involved has made good on the order. The firms listed below have learned through experience how to wrap plants for rough handling and they are eminently fair people, ready to hear from you, the buyer, if you have a problem.

Like seed companies, no two nurseries are alike. Each firm will have a few unusual things to offer. I have not listed fees because they continue to change so drop the supplier a note asking for the catalog and fee.

Alpenflora Gardens, 17985 40th Avenue, Surrey, BC, Canada V3S 4N8. A large selection of rock garden and alpine plants.

Appalachian Gardens, P.O. Box 82, Waynesboro, PA 17268. A good list of hardy ornamental trees and shrubs.

B & D Lilies, 330 P Street, Port Townsend, WA 98368. Large selection of hybrid and species lilies.

Bernardo Beach Native Plant Farm, Star Route 7, Box 145, Vesquita, NM 87062. Perennials, vines, and other plants especially for southwest gardens.

Kurt Bluemel, Inc., 2543 Hess Road, Fallston, MD 21047. World's largest selection of ornamental grasses.

The Bovees Nursery, 1737 S.W. Coronado, Portland, OR 97219. Species and hybrid rhododendrons.

Coastal Gardens & Nursery, 4611 Socastee Boulevard, Myrtle Beach, SC 29575. Large selection of hostas and irises.

Charley's Greenhouse Supplies, 1569 Memorial Highway, Mount Vernon, WA 98257. All kinds of greenhouse and garden supplies.

Daylily Discounters, Rte. 2, Box 24, Alachua, FL 32615. Many, many attractive daylilies.

The Garden Place, 6780 Heisley Road, P.O. Box 83, Mentor, OH 44061. Large selection of perennials.

Glasshouse Works, Church Street, P.O. Box 97, Stewart, OH 45778. Plants for indoors and out.

Holbrook Farms and Nursery, Route 2, Box 223B, Fletcher, NC 28732. Many unusual perennials and wildflowers.

Lilypons Water Gardens, 6800 Lilypons Road, Lilypons, MD 21717. Plants for pool and pond.

Logee's Greenhouses, Danielson, CN 06239. A vast selection of plants for garden and greenhouse.

Magnolia Nursery & Display Garden, 12515 Roberts Road, Chunchula, AL 36521. Large selection of magnolias.

McClure & Zimmerman, 108 W. Winnebago, P.O. Box 368, Friesland, WI 53935. A major supplier of bulbs.

Milaeger's Gardens, 4838 Douglas Avenue, Racine, WI 53402. Large collection of perennials.

Mellinger's Inc., 2310 W. South Range Road, North Lima, OH 44452. Plants, seeds and garden supplies.

Montrose Nursery, P.O. Box 957, Hillsborough, NC 27278. Plants for the Southeast.

Walt Nicke Company, 36 McLeod Lane, P.O. Box 433, Topsfield, MA, 01983. A houseplant and garden supermarket of supplies.

Niche Gardens, Rte. 1, Box 290, Chapel Hill, NC 27516. Many nursery propagated wildflowers of the Southeast.

Prairie Nursery, P.O. Box 365, Westfield, WI 53964. American grasses and wildflowers.

Rocknoll Nursery, 9210 U.S. 50, Hillsboro, OH 45133. Rock garden plants and perennial flowers.

Sandy Mush Herb Nursery, Rte. 2, Surrett Cove Road, Leicester, NC 28748. Herbs and garden perennials.

John Sheepers, Inc., Phillipsburg Road, RD 6, Middletown, NY 10940. A large selection of lilies and bulbs.

Andre Viette Farm & Nursery, Rte. 1, Box 16, Fishersville, VA 22939. Daylilies, hostas, ornamental grasses, and more.

Washington Evergreen Nursery, P.O. Box 388, Leicester, NC 28748. A huge selection of dwarf conifers and evergreens.

Wayside Gardens, Hodges, SC 29695. Perennials, shrubs, and trees.

We-Du Nurseries, Rte. 5, Box 724, Marion, NC 28752. Many unusual American wildflowers.

White Flower Farm, Litchfield, CT 06759. A large selection of perennials.

Woodlanders, 1128 Colleton Avenue, Aiken, SC 29801. Many fine wildflowers and native trees and shrubs.

Appendix C: Climate Map of the United States

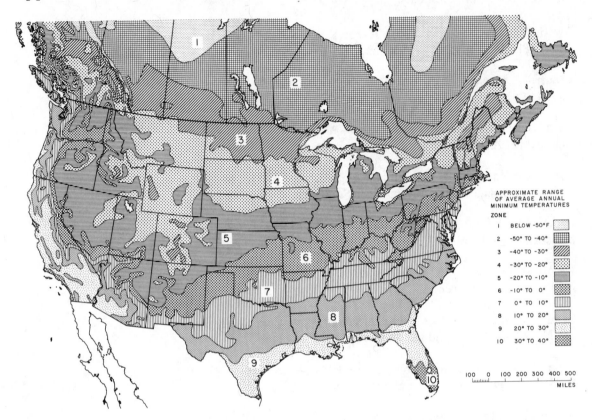

APPROXIMATE RANGE
OF AVERAGE ANNUAL
MINIMUM TEMPERATURES

ZONE	
1	BELOW -50°F
2	-50° TO -40°
3	-40° TO -30°
4	-30° TO -20°
5	-20° TO -10°
6	-10° TO 0°
7	0° TO 10°
8	10° TO 20°
9	20° TO 30°
10	30° TO 40°

100 0 100 200 300 400 500
MILES

Index

Bold type denotes illustrations